Globalisation and Governance in India

This book examines the impact of globalisation on some vital aspects of Indian politics – its structures and processes – and identifies the challenges to globalisation itself in order to highlight India's complex and fascinating story. In 1991, India officially embraced the policy of neo-liberal reforms by signing the General Agreement on Trade and Tariff (GATT), which exposed the country, its society, culture, and institutions, to the various forces of globalisation. Globalisation as such may not be new to India, for the country has been experiencing the impact of external cultures and civilisations for millennia, but the post-1991 reforms policy marked a significant shift from a predominantly social welfare state and a command economy to a predominantly market-driven one.

Through a range of disciplinary perspectives, the authors analyse how India's version of secularism, communal harmony, nationhood, the public sphere, social justice, and the rights of aboriginal communities came under attack from the forces of the new dispensation. The book goes on to show how globalisation in India has posed fresh challenges to the political economy, democracy, federalism, decentralisation, the parliamentary system, the judiciary, and the parliamentary Left.

Critically reflecting on themes in the context of India's globalisation that are local, regional, national, and global, this book will be of interest to those in the fields of South Asian politics, globalisation, and international relations.

Harihar Bhattacharyya is Professor of Political Science, The University of Burdwan, India.

Lion König is Adjunct Faculty at the Centre for Culture, Media and Governance, Jamia Millia Islamia, New Delhi.

Routledge Advances in South Asian Studies
Edited by Subrata K. Mitra, *South Asia Institute, University of Heidelberg, Germany*

South Asia, with its burgeoning, ethnically diverse population, soaring economies, and nuclear weapons, is an increasingly important region in the global context. The series, which builds on this complex, dynamic, and volatile area, features innovative and original research both on the region as a whole and on the countries. Its scope extends to scholarly works drawing on history, politics, development studies, sociology, and economies of individual countries from the region, as well as those that take an interdisciplinary and comparative approach to the area as a whole or to a comparison of two or more countries from this region. In terms of theory and method, rather than basing itself on any one orthodoxy, the series draws broadly on the insights germane to area studies, as well as the toolkit of social sciences in general, emphasising comparison, the analysis of the structure and processes, and the application of qualitative and quantitative methods. The series welcomes submissions from established authors in the field, as well as from young authors who have recently completed their doctoral dissertations.

1 **Perception, Politics and Security in South Asia**
The compound crisis of 1990
P.R. Chari, Pervaiz Iqbal Cheema and Stephen Philip Cohen

2 **Coalition Politics and Hindu Nationalism**
Edited by Katharine Adeney and Lawrence Saez

3 **The Puzzle of India's Governance**
Culture, context and comparative theory
Subrata K. Mitra

4 **India's Nuclear Bomb and National Security**
Karsten Frey

5 **Starvation and India's Democracy**
Dan Banik

6 **Parliamentary Control and Government Accountability in South Asia**
A comparative analysis of Bangladesh, India and Sri Lanka
Taiabur Rahman

7 **Political Mobilisation and Democracy in India**
States of emergency
Vernon Hewitt

8 **Military Control in Pakistan**
The parallel state
Mazhar Aziz

9 Sikh Nationalism and Identity in a Global Age
Giorgio Shani

10 The Tibetan Government-in-Exile
Politics at large
Stephanie Roemer

11 Trade Policy, Inequality and Performance in Indian Manufacturing
Kunal Sen

12 Democracy and Party Systems in Developing Countries
A comparative study
Clemens Spiess

13 War and Nationalism in South Asia
The Indian state and the Nagas
Marcus Franke

14 The Politics of Social Exclusion in India
Democracy at the crossroads
Edited by Harihar Bhattacharyya, Partha Sarka and Angshuman Kar

15 Party System Change in South India
Political entrepreneurs, patterns and processes
Andrew Wyatt

16 Dispossession and Resistance in India
The river and the rage
Alf Gunvald Nilsen

17 The Construction of History and Nationalism in India
Textbooks, controversies and politics
Sylvie Guichard

18 Political Survival in Pakistan
Beyond ideology
Anas Malik

19 New Cultural Identitarian Political Movements in Developing Societies
The Bharatiya Janata Party
Sebastian Schwecke

20 Sufism and Saint Veneration in Contemporary Bangladesh
The Maijbhandaris of Chittagong
Hans Harder

21 New Dimensions of Politics in India
The United Progressive Alliance in power
Lawrence Saez and Gurhapal Singh

22 Vision and Strategy in Indian Politics
Jawaharlal Nehru's policy choices and the designing of political institutions
Jivanta Schoettli

23 Decentralization, Local Governance, and Social Wellbeing in India
Do local governments matter?
Rani D. Mullen

24 The Politics of Refugees in South Asia
Identity, resistance, manipulation
Navine Murshid

25 The Political Philosophies of Antonio Gramsci and Ambedkar
Subalterns and dalits
Edited by Cosimo Zene

26 **Suicide Protest in South Asia**
Consumed by commitment
Simanti Lahiri

27 **E-Governance in India**
Interlocking politics, technology and culture
Bidisha Chaudhuri

28 **Globalisation and Governance in India**
New challenges to society and institutions
Harihar Bhattacharyya and Lion König

Globalisation and Governance in India

New challenges to society and institutions

Edited by Harihar Bhattacharyya and Lion König

LONDON AND NEW YORK

First published 2016 by Routledge

2 Park Square, Milton Park, Abingdon, Oxfordshire OX14 4RN
711 Third Avenue, New York, NY 10017

*Routledge is an imprint of the Taylor & Francis Group,
an informa business*

First issued in paperback 2018

Copyright © 2016 selection and editorial material, Harihar Bhattacharyya and Lion König; individual chapters, the contributors

The right of Harihar Bhattacharyya and Lion König to be identified as authors of the editorial material, and of the contributors as authors of their contributions, has been asserted by them in accordance with sections 77 and 78 of the Copyright, Designs and Patents Act 1988.

All rights reserved. No part of this book may be reprinted or reproduced or utilised in any form or by any electronic, mechanical, or other means, now known or hereafter invented, including photocopying and recording, or in any information storage or retrieval system, without permission in writing from the publishers.

Notice:
Product or corporate names may be trademarks or registered trademarks, and are used only for identification and explanation without intent to infringe.

British Library Cataloguing in Publication Data
A catalogue record for this book is available from the British Library

Library of Congress Cataloging-in-Publication Data
Globalisation and governance in India : new challenges to society and
   institutions / edited by Harihar Bhattacharyya and Lion König.
      pages cm. — (Routledge advances in South Asian studies)
   1. India—Economic policy—1991– 2. India—Politics and
government—1977– 3. Neoliberalism—India. 4. Globalization—India.
I. Bhattacharyya, Harihar. II. König, Lion.
   HC435.3.G655 2016
   306.20954—dc23
   2015007026

ISBN: 978-1-138-85323-2 (hbk)
ISBN: 978-1-138-32007-9 (pbk)

Typeset in Times New Roman
by Apex CoVantage, LLC

Contents

List of illustrations	ix
List of abbreviations	x
Glossary	xii
Preface and acknowledgements	xiii
Foreword by Sudha Pai	xv

Introduction   1
HARIHAR BHATTACHARYYA AND LION KÖNIG

1 **The globalisation–decentralisation nexus: the Indian predicament**   16
MOHIT BHATTACHARYA

2 **Changes in Indian politics until the 1990s: issues and trends**   30
T. R. SHARMA

3 **Cultural globalisation in India: towards a 'third space'**   42
LION KÖNIG

4 **Challenges to democratic governance in India since the 1990s: an 'unfinished symphony'**   55
ASOK KUMAR MUKHOPADHYAY

5 **The new political economy of judicial review in India**   68
MAHENDRA PAL SINGH

6 **Globalisation, extremist violence, and the Indian Left: a critical appraisal**   78
SOBHANLAL DATTA GUPTA

7	**Policing in India: a failed case of institutional reform?** SURAJIT C. MUKHOPADHYAY	89
8	**The problems of Statehood in Indian federalism: a case for territorial pluralism** REKHA SAXENA	98
9	**Regional movements in India: evaluating Telangana and Uttarakhand** JHUMPA MUKHERJEE	110
10	**Governing India's localities: limits of structural and governance reforms** HARIHAR BHATTACHARYYA	125
11	**Conclusion: India's second 'tryst with destiny'** HARIHAR BHATTACHARYYA AND LION KÖNIG	138
	List of contributors	149
	Bibliography	153
	Index	169

Illustrations

Figures

3.1	Covers of the German editions of international magazines on Indian film	50
4.1	India GDP growth rate, 2007–11	59

Tables

2.1	Popular participation in the Indian parliamentary elections (1952–2004)	34
8.1	States reorganised in 1956	103
8.2	States and Union territories in India (2014)	106
9.1	Human development indicators in the regions of Andhra Pradesh	113
9.2	Lok Sabha election results in Andhra Pradesh	118

Abbreviations

ADB	Asia Development Bank
ADC	Autonomous District Council
AIADMK	All India Anna Dravida Munnetra Kazhagam
AIR	All India Reporter
APEC	Asia Pacific Economic Cooperation
ASEAN	Association of South-East Asian Nations
BALCO	Bharat Aluminum Company
BJP	Bharatiya Janata Party
BRICS	Brazil, Russia, India, China and South Africa (Association of Emerging Economies)
CCDI	Comprehensive Composite Development Index
CMP	Common Minimum Programme
CNPC	China National Petroleum Corporation
CPI (M)	Communist Party of India (Marxist)
CPI (ML)	Communist Party of India (Marxist-Leninist)
CPI (ML, Liberation)	Communist Party of India (Marxist-Leninist, Liberation)
CPI	Communist Party of India
DMK	Dravida Munnetra Kazhagam
FDI	Foreign Direct Investment
FEMA	Foreign Exchange Management Act
FERA	Foreign Exchange Regulation Act
FICCI	Federation of Indian Chambers of Commerce and Industry
GAIL	Gas Authority of India Limited
GATT	General Agreement on Trade and Tariff
GDP	Gross Domestic Product
HDI	Human Development Index
ICHRP	International Council for Human Rights Policy
IMF	International Monetary Fund
JNNURM	Jawaharlal Nehru National Urban Renewal Mission
LFG	Left Front Government
LNG	Liquefied Natural Gas
MNC	Multinational Corporation

MNREGA	Mahatma Gandhi National Rural Employment Guarantee Act
NDA	National Democratic Alliance
NEFA	North-East Frontier Agency
NEP	New Economic Policy
NGO	Non-Governmental Organisation
NRIs	Non-Resident Indians
OBC	Other Backward Class
PEPSU	Punjab and East Punjab States Union
PIL	Public Interest Litigation
PPP	Public-Private Partnership
RSS	Rashtriya Swayamsevak Sangh
RTE	Right to Education
RTI	Right to Information
SAARC	South Asian Association for Regional Cooperation
SAP	Structural Adjustment Programme
SC	Scheduled Caste
SCO	Shanghai Cooperation Organization
SEZ	Special Economic Zone
SIPRD	State Institute for Panchayats and Rural Development
SRC	States Reorganisation Commission
ST	Scheduled Tribe
TMC	Trinamool Congress
TRIPS	Trade-Related Aspects of Intellectual Property Rights
UFCs	Union Finance Commissions
ULB	Urban Local Bodies
UNDP	United Nations Development Programme
UPA	United Progressive Alliance
USAID	United States Agency for International Development
WTO	World Trade Organization

Glossary

Adivasis   Literally, original inhabitants; India's aboriginal communities
Anaganaga O Dheerdu   *Once Upon a Time There Was a Warrior*, the first Oriya film co-produced by Disney in 2011
Ayudhapuja   An integral part of the Hindu Navratri festival. It entails the veneration of implements, machines, weapons, books, and musical instruments.
Chakalis   A sub-caste of the *dhobi* caste.
Dalits   Former 'Untouchable' communities in India, usually known as Scheduled Castes; nowadays, the category is used to include India's aboriginal peoples
Dhobi   Caste of washers
Doordarshan   Indian Public Broadcaster
Gram Sabha   Assembly of all voters of a village (Gram)
Gram Sansad   Literally 'village parliament'; a constituency-based assembly of voters under *panchayats* in West Bengal since 1994
Jal jangal jameen   Water, forests, land
Katikaparlu   A caste engaged in burying the dead
Kaun Banega Crorepati   The Indian version of the TV show *Who Wants to Be a Millionaire?*
Malguzaree   A land revenue system introduced by the British colonial authorities
Mazdoor Kishan Shakti Sangathan   An organisation of peasants and workers
Mulki   An Urdu word meaning 'residents of a nation'
Panchayati raj   Rule of *panchayats*
Panchayats   Local rural self-governing institutions in India
Reiats   Also known as 'ryots'. Tenant farmers who provided the government with a fixed rent from the produce of the land.
Salwa Judum   'Peace March' or 'Purification Hunt' in the Gondi language; nowadays referring to a militia targeting Naxalite violence in some Indian States at the connivance of some State authority.
Zindegi Na Milegi Dobara   A 2011 Bollywood film set in Spain which was a box office hit.

Preface and acknowledgements

Sea changes have taken and are continuing to take place in the Indian polity, its structures, institutions, and processes, as well as in its society and culture, due to the interrelated processes of globalisation and economic liberalisation. In the crucial post-1991 phase, globalisation triggered changes in different aspects of the political life of this most complex federal democracy in the world. The most distinctive aspect of this phenomenon is that India has opened up while being governed democratically, not simply at the national level, but also at the level of States and localities. Although the structural arrangements of governance in India are in flux, the democratic processes from below have been increasingly assertive. Added to this is the country's diversity, its identities, castes and communities, and its inequalities and hierarchies, which do not constitute fertile grounds for working out the processes of globalisation. The story of making globalisation work in India is therefore very complex and wrought with a host of intricate problems and obstacles. The conventional texts on Indian politics, in most cases, are insufficient, if not inadequate, to comprehend this fast-changing scenario.

This collection of chapters written by both well-established scholars in the field, and young ones with detailed knowledge on the subject is the first attempt ever made to examine the impact of globalisation on some vital aspects of Indian politics, its structures, and processes, and to identify the challenges to globalisation itself in order to bring to the notice of informed observers and the policy community India's complex and intriguing story of globalisation. The book brings together different perspectives on the subject: political science, sociology, public administration, juridical, and cultural, which has added interdisciplinary breadth to the endeavour.

The foreword to the book, written by Sudha Pai, Professor of political science, Centre for Political Studies, and Rector, Jawaharlal Nehru University, has added further strength to the collection. She deserves our sincere thanks and gratitude for agreeing to write it for us.

In the course of preparing the book over the last year and a half, we have incurred our debt to many institutions and persons. We are thankful to our authors for the patience that is required in such efforts and for complying with our requests for revisions. We are particularly thankful to authors who responded positively to our invitation to contribute and responded to our queries of many sorts with grace.

We also wish to extend our gratitude to Subrata K. Mitra, Professor Emeritus, Department of Political Science, South Asia Institute, Heidelberg University, Germany, for his inspiration and help at critical stages of the editing process.

The job of editing books is onerous, particularly so when one has had to do it without any sabbatical or leave and in the midst of carrying out the daily tasks of semester-based teaching, marking, and other related activities. Needless to say, the family pays some price for it at the end of it all. We crave forgiveness!

Last, but certainly not least, we also wish to extend our sincere thanks to Jillian Morrison of Routledge (London) for her patience and support.

Harihar Bhattacharyya
Department of Political Science
The University of Burdwan

Lion König
Centre for Culture, Media and Governance
Jamia Millia Islamia
26 January 2015

Foreword

Globalisation has been a dominant force worldwide since the 1980s, although its impact on the Indian polity has been felt to a greater extent since the 1990s. Globalisation has had both a multi-dimensional and multi-level impact on India's institutions and processes; in addition, it is taking place in a society characterised by mass poverty and regional and social inequalities, making it complex and uncertain. Much scholarly attention has been directed to understanding the direction, pace, and extent of change that globalisation has introduced in India. The essays in this volume examine the impact of globalisation on our democratic system, ranging from decentralisation, various aspects of governance, regional movements, cultural change, politics of identity, policing, judicial review, and extremist violence. However, a common denominator running through the essays is globalisation, which constitutes the overarching phenomenon within which all other changes are seen as occurring.

Globalisation is a concept that stands for tremendous diversity of issues and problems and has been interpreted from a variety of theoretical and political positions. Yet, both modern and post-modern theorists recognise that the world today is increasingly organised according to the terms set by globalisation, which is strengthening the dominance of a world capitalist economic system, supplanting the primacy of the nation-state by transnational corporations and non-governmental organisations (NGOs), and eroding local cultures and traditions through a global culture. Some scholars see it as a central and irreversible process, a new epoch of history in which traditional nation-states can no longer function independently of one another. A more balanced view believes that globalisation is 'transforming' the world, seeing it as a driving force behind the rapid social, political, and economic changes that are reshaping modern societies and the world order. There has also been a resurgence of ethnic identities in the political arena based on language, tribe, and community, not only in countries of the developing world, including India, but also in many developed countries. Globalisation promotes a global culture, whereas ethnic identities promote the local, the parochial, the 'other'. It is a two-way process with outside forces impinging on the country along with changes within.

In India, the process of globalisation has some distinctive features and characteristics, some of which are explored in this volume. What is unique is that together with globalisation, some fundamental shifts in various areas of our democratic life have taken place simultaneously and have affected all sections of society, not merely the elite: heightened political awareness, encouraged civil society activists, and social media sites. Two key processes of democratisation and regionalisation of politics – which have been active since independence – have affected the functioning of our democratic polity. These accelerated in the 1980s, contributing to the breakdown during the tumultuous decade of the 1990s of the cardinal features of the Nehruvian period: the single-party system, secularism, and socialism. These changes provided room for the rise of narrower parties based on identity and coalition governments at the centre and the States. Consequently, the 1990s constituted a decisive shift, a period of transition, when the collapse of the older polity triggered a number of changes with enormous implications for national and State politics. Because these developments took place at the same time as globalisation, the two processes have closely interacted with each other. Primordial identities based on caste and community drove mass politics as political parties mobilised along the lines of social cleavages dividing the electorate. An upsurge from below created a new identity for the *dalits*, brought the Other Backward Classes (OBCs) into politics, and questioned the position of the higher castes – developments that led to a considerable deepening of democracy and the rise of lower-caste parties. The construction of the ideology of Hindutva by the Bharatiya Janata Party (BJP) and the politicisation of the Ram Mandir issue created communal conflict and violence. The reappearance of communal conflict in Uttar Pradesh since 2012 has once again created insecurity. A number of protest movements have also taken place in the 2000s, such as the farmers' movements against land acquisition for Special Economic Zones (SEZs), movements against big dams and nuclear plants, and, more recently, the Anna Hazare movement against corruption.

Yet at the same time since the early 2000s there has been a weakening of primordial identities in the Hindi heartland leading to demands for development. The BIMARU States are now keen to catch up with the faster-growing States of western and southern India, although this process will take time and considerable effort due to decades of neglect. The context in which globalisation is taking place has changed. A new, post-Congress polity has emerged in which multi-party competition has changed the structure of electoral competition, provided space for the rise of new social identities that have played a greater role in national politics, and loosened the tight mould of federalism cast at independence.

With globalisation, the rise of neo-liberalism, and the adoption of economic reforms, a different understanding of governance has appeared in the discourse on development since the 1990s in India, which contributors in the volume critically analyse. Notions of Good Governance mooted by the World Bank – which advocate a single fit for all polities – have been challenged by attempts to build governance systems more suited to Indian working conditions. There is also a growing recognition that the process of governance is not neutral, but affected by culture, which can impede or assist the process of reform. Although the role of the Indian state as an interventionist and welfare state has come to be undermined with the play of market forces, welfare programmes have not been abandoned and new ones have appeared. As a result, despite the advocacy of a more broad-based model of governance – which provides greater room for market forces and civil society – the state remains central to the process of development. It needs to provide law and order, rules and regulations, and maintain control over competitive market forces.

At the same time, globalisation has political and sociological aspects which many essays highlight. Together with regionalisation, it has affected the relationship between the centre and the States, affecting the functioning of our federal polity. Regional parties are now competing in many States with national parties and, as members of central coalitions, have also become partners in national governance. As a result, national parties, particularly the Congress, have found it difficult to run a coalition government. Methods of democratic governance under the Congress-led United Progressive Alliance (UPA) underwent a marked change with the creation of the National Advisory Council (NAC) and Empowered Groups of Ministers (EGOMs) replacing the conventional working of a Cabinet or prime ministerial form of government. At the same time, the Prime Minister's office (PMO) is becoming very powerful. India is slowly evolving its own system of coalition governments, which, it is hoped, will provide greater stability and effective policy making.

A major outcome of these developments to which the volume draws attention is the seminal position occupied today by the States of the Indian Union in national politics. The States have become conscious of their autonomy and collective voice against the centre; following liberalisation they have achieved greater financial freedom; with the establishment of a market economy, there is greater competition over access to common resources or in attracting private investment – both domestic and international. Under the constitutional division of powers, decision-making related to the sectors that are central to the reform process – infrastructure, power, agriculture, education, and so on – lie with the States. With the dismantling of centralised planning and controls, there has been a progressive devolution of power to the States, which makes gaining their support crucial for the successful implementation of reforms. Consequently, there is a growing consensus that if economic reform is to succeed, it must be properly implemented in the States. However, this is not easy, as different parties are in power in the States; State governments are much closer to the electorate and more vulnerable to instability arising out of pressures by economic interests, conflicting pressures, and diverse local interests. Accordingly, the process of economic reform has shown immense regional variation in terms of pace, extent, and direction, with states being categorised as fast reformers, intermediate reformers, and lagging reformers.

Studies also indicate that India's developmental failure or recent successes cannot be credited to the policies framed by the central government; due to the federal structure, it is as much the result of varying political choices by regional elites and regional political competition. The two simultaneous shifts in the 1990s – liberalisation and the emergence of a regionalised multi-party system – have resulted in the gradual creation of a federal market economy. In this the States enjoy a greater share of economic sovereignty while the centre is moving from an interventionist to a regulatory state that enforces fiscal discipline, accountability, and transparency. Consequently, performance by the States now depends on themselves to a much greater extent. They need to address the major challenges posed if liberalisation is to succeed. The most pressing tasks include the improvement of the policy environment, and the development of infrastructure and human resources to attract investment, while at the same time ensuring the necessary measures of fiscal discipline imposed by the centre, as well as by international and domestic credit-rating agencies. The States are on a learning curve, gradually realising that both competition and cooperation are required in the new federal dispensation.

These multi-faceted changes since the 1990s have encouraged demands for the creation of smaller States out of the large ones created by the States Reorganisation Commission at independence. The rise of new elites from among the newly emerged middle and lower castes/classes has created a highly competitive electoral politics within which regional/state-based political parties have staked their specific demands for political power. Earlier, 'reorganisation' was situated in the context of a socialist state with centralised planning. Presently, liberalisation and the emergence of a market economy have given greater room to the private sector and financial autonomy to these ruling elites. Consequently, whereas many unresolved issues led to demand for the creation of new States earlier, today as many as thirty such demands are pending for consideration before the central government. With the creation of three new States in the year 2000, demands for several other States have begun to voice their agitation more explicitly. These demands indicate a shift away from language and culture that shaped the earlier process of reorganisation to one driven by the needs of economy, better governance, greater accountability, and desire for greater political participation. These developments underlie the demand for a second States Reorganisation Commission that could redraw the federal map of India in keeping with the needs and aspirations of the new regional elites.

Against this backdrop attention has been focused on the sharpening of regional disparities and their relationship to economic reform. Although some scholars argue that regional disparities are a result of the unequal patterns of investment in the colonial period that the post-independence state has not been able to remove, others point out that liberalisation has increased these differences as the better-off States have made use of opportunities under globalisation and moved ahead faster. This has sparked a debate over whether there is evidence of 'convergence' in development among the States or 'divergence' due to accentuation of regional disparities in social and economic development. Regional disparities are also responsible for conflicts and movements against the state, including the Maoist movements in parts of the country. Nevertheless, globalisation can function as a positive force; dilution of controls and a variety of tax reforms have created a national market and generated revenue for loan waivers and welfare programmes such as the Mahatma Gandhi National Rural Employment Guarantee Act (MGNREGA) in the States. Over the last decade India has entered a higher growth path, but scholars remain divided over its sustainability and whether the benefit of this change has reached the poorer sections.

A closely related development has been the emergence and growing significance of a new urban middle class which has begun to assertively claim a role as the agent of globalisation in India. This has created a desire among the newly emerged better-off groups, agricultural and industrial, in the smaller metropolises to emulate and join the privileged lifestyle and patterns of consumption depicted in the media and associated with English-educated professional classes. Economic reform has also been described as one of the 'elite revolts' – carried out by or on behalf of urban, industrial, and even agricultural and political elites – against the earlier model of state-directed economic development. Some scholars point to a close nexus between economic reform and organised business classes that have actively lobbied and been responsible for policy debates in favour of reforms, as well as the role played by elites in pushing forward reform processes and in mediating the relationship between State politics and mass political responses. Thus, there is a close relationship between the political processes of democratisation, which have spawned new classes, and the consolidation of economic reform over the last two decades.

The volume has well-researched essays by eminent scholars who have explored various facets of the new politics emerging at the interface of globalisation and governance. Their contributions suggest that older explanations regarding Indian politics are no longer valid. Today, fundamental issues such as the role of the state and the market, new forms of governance (both administrative and judicial), social and political identities, federal relations, and States reorganisation – in sum, what holds India together – is being rethought. Fresh research and new explanations are required, some of which this volume offers. The larger question that is collectively raised is how the Indian State and the States in the Union will adapt to the new context and the challenges presented by globalisation. Will they follow the old paths or allow for new values, norms, and practices and build a new national consensus that will take Indian democracy forward?

Sudha Pai

Introduction

Harihar Bhattacharyya and Lion König

Globalisation, by no means a new phenomenon, but increasingly assertive since the 1980s, is a multi-dimensional process that interconnects the whole world for various purposes, such as economic transactions, communications, cultural interaction, and political exchanges. It is in the process of globalisation that "the local and the global intertwine, forming a web in which both elements are transformed as a result of their own interconnections" (Guibernau, 2001: 244). There are considerable differences of opinion regarding its origin, antiquity, nature, direction, impact, and the challenges that it poses (e.g. Sen, 2005, 2007; Friedman, 2000; Fukuyama, 1992; Gilpin, 2000; Ohmae, 1990; Stiglitz, 2007, 2003; Bhagwati, 2007, 2004; Friedman, 2005; Amin, 2004). Amartya Sen (2005: 344–346) defines globalisation as "[a] diverse basket of global interactions that are put under this broad heading, varying from the expansion of cultural influences across borders to the enlargement of economic and business relations throughout the world". For Sen, globalisation is not new, in the sense of a movement of ideas. What is particularly new for him is the "global movement of ideas, people, goods and technology" (Sen, 2005: 345; Sen, 2007: 117). Second, the direction of today's globalisation, according to Sen, is very different; he points out that around 1000 CE, the dominant direction of movement was from the East to the West, when the "globalization of science, technology and mathematics was changing the nature of the old world" (Sen, 2005: 345).[1] He further adds that India has been an integral part of this process since the beginning of the first millennium (Sen, 2005: 345). Unlike Bhagwati (2007), who defends globalisation, Sen's position is critical and more nuanced: To reject globalisation in favour of insularity and isolation would be a great mistake. And yet, there are important issues of equity and fairness that have to be addressed by each country and by the global community. Sen (2006: 120) acknowledges the ways in which globalisation has created "massive inequalities in the opportunities different people have" and is unsure if globalisation has the ability "to serve the interests of the underdogs" (Sen, 2007: 117). Sen (2007: 117–132) has raised a number of very interesting issues with policy implications: globalisation's relation with development; democracy, equity and fairness; reduction of poverty; distributional issues; and the appropriate institutional arrangements at domestic and global levels. Does globalisation mean economic growth, which means reduction in poverty? Do the globalisers believe more in democracy than in 'ordered autocracies'? Are the global institutional arrangements, as well as those at the domestic front, designed to cater to the needs for equity and fairness? What about the effects of global trade in arms monopolised (81 percent during 1996–2000) by the permanent members of the UN Security Council and its effects on people's livelihood? If G-8 countries sold 87 percent of the total arms to the entire world (Sen, 2007:131), one needs to re-think the real meaning of the so-called 'war on terror' campaign originating mostly from the West itself. Or take the example of the United States, which since 9/11 has given a clarion call for a 'war on terror', when its own share during the same period in the global arms sale was 50 percent (Sen, 2007: 131).

The main propeller of the process of globalisation today is world capitalism, which believes in a free market (albeit with the help of the state!) and a lesser role for the social welfare state so as to enlarge the market's space. If we take the view that globalisation refers to a capitalism that wants a border-free movement, then there is nothing particularly new about this view because free trade has been intellectually defended by thinkers such as Adam Smith and David Ricardo since the eighteenth century. Even then a free market was not embraced wholeheartedly, and Karl Marx and Friedrich Engels wrote of the nature of capitalism: "[I]t must nestle everywhere, settle everywhere, and establish connections everywhere" (Marx and Engels, 1975: 46). What was this but the global character of capitalism and its global vision that the founders of Marxism were clearly hinting at? The first chapter of the aforementioned classic in Marxist literature is replete with the globalising zeal, activities, and spread of capitalism in the West.

The leading sociological accounts of globalisation (e.g. Waters, 2002; Giddens, 1994) go beyond the primarily economic meaning of globalisation in order to highlight the effects of technological innovations and revolutions in communications. Giddens argues that globalisation should not be seen as a primarily economic phenomenon; neither should it be equated with the emergence of a 'world system' (Wallerstein, 1974 and Balibar and Wallerstein, 1993); rather, it should be understood as being "about the transformation of time and space" (Giddens, 1994: 4).[2] Giddens thus defines globalisation as "action at distance" and relates its intensification in recent years to "the emergence of means of instantaneous global communication and mass transportation" (Giddens, 1994: 4). According to Giddens, the challenges that globalisation holds for cultures and societies are immense. First, it leads to a revival of local nationalism in the form of regional and ethnic movements and an accentuation of local identities. Second, it gives birth to *post-traditional* societies, not in the sense of the loss of tradition, but in a situation when traditions have to explain themselves "to become open to interrogation or discourse" (Giddens, 1994: 5).

Although globalisation affects the nation-state, society, and culture and institutions of governance, the process is not one-way. The impact upon the nation-state and its system of governing the country is more directly affected, and as we shall see shortly, society and culture may not as easily be amenable to it or to imbibe the change. There is above all the question of multiple cultures within a particular nation-state boundary. Thomas Friedman in *The World Is Flat* (2005) cautioned about the cultural factors which play a critical role in globalisation. In a section appropriately titled "Culture Matters: Glocalization" (Friedman, 2005: 124–129), he argues that it is insufficient to analyse a country's economic performance without reference to culture. A country's cultural endowment is a key factor in economic development via the adoption of new technology, change, and gender equality (Friedman, 2005: 124). Friedman draws particular attention to two aspects of culture relevant in this context of 'glocalization'. First, the culture could be open to foreign influences and ideas, that is, outwardly looking. Second, there could be an inwardness of culture: to what degree is there a sense of national solidarity and a focus on development, to what degree is there trust within the society for strangers to collaborate (Friedman, 2005: 324–325)? Incidentally, Friedman has recognised that Indian culture is one of the few which has "the natural ability to glocalize" (Friedman, 2005: 325). In effect, what Friedman stresses here is the 'culture of tolerance' that is of paramount importance in economic development (Friedman, 2005: 327).[3]

This analysis suggests that if a country formally adopts the macro-level policy of reforms, or economic globalisation, this does not mean it will succeed. Globalisation is not a culture-blind process. The social and cultural ethos that goes with globalisation may come into conflict with the host culture if the latter is not liberal enough to adapt to it. Even the very concept of economic development or growth is value laden and political, if not in design certainly in terms of results. Nowhere has globalisation-propelled growth benefitted all sections of society equally, and Amartya Sen has noted that the social underdogs pay the "penalties of globalization" (Sen, 2006: 121). Therefore, society and culture become a domain of contestation as far as the process of globalisation in a particular country is concerned. Whereas globalisation, leading to macro-economic reforms, has an impact of a varied nature, its interactive space with the surrounding context remains uncertain. Often, the former may not produce any impact at all! For example, the current notion of economic reforms, or globalisation (they are used interchangeably here), primarily insists upon market equality as its dominant ethos, but its sway may be limited by the large-scale and often very rigid pre-existing social hierarchies and discrimination.

The interplay of globalisation, government, and governance

The most profound impact of globalisation is in the realm of governance, which was traditionally closely and almost entirely associated with government, but is nowadays increasingly dissociated with from government. Conventionally, governance was understood to be the effect of government, that is, the outcome of government action in terms of the delivery of services, and the realm of law and order. In the current phase of neo-liberal globalisation, this law-and-order function of the state remains the *conditio sine qua non* and is being strengthened, paradoxically, for greater protection to the market. However, this means we are moving towards a strong state that governs at a minimum. Who is then responsible for governance and what does it imply? We are tempted here to refer to an expression of India's current Prime Minister Narendra Modi (an unrepentant advocate of neo-liberal reforms in India) who, on being sworn in, declared that India under him would experience 'less government, more governance'.

The term 'governance' is most often conflated and confused with 'government'. The processes of globalisation in its current reincarnation seem to have made the term so popular that students of government and politics tend to forget their age-old subject of 'Government'. Has 'governance' then replaced 'government'? What is the difference between the two? What is the politics of this renewed emphasis on 'governance'? Has it anything to do with the neo-liberal globalisation agenda? The simple dictionary meaning of the term 'government' refers to a system of governing, that is, a form of organisation of the state. The *Concise Oxford Dictionary* defines it as "a group of persons governing a state". In ordinary parlance then, 'government' refers to a whole set of organs and institutions, rules and procedures, control, regulation, sovereignty, and above all, the rulers (Bhattacharyya, 2007: 3; Bandopadhyay, 2007: 190–203).[4] Governance in this sense would refer to the manner, act, or functions of government, and therefore could be seen as the offshoot of government, the effect of the former. Thus understood, government is an independent variable whereas governance is a dependent one. If looked at from the positivistic angle, as Subrata Mitra has done (1997: 1–7, 17–50), the absence of governance is indicated by empirical indicators such as "violent deaths, criminal damage to property, riots, lawlessness, man/woman days lost in illegal strike".

Since the term 'governance' today has become entangled with the neo-liberal globalisation agenda, it requires some further conceptual clarifications. It is now almost a truism that the social interventionist welfare state the world over has been heavily affected by today's globalisation. The 'rolling the state back', Structural Adjustment Programme (SAP), 'governance reforms', and cuts in public expenditures are terms used to indicate, if not to conceptualise, the ideological shift. Today's market-centric globalisation suggests a lesser role for the state, or the government, as the deliverer of public goods, while more and more space is cleared for the market, which, however, does not move alone, but takes the help of what is styled the 'strong state', a state of law and order, well equipped with the means of protecting the market.

Does then 'governance' belong to the state or to civil society? Who is in charge of governance, and who is to deliver, if at all, public goods and welfare? Any knowledge of the history of government would suggest that even in the days of the minimal state, the state interfered in societal matters, and civil society learnt to manage its own affairs independent of the state in significant respects, even long before the notion of such a state came into being (Putnam, 1993).[5] In fact, India's tradition of social thought is replete with examples of self-governing society (Bhattacharyya, 2007; Bhattacharyya, 2010). Therefore, it can be argued that governance belongs to the spheres of both state and society. However, the globalisation-propelled meaning of governance is more inclined to civil society in ways that, as will be pointed out later, hardly aim at reforms of society in terms of addressing inequalities and hierarchies,[6] but seek to leave things to the market as the deliverer.

Structural adjustment and governance reforms: Changing global perspectives

From the perspective of globalisation, the expression 'governance reforms' has replaced, as it were, 'structural reforms', or the SAP, which received greater attention in the earlier years of globalisation and aimed at clearing more space for the market. As elsewhere, market reforms failed in India, a society marked by extremes of unevenness, inequalities, and hierarchies of sorts, on the one hand, and heavily entrenched structures of government designed to serve the public purposes and the complex institutional and political arrangements of a federal democracy (with very deep identification with ethno-regional identities), on the other (Guhan, 1995; Williams, 1997: 235–238; Nayar, 2008; Rudolph and Rudolph, 2008; Govinda Rao and Singh, 2005). The shift then from market reforms to 'governance reforms' with the central focus on the capacity of the state and its institutions to make globalisation work since the late 1980s globally, and about a decade later in India, was predictable. However, this shift did not signify a complete break with the role of the state or doing away with the state. On the contrary, the state is also needed very much, albeit in a newer role as facilitator of the development of the market. David Williams, with an insider's view of the World Bank, wrote that

> ... during the same period (late 1980s) the World Bank was reconsidering the role of the state in development more generally, and by the late 1980s the minimalist state view was giving way to a more nuanced account of the relationship between state and market.
>
> (Williams, 1997: 236)

As the World Bank's view further crystallised, so remarks Williams:

> In a sense the Bank has simply come to realize what classical economists had always said: market led economic development requires a strong and effective state to create the conditions for capitalist development and mould a sustaining environment for private enterprises.
>
> (Williams, 1997: 237)

Those familiar with the ongoing debates on the impact of globalisation on the nation-state are aware that the classical nation-state is now giving way to a reformed one styled as 'post-classical' or 'post-traditional' (Guibernau and Hutchinson, 2002: 247)[7] with a much reduced role not inimical to the market.[8] Thus, 'governance reforms', that is, the reforms of the state institutions, became a necessity (Bandopadhyay, 2007; Corbridge *et al.*, 2005; Ramesh and Fritzen, 2009). It was this new role of the institutions that prepared the grounds for the rise of the phenomenon of the so-called Public-Private Partnership (PPP) model of development (Mukhopadhyay, 2011: 9–25).

Deeply connected with globalisation and its market-equality zeal is the renewed international emphasis on democracy, local self-government, and empowerment, especially of the weaker sections of society. In the days of the Cold War, when international politics was conducted in a predominantly bipolar mode, those ideals and principles had a very poor following among the international actors, public and private. Therefore, it was not surprising that 'hard dictatorships' across the so-called Third World took shape accompanied by the gross violations of human rights and the encouragement for the misuse of democratic institutions. The rise of a multi-polar international world after the Cold War and of manifold actors, agencies, institutions, and associations has served to pave the basis for a renewed emphasis on democratisation, participation, and empowerment (Ramesh and Fritzen, 2009; Hale and Kienle, 1997[9]; Kothari, 2012). Reflecting quite early on this change, David Williams, arguing that something had gone wrong with the political system in Africa, for example, wrote that "USAID has committed itself to supporting sustainable African led initiatives for democratic institutions and improved governance. This is manifested in its focus on broadening participation in development at all levels of society, and supporting human rights activities" (Williams, 1997: 229).

The current inquiry, however, focuses more on the 'loose concept of governance' than on government (Stubbs and Underhill, 2005: 32–33) in order to overcome the so-called gap between formal and informal frameworks of government, a hypothesis which connects itself to a theoretical tradition in comparative politics recently advanced by Putnam and others in terms of the reformulated seminal concept of 'social capital' (Putnam *et al.*, 1994).

Exploring the Indian engagement with processes of globalisation

Although India has been part of the process of globalisation since the first millennium, as Amartya Sen notes, India's signing of the General Agreement on Tariffs and Trade (GATT) in 1991 was a major step in opening up parts of the national economy to the world economy. India's adoption of neo-liberal market reforms since 1991, although the economic background of the same had been prepared at least two decades earlier under the guise of liberalisation, was not to be seen simply as economic reforms because such reforms, as has been indicated earlier, do not emerge in a vacuum. The impact of this multidimensional process on India's society, political system, its structures, and institutions and processes remains varied and very complex, and the multi-level interactions between reforms, on the one hand, and the whole gamut of society and culture and various institutions of the state, on the other, are no less complex and uncertain. Kaviraj (2010: 233–271) has brought out the various aspects of this complexity from a political theoretical point of view not warranted in the existing account of the subject (e.g. Nayar, 2007; Corbridge and Harriss, 2000; Kohli, 2009; Tendulkar and Bhavani, 2007; Govinda Rao and Singh, 2005). The post-liberalisation reforms have affected the sense of identity and citizenship and raised questions about the effectiveness of the existing constitutional arrangements to cope with changes. India's federalism, particularly the role of the States in the reform process, has come under scrutiny, and the very definition of the state itself as a predominantly social welfarist/interventionist player and a caring *sirkar* or *mera baap* has been questioned (Morris-Jones, 1967). One significant change that has taken place in India's party system is that most political parties, ideologically speaking, have turned 'pragmatic'. Bhattacharyya (2012) has argued that in this vastly changed social and cultural space, new areas of tensions have arisen between the need for a 'national identity' for citizenship, as a political identity, on the one hand, and the fragmented society of continuously proliferating identities of varying sizes and import, on the other – a framework in which the newly emerging concept of market-friendly consumerist citizenship does not seem to find a hospitable home.

It must, however, be kept in mind that macro-economic reforms have been set motion in India today in a vastly different and very often predictable and challenging context. In the earlier days, the scope of the process was limited and the impact was felt, if at all, first mostly among the ruling elites to be percolated down to the masses after quite some time. But today, it is played out in conditions of mass society (and mass poverty), democracy (parliamentary with many layers) (with large illiteracy) with increased awareness of the people about their various rights, civil society of sorts, web-based social media, and a very sensitive and often aggressive mass media. In other words, there is, as it were, a built-in transparency in the process itself, which is unavoidable in the medium-term if not in the short-term perspective. To cap it all, in this "reflexive society" of ours, to use a term by Anthony Giddens (1994), developments in the economy, society, and polity are instantly discussed, commented upon, and judged in various discursive modes, leading to a dialectical process. To give but one example: the acquisition of land for setting up industries and the Special Economic Zones (SEZs) for carrying out SAP in some States in India was resisted quite successfully by opposition parties, various civil society organisations, and media, resulting in the withdrawal of the projects; the game is played out in the reverse as well.[10] In another respect, that is, 'governance reforms', much emphasis has been put on local government reforms, participation, empowerment of the weaker sections of society, accountability, and transparency in India. Although this has at least formally empowered the vast number of socially underprivileged citizens, the old society of hierarchies and discrimination has revolted and served to curtail the very basis of such efforts. At the same time, those discriminated against along caste lines have learnt to make skilful use of their caste identities as a weapon against higher caste domination and to demand more social welfare benefits accruing from quota and reservation. As a result, India's proverbial caste system was reinforced rather than weakened, much to the irritation and dismay of the theorists of the modernisation mode of thinking since the 1950s (Singer, 1972; Rudolph and Rudolph, 1967; Srinivas, 1952; Parsons and Shils, 1951; Shils, 1965). Thus, Rudolph and Rudolph (2008: 100–118) revisited many of the categories used to understand Indian society and politics. In a very incisive yet self-critical essay, they interrogate the basic assumptions of Lockean universalism and liberalism, as well as those of modernisation theory, and plead for a case of "cultural relativity" and an approach that is no longer "indifferent to difference" (Rudolph and Rudolph, 2008: 118). The painful fact remains though: India's adoption of such a major macro-economic policy step lacked the democratic legitimacy required because such a move was not democratically mandated; like the Constitution itself, it was superimposed upon the people.

At another level, the effects of reforms have meant that newer modes of identity articulation have taken place, and the many erstwhile regional movements have retuned themselves, asking now for more development, investment, and market opportunities. Although most of the linguistic issues in India have been sorted out in phases of reorganisation of States, this has not, arguably, done away with the many still-unresolved issues: regional, sub-regional, caste, sub-caste, and significantly religious identities that seek political recognition and empowerment. Although the existing institutional arrangements have done their best in responding to such questions, the latter have called for revision of such arrangements designed and devised some half a century back to serve basically a socialistic, public-sector–oriented society.

Another major area of concern in India in the context of the new political economy is federalism, constitutionally still highly centralised but administratively decentralised. Is a centralised federalism more congenial to economic liberalisation? Does a decentralised federalism serve to derail the process of SAP? The existing literature on India's new political economy suggests that in the beginning, that is, in the first half of the 1990s, the international multilateral agencies seeking to invest in India preferred to have policy dialogues with the centre alone (Guhan, 1995). This did not work well, however, because India's globalisation was to take place in the States, and also, per the Indian Constitution, most powers and functions relating to implementing such programmes lie with the States. Therefore, the role of the States in the reforms process was thought to be crucial. Rudolph and Rudolph (2008: 313) thus write on the "emergence of the States as crucial actors in economic reforms and growth", a phenomenon which they consider to be quite challenging to Indian democracy. But it must not be forgotten that not all the States were very eager to involve themselves in the process, and also not all the States were equally attractive destinations for investment, trade, and commerce for a variety of reasons (Bhattacharyya, 2009a; Bhattacharyya, 2010, 2012). But two things in this respect have become evident. First, some States readily got themselves involved in the process and reaped considerable benefits out of it. Second, even within the existing constitutional set-up, the States have been allowed, by way of 'executive federalism', more freedom of action in matters of attracting investment and for engaging themselves in trade and commerce even with foreign companies and countries. Quite predictably, this has served to pave the basis for demanding States' rights anew in India (Bhattacharyya, 2009a). And yet, this has resulted in a new inequality among the States in India: between forward and backward States in terms of the human development index (Sáez, 2002; Tremblay, 2005: 341–342), which, if not adequately attended to, may serve to exacerbate ethnic conflicts within the States.

India has eked out a new model of globalisation-propelled growth, which is integrated with the world economy but not fully – one of the reasons why, despite the recent and the current depression in the world economy, India shows some signs of resilience and does not collapse. India still has a considerable stake in the public sector, although the thrust is more and more on the market. Be that as it may, globalisation has brought fresh challenges to various movements, left and right, old and new, in which the new problems and issues are being articulated. It is also true that while India's globalisation, coupled with some local factors, has served to give birth to Left extremist movements, the mainstream Left in India has been put in a dilemma: it could neither say 'no' to globalisation nor say 'yes'! Electorally, the costs have been heavy for them.[11]

Without a doubt, it is a time of great transformation in India for her economy, structures of governance, and social structures of castes and communities, the latter having found a new space for negotiation, more openly and often brazenly. When that is the case, then the question is what holds India together today and tomorrow? What constitutes India's national identity? As Bhattacharyya (2012: 1–23) has argued, in the changed context marked, among other things, by a shift from the social interventionist state to a free market economy, it now seems difficult to obtain a "nation of citizens in a fragmented society". This question acquires special poignancy in the sense that despite a sustained period of growth for over two decades since the 1990s, two ominous signs, as pointed out by Rudolph and Rudolph, are worth mentioning here. First, India's federal government has been ridden with deficit so that it can no longer run a planned development. Second, the central government's gross assistance to the States' capital formation has declined perceptively: 12 percent in 1990–91 to 9 percent in 1998 (Rudolph and Rudolph, 2008: 119).

How do the governing structures of India adapt themselves to such challenges? Although the particular chapters in the volume deal with this question in greater detail, the general comment that can be made here is that such governing structures have assumed more importance today; they need to reform themselves and adapt to changing scenarios.

Our book is thus the first attempt to examine the impact of India's globalisation and its economic reforms on some vital aspects of India's society, culture, and political institutions. As indicated earlier, the relations between India's reforms, on the one hand, and its society and institutions, on the other, are heavily interdependent. India's globalisation has been responsible for far-reaching changes in Indian politics, its structural arrangements, and political dynamics. Since the early 1990s, when India embraced a certain kind of globalisation, pro-capitalist and market-driven, replacing gradually a welfare state with a neo-liberal one, political economy, the polity and the political processes, began to take on a different meaning. The prevailing structures began to revise themselves in tune with the demands for change, and the old ideas and principles began to acquire negative connotations. India's version of secularism, communal harmony, nationhood, the public space, social justice, and the rights of aboriginal communities came under attack from the forces of the new dispensation. India's globalisation has posed fresh challenges to the political economy, judiciary and the police, democracy, federalism, decentralisation, parliamentary system, and the parliamentary Left.

Protests against this form of globalisation have often taken on a violent character. The challenges have been so devastating that India's parliamentary-federal democratic system is today confronted with the questions doubting the very legitimacy of the system itself.

The chapters that follow critically examine only some important aspects from among the gamut of society, culture, and public institution–related issues which pose challenges to India's reform process. The chapters are arranged in such a way that the questions, as noted earlier, are addressed from the pan-Indian, regional, and local levels.

In the first chapter, Mohit Bhattacharyya analyses the nexus between 'globalisation' and 'decentralisation' against the global and the Indian perspective. Currently, developing countries like India have been actively engaged in the experimentations of 'decentralised' grassroots governance with citizens – men and women – actively participating in the planning, implementation, and evaluation of questions of local development, including local natural resources management. The chapter takes into consideration the paradigm shift from over-reliance on bureaucratic management to what is called 'participatory development management'. Bhattacharyya discusses the impact of the process at length and comments on the prospect, with the concept of 'glocalisation' being pivotal to his discussion.

The contribution by T. R. Sharma provides a critical outline of the various shifts and turns in Indian politics up to the 1990s, which offers, as it were, the background against which the process of globalisation was set. His analysis includes such broad issues as alterations of the federal setup; newer dimensions of caste, communal politics, and regionalism for the purpose of gaining votes and political power, as well as the changing role of the Indian judiciary. Sharma also discusses coalition politics and changes in the structures and functioning of the local political institutions that have shaped Indian politics in the decades after liberalisation.

Providing an overview from the Nehruvian to the post-Nehruvian Indian polity, the chapter argues that the political system remains rather insensitive towards people's needs so long as they remain peaceful and responds only when they turn violent. The chapter highlights the resilience of the Indian political system nonetheless, born of built-in checks and balances that seem to withstand major external challenges such as globalisation.

Lion König, in exploring the analytical category of 'cultural globalisation', stresses the multi-dimensional character of the phenomenon and argues against the conventional understanding that globalisation, at least in so far as culture and cultural identity are concerned, has encouraged monolithisation, with Western cultural achievements dominating the rest. Rather than invoking the spectre of cultural uniformity and a 'communication imperialism', this chapter argues that the processes of globalisation have in the past contributed to a strengthening of cultural identity by preserving cultural artefacts rather than extinguishing them and by introducing techniques which were used for political ends by Indian agents of change. On the basis of a historical narrative that takes into account the introduction of the printing press in India, the use of the same by the Indian nationalists fighting for liberation, the developments in telecommunications, and the role of the government-controlled *Doordarshan* and All-India Radio in nation building, this chapter takes full cognizance of the proliferation of print and electronic media in recent times and their role vis-à-vis India's indigenous cultures and traditions. König comments also on the character of the media in India vis-à-vis endogenous themes and values. König's central argument is that globalisation is hybridising, socially and culturally speaking, thus providing space for the negotiation and articulation of 'hitherto silenced identities'.

In the following chapter, 'Challenges to Democratic Governance in India: An "Unfinished Symphony"', Asok Kumar Mukhopadhyay's subject matter is India's democratic governance. He casts a critical light on the recent shifts in Indian politics and society caused by globalisation, arguing that after achieving some successes and considerable failures, Indian democracy is now witnessing three basic trends which desperately need a successful reconciliation: the aspiration for quick economic gain among the upper classes, the strong demand for inclusive growth, and the rising power of the people's voice. It is argued here that politics in India since the 1990s has hardly produced any optimism in the minds of India's present generation because the government's development policy has been found to be insensitive to people's needs. Thus, this chapter intends to identify and analyse the challenges to democratic governance in India that have emerged since the invocation of the neo-liberal reforms in the early 1990s, and sets agenda points for the future.

The judiciary as a very important organ of the polity assumes added significance in the wake of a country's reforms. The subject acquires special significance in India because it was designed and developed in the days of the Raj (British colonial rule), and then reoriented to serve a different purpose in the post-independence period when the country's leadership embarked on a nation-building project that entailed both capitalism and socialism. Since the early 1990s, when India adopted the reforms programme of increasingly clearing the space for the market, both Indian and foreign, often at the cost of the social welfare state (of whatever variety, extent, and quality, of course), the Indian judiciary faced apparently newer challenges to retune itself, as it were, with the new dispensation.

In Chapter 5, 'The New Political Economy of Judicial Review in India', Mahendra Pal Singh, a leading constitutionalist of India, argues that in the light of the comparative constitutional and the Indian judicial tradition, there is apparently no conflict between the provisions of the Indian Constitution, on the one hand, and the requirements of the New Economic Policy (NEP) in India, on the other, given the written constitution in the common law traditions. In the backdrop of the critical discussion of the evolution of the role of the higher judiciary with respect to law and policy, Singh argues that now that the political ideology of socialism has been removed thanks to reforms in India, the gap between the judiciary and the legislative-executive wings of the state has been much narrowed, and the higher judiciary is more concerned with the liberal foundations of the Constitution and various claims of individuals.

India's reforms, without a doubt, have been the most challenging to the Indian Left of all varieties which has so far stood for various kinds of alternative routes to development based on different versions of socialism. With the decline of 'socialism' in the Soviet Union and Eastern Europe and China predominantly taking on a capitalistic line of development, the ideological basis of the Indian Left has also been dampened. Added to this are electoral compulsions when various promises of pro-poor policies backed up by a social welfare state are most often propagated. In other words, India's globalisation has served to prepare, as it were, the basis for an ideological crisis of the Left as a whole.

It is in this context that Sobhanlal Datta Gupta critically examines the dialectics of the Indian Left and India's globalisation. According to him, the mainstream Indian Left has viewed globalisation on two levels. On one level, despite initial reservations, its technological dimension is appreciated and utilised, while on another level, its socio-economic and cultural dimension has been a target of fierce criticism. Consequently, the anti-globalisation movements have been supported by the mainstream Left. But when the counter globalisation movements, in contesting the homogenising forces of globalisation, focus on a celebration of identity politics and tradition, it does not augur well with the mainstream Left in terms of its political and ideological implications. Consequently, the mainstream Left's position on globalisation is quite different from that of the extreme Left (i.e., the Maoists). The Indian Left, therefore, remains sharply divided on the question of countering the phenomenon of globalisation. This chapter discusses the aforementioned contentious issues for the Indian 'mainstream' and parliamentary Left on the basis of a critical examination of the substantive evidence. In the concluding part of his discussion, Datta Gupta brings in the larger theoretical question of the nexus between modernity and democracy in the context of globalisation and points out rather sharply that in the extremist left paradigm democracy is a casualty in a country where the norms of a constitutional democracy are more or less operative.

Surajit C. Mukhopadhyay has taken up for critical examination a strategically, very significant institution, namely, the police. The author argues that policing in India has swayed between two models in the face of the newly emerging sociopolitical concerns. One model largely retains the historically derived colonial system that relies heavily on armed policing response, and the other has tried several ways, not with any great deal of success, to implement community-oriented policing.

The spate of terrorist attacks within India and the resurgence of extreme Left militancy have greatly strengthened the resolve of the government for an armed police response that draws sustenance from the colonial model of armed policing. This has in some way put the pro-community-oriented police reforms on the back burner and effectively buried the hopes of creating a modern Indian police system that is responsive to community concerns.

In the backdrop of a global trend in militarisation of the police today, this chapter explores the manner in which policing has evolved and is continually evolving in India in tandem with the unfolding of globalised administrative practices in a global polity of nations and draws attention to the widening gap between the state (as represented by the police force) and the citizens. The overall scenario for Mukhopadhyay as far Indian policing is concerned is not optimistic at all.

Rekha Saxena analyses the federal setup in India in the face of globalisation. Two things are of special importance here. First, India's reforms are to take place in India's States. Second, as per the Constitution of India, many of the important functions to be performed for the setting up of industries and companies in the framework of SEZs fall within the competence of the States, so the States cannot be ignored in the reform process. The chapter examines the impact of India's globalisation on India's federal governance and argues that India's reforms have allowed a new space for the States in matters of development and growth, giving birth to what may be called a 'decentralised federalism'. It is further argued that this process has also encouraged the forces for further reorganisation of the Indian federal territory in favour of smaller States for growth and development in which she finds what is called 'pluri-national' moorings.

In Chapter 9, Jhumpa Mukherjee critically assesses the impact of India's globalisation on regional movements and shows with the help of two case studies of the States of Telangana and Uttarakhand how such movements have shifted to a newer articulation of regional autonomy and identity demands. Her chapter contains a discussion of the various phases of regionalism. However, since the 1990s, the character of conflicts has changed. One finds a considerable interweaving of linguistic, cultural, political, economic, and geographic issues in the current wave of demands for regional autonomy, Statehood, and the development of backward regions. In other words, globalisation has resulted in re-creating fresh bases of ethno-regional conflicts in India.

In the final chapter of this volume, Harihar Bhattacharyya analyses India's localities (villages and regions) where the overwhelming majority of citizens live and which therefore hold the real key to the success or failure of globalisation in the country. Enconsced within a critical discussion of the national, international, and institutional contexts, Bhattacharyya's argument is that since globalisation and the socio-economic reforms in India that are linked to it are manifesting themselves within a democratic framework where citizens are increasingly conscious of their rights and entitlements, India's localities can hardly be ignored. He points out that the perception of 'reforms' for India is too limited to take into consideration a society of hierarchies and inequalities, of castes and sub-castes, in which the so-called 'market equality', as propagated by the World Bank, sounds hollow. Bhattacharyya also makes a brief critical reference to the current thrust on (non-governmental) 'governance' for a country where government is needed more for delivery of goods and services for the socially disadvantaged. His chapter focuses on two types of case study materials on how India's rural society is governed nowadays through *panchayats*, and shows the various limits to the realisation of self-governance in the villages – stemming from local party oligarchies (where the political party has sway over them) and social oligarchies originating from various forms of social discrimination currently in vogue.

Seen in its entirety, this collection highlights the most relevant aspects of globalisation, its challenges, and its opportunities in contemporary India. Globalisation is a multi-dimensional process which, in order to become successful, requires the concerted effort of state, market, and society. In the concluding chapter of this volume, the findings of the chapters are summarised, the implications of the findings for further research and policy are assessed, and the challenges that lie ahead are identified. With the change of guards at New Delhi in 2014, the political stability has been assured for the next five years, which provides a congenial environment for development. The concomitant policy shift in favour of reforms may produce far-reaching consequences and hold surprises, good or bad, for a society still struggling with mass poverty, regional disparities, and illiteracy.

Notes

1 Samir Amin would have us believe, though, that globalisation has been the other name for imperialist expansion and consequently has been a devastating process. Thus, post-1492, the conquest of America during the heydays of the mercantilist system of the Atlantic Europe led to the destruction of the Native American civilisations and the Hispanicisation-Christianisation of the indigenous peoples in the Americas. According to him, since 1492 the imperialist dimension of conquest and devastation has remained the dominant ideology of the world system (Amin, 2004: 71).
2 The closely related terms used are 'time-space compression', 'accelerated interdependence', 'shrinking world', and 'global integration'. The 'Global Village' is an older term used to refer to the same phenomenon (Guibernau, 2001: 244).
3 Although Indian culture has been the culture of tolerance for millennia, the forces of Hindutva, represented politically by the Bharatiya Janata Party (BJP) (now in power in Delhi leading the National Democratic Alliance [NDA] government), stand opposed to this synthetic culture of India. The apparent paradox is that in this case the so-called 'developmentalism' goes along with the Hindutva agenda. As Ramakrishnan (2014) has pointed out in detail, the Sangh Parivar (nucleus of the various outfits of the BJP), after having gained political power at the centre, has started pushing its various communal agendas and projects in various spheres of life. (Ramakrishnan, 2014 'Now the Real Agenda', *The Frontline* 31(25): December 26, 4–8. This serves to caution about taking the culture of tolerance too uncritically.
4 Bandopadhyay (2007: 191) has described this market-centric, NGO-oriented, and corporate-style governance, known as 'Good Governance', as the "symbol of re-colonisation and neo-imperialism".
5 Putnam and others (1993) pointed out that from around the twelfth century onwards, many co-operatives that had sprung up in north and central Italy were quite successful in collective action solutions, and thus prepared the bedrock of civic traditions in Italy.
6 Any casual look at the five principles of 'Good Governance' propagated by the United Nations Development Programme (UNDP) will testify that these principles are (1) legitimacy and voice (equal participation of men and women in decision making premised on the freedom of speech and association, and on broad consensus; (2) direction (referring to the strategic vision of leaders and the public on Good Governance and development with due knowledge of the historical, social, and cultural contexts); (3) performance (meaning that all stakeholders are responded to); (4) accountability, that is, decision-makers in government, the private sector, and civil society organisations are accountable to the public and to institutional stakeholders; and (5) fairness, that is, equity and the rule of law (all men and women have opportunities to improve their lot, and the legal framework to be fair and impartial) (Graham, John, Bruce Amos, and Tim Plumptre, 2003. 'Principles of Good Governance in the 21st Century', *Institute on Governance Policy Brief* No.15, August). This set of formal instrumentalities is based on pious hope and optimism, but seems quite hollow in a land of abject poverty, illiteracy, and extremes of gender inequalities.

7 For further details, see, Guibernau, 'Globalization and the Nation-State', in: Guibernau and Hutchinson, 2002: 242–268.
8 See, for further discussion, on the reduced but strategically significant role of the transformed state, Guibernau 2001: 242–269.
9 See especially Chapters 7–11 for an early statement on the issues.
10 The fiasco of the proposed small car factory in Singur (West Bengal) on this contentious issue is now known the world over. The current Trinamool Congress (TMC)-led coalition government in West Bengal is confronted with similar challenges in other areas of land acquisition.
11 In 2011 the CPI (M) conceded defeat in their strongholds in West Bengal, where they had been in power for over three decades, and Kerala, which had installed the world's first elected Marxist government way back in 1957!

1 The globalisation–decentralisation nexus

The Indian predicament

Mohit Bhattacharya

Today, 'globalisation' is a buzz word used in different forums by academics, administrators, and even the non-governmental organisations (NGOs). The phenomenon of globalisation is characterised by increasing integration of the international economy through trade and relatively free cross-border flow of factors of production, as well as new information and communication technologies facilitating speedy exchange of information among nations. The world economy is being restructured not only by technological changes, but also by the geographic movement of all factors of production. This mobility has been changing the location of production and the direction and volume of flows of trade and investment among urban and regional centres as local autonomy units. No government today can ignore or escape the consequences of this phenomenon of globalisation. Expressed slightly differently, the global economy has in recent years been consistently unleashing economic and political forces strengthening both global and local pressures at the expense of the traditional nation-state. Defined narrowly as increasing economic integration of the international system, globalisation has created pressures for relocation of decision-making authority away from the state. There is a change in location or site of governance. States are willy-nilly delegating more responsibility over decision making upwards to supranational institutions or devolving decision-making powers downwards to sub-national political units. For a variety of reasons, there has been a noticeable move towards decentralisation of fiscal, political, and administrative responsibilities to lower-level governments in many countries of the world today, as governments have been seeking new ways of service delivery in response to rising public demands for public services. It has thus become essential to situate the debate on decentralisation in the context of globalisation. Until the mid-1980s the major debate was whether or not to decentralise. Today, this is no longer relevant. The question at the centre of the decentralisation debate today is how to decentralise, or in other words, what are the competing approaches for designing decentralisation?[1]

Globalisation of the world economy has been impelling cities and metropolitan areas to adapt their economic bases and cultures to the needs of international competition since the 1990s and the early years of the present century.

Against this background, many governments in the developing world started experimenting not only with new approaches to development, but also with new political, administrative, and global managements for planning and managing space-specific development programs and projects.

Decentralising authority

At the other end, the increasing interest in 'decentralising' authority for planning and administration to regional and local agencies, local governments, and special-purpose organisations arose from four converging forces:

(1) Disillusionment with the results of central planning and control of development activities during the 1950s and 1960s;
(2) The implicit requirements for new ways of managing development programs and projects that were embodied in growth-with-equity strategies that emerged during the 1970s;
(3) The growing realisation during the 1980s and 1990s that with increasing social complexities, expanding government functions, and the need to respond to globalising influences, it becomes increasingly difficult to plan and administer all development activities effectively and efficiently from the central government level; and
(4) Higher government's positive response to vociferous demands for 'autonomy' and 'participation' in local developmental decisions emanating from localities and regions.

Multiple sources

The contemporary decentralisation discourse is the result of a convergence of multiple ideas. In a sense, it is a revival of the old libertarian view of local institutional development à la Mill, Tocqueville, Bryce, and others. The other impulse can be traced to the contemporary 'democracy wave' sweeping the globe as described by Huntington. Another motivating factor is our increasing concern today about the environment and natural resources conservation which, as revealed by many research evidences, need to be locality and people based. Also, there is now a worldwide shift of emphasis in the governance process from bureaucracy to people, implying a call for a new mode of participative, accountable, and transparent governance. Last, but not the least, even in terms of efficiency, the donor agencies and development consultants are increasingly advocating more and more people-driven, inclusive and participative management of local development projects.

Pranab Bardhan (2002) notes that decentralisation is the rage in today's world. The important reasons suggested by him in this context are loss of legitimacy of the central state and a corresponding belief that decentralisation (as against the predatory state) can bring a range of benefits directly to the local people. It is good to have more intergovernmental competition and attendant checks and balances. In this view, decentralisation is supposed to make government more responsive and efficient. Bardhan also points out that technological changes have made it easier to arrange supply of services in smaller market areas, and that transaction costs are much lower in decentralised operations.

Bardhan and Mookherjee have further elucidated decentralisation in terms of 'participatory democracy'. As they have argued:

> From the standpoint of politics, decentralisation is typically viewed as an important element of participatory democracy that allows citizens to have an opportunity to communicate their preferences and views to elected officials who are subsequently rendered accountable for their performance to citizens. Apart from actual outcomes in terms of policies, their detailed implementation, and their impact on economic well-being, popular participation is valued for its own sake for a variety of reasons. It can promote a sense of autonomy in citizens, enhance social order by promoting the legitimacy of the state, and limit pressures for separatism by diverse regions or ethnic groups.
> (Bardhan and Mookherjee, 2007: 4)

Glocalisation

In this connection, a hybridised term called 'glocalisation'[2] has emerged in many quarters to signify a global-local mix. Marketing departments of many international corporations have come out with the latest slogan: 'Think Globally, Act Locally'. In current usage, glocalisation has come to mean 'the way in which ideas and structures that circulate globally are adapted and changed by local realities', and Roland Robertson conceptualised it as "the universalization of particularization and the particularization of universalism" (Robertson, 1992).

According to the observers of the contemporary phenomenon of globalisation, the global economy has in recent times unleashed economic and political factors, strengthening both global and local pressures at the expense of the traditional nation-state.

Unlike the past fashion of dichotomisation, the decentralisation discourse today is no longer put against centralisation. The debate, instead of continuing with the old refrain of centralisation vs. decentralisation, focuses on the complementary role of the two. The final aim is not to decentralise just for the sake of it, but to ensure good governance.

However, the context of glocalisation has pronounced the dilemma of balancing the contrasting forces of centralisation and decentralisation. Decentralisation is no longer an alternative to centralisation. Both have their respective strong and weak points and should be considered together. The complementary roles of national and sub-national actors should be determined by analysing the most effective ways and means of achieving a desired objective. It does not make much sense to hope for any sort of bottom-line presumption in favour of 'more centralisation' or 'more decentralisation'. Research shows that glocalisation is generating tendencies in both directions of centralisation and decentralisation with the aim of providing good governance and a stable, secure, and just government. It has been argued that centralising tendencies are likely to be more salient in countries like the United States where intrastate authority was initially more decentralised, whereas decentralising tendencies are likely to be more salient in other states that were initially more centralised like China and India. Glocalisation is creating incentives for sub-national governments to play a more active role in attracting foreign investment, promoting trade, providing infrastructure, and enhancing human capital; yet on the other hand, it is promoting various forms of centralisation by increasing the importance of macro-economic policy levers, especially monetary policy and other central bank–sponsored fiscal policies.

Globalisation–decentralisation: pros and cons

In this respect, one has to appreciate that the parallel between globalisation and decentralisation is quite close. The management of decentralisation calls for strong national action, just as the management of globalisation requires strong international interventions. Also, like globalisation, decentralisation carries a potential for large overall benefits, as well as risks and losses for the more vulnerable areas and groups. Internally as well as externally, the intermediate administrative space is shrinking. In the nineteenth-century state, this space was normally occupied by the province, acting as intermediary between the national government and the local ones. The intermediate administrative entity typically enjoyed a double monopoly position: as the sole interpreter of government policy vis-à-vis local governments, and as the sole provider of information and of upward feedback to the centre. With the reduction in economic distance within countries, this state of affairs has been changing.

Usually, decentralisation is looked at from the 'supply' side of the spectrum – how does the centre delegate or devolve powers and resources to decentralised units. But an enduring and sustainable scheme of decentralisation has to be demand driven, or, in other words, there has to be an effective demand from the local populace for a decentralised system of administration which the people would like very much to operate themselves zealously and fairly autonomously. Thus, the understanding of only the national context of decentralisation, as has been the practice in the past, is not enough under today's circumstances. The contemporary situation calls for a greater understanding of the sub-national (especially the local) context. In this respect, however, there is little understanding at higher levels of how policy processes and decision-making take place at the local level. It is an imperative necessity, therefore, to probe into the 'anthropology of the local state' by gathering empirical data on the variations among local political structures, leaderships, and institutions. This would apply to both urban (municipal) and rural (*panchayat*) local government institutions.

The impact of globalisation

The literature on globalisation and its impact on country situations is vast.[3] The theme of the globalisation–decentralisation nexus has also been critically reviewed by many researchers.[4] Regarding the impact of globalisation,[5] there have usually been two major concerns. The first major concern is that globalisation leads to a more iniquitous distribution of income among countries and within countries. In this respect, one has to be more cautious in making any sweeping a priori judgment. As Pranab Bardhan (2007: 3852) comments while comparing the impact of globalisation on Chinese and Indian economies, "It is time for a great deal of caution and reasoned and rigorous empirical analysis before we pronounce judgments on the effects of globalisation on poverty and inequality [. . .]". Bardhan particularly refers to the paucity of "reliable studies" in both China and India, testing "a causal model liking globalization with inequality". Pointing out methodological problems in this regard, Bardhan argues:

> At least two major problems beset the empirical analyst in this matter. One is that so many other changes have taken place in the last quarter century in these two countries, it is difficult to disentangle the effect of globalization from that of other ongoing changes (like technological progress – often skill-biased – demographic changes or regulatory and macroeconomic policies). Secondly, in both countries there are reasons to suspect that economic inequality (or its rise) is underestimated because of a widely-noted fact facing household surveys (in many countries) of large (and increasing) non-response by rich households. It is also difficult to compare China and India, as most of the inequality data that are cited in this context usually are for income inequality for China and consumption expenditure inequality for India (as the NSS does not collect income data). The latter two disparate sources do show a rise in expenditure inequality in both countries in the last decade or so. But, as we have suggested, this rise may be an underestimate, and there is very little analysis as yet to show that this rise is primarily due to globalization.
> (Bardhan 2007: 3851)

Globalisation's second 'discontent' is related to the fear about loss of national sovereignty, and it is not wholly wrong to suggest that today most countries are finding it increasingly difficult to follow independent domestic policies.

The argument that globalisation leads to inequality is based on the premise that since globalisation emphasises efficiency, gains will accrue to countries – particularly advanced Western industrialised countries – which are favourably endowed with natural and human resources. The technological base of these countries is wide and highly sophisticated. Although trade benefits all countries, greater gains accrue to the industrially advanced countries. This is the reason why even in the present trade agreements, a case has been built up under the World Trade Organization (WTO) regime for special and differential treatment in relation to developing countries.

There are two changes with respect to international trade which may work to the advantage of the developing countries. First, for a variety of reasons, the industrially advanced countries are vacating certain areas of production. These can be filled in by developing countries, pursuing a more efficient cost-minimising production process. Second, international trade is no longer determined by the distribution of natural resources. The role of human resources has emerged as more important. Specialised human skills aided by improved information technology are going to be the determining factor in the coming decades.

Productive activities are becoming 'knowledge intensive' rather than 'resource intensive'. Although there is a divide between developing and advanced countries even in this area – sometimes called the digital divide – it is a gap which needs to be bridged. In the context of the globalised economy, developing countries like India have to pursue an imaginative policy of creating and fostering the requisite specialisation to ensure improved productivity and faster growth.

Fears have been expressed that globalisation will lead to widening income gaps within the countries as well. This can happen both in the developed and developing economies. Even within a country, globalisation may benefit differentially those who have the skills and the technology. A higher overall growth rate in an economy can be achieved at the expense of declining incomes of people in 'depressed regions'. If the growth rate of the economy accelerates sufficiently, then part of the resources so generated can be diverted in a planned way to modernise and re-equip people in poorer or lagging regions.

Fear of loss of national autonomy in the pursuit of economic policies in a highly integrated world economy is not without justification. Capital, technology, and skilled manpower are fluid; they will move where the benefits are greater. In a globalised world, as the nations come together in the political, social, or economic arena, there is bound to be some sacrifice of sovereignty. The constraints of a globalised economic system on the pursuit of domestic policies have to be recognised. In fact, domestic policies need to be carefully framed in the new context of a globalised and economically integrated existence.

Greater freedom of movement of skilled manpower has to be ensured. At the same time, appropriate attempts should be made to ensure that India continues to remain a leader in the area of skilled manpower. India can attract greater foreign investment if growth is accelerated with stability. In this context, stability means reasonable balance on the fiscal and external accounts. The country must maintain a competitive environment domestically, taking full advantage of wider market access. Within the extended time granted to the developing countries, selective dismantling of trade barriers needs to be ensured. Wherever legislations are required to protect sectors like agriculture, they need to be enacted quickly. As experts point out, India took a long time to pass the Protection of Plant Varieties and Farmers' Rights Act, 2001. The country must also be active in ensuring that its firms make effective use of the new patent rights on the lines of South Korea and China.

A greater integration of the Indian economy with the rest of the world is unavoidable. It is important that Indian industry be forward looking and get organised to compete with the rest of the world at levels of tariff comparable to those of other developing countries. The government should take advantage of the safeguards available in the WTO agreement to ensure that Indian industries do not fall victim to unfair trade practices.

India is no longer a country producing goods and services for the domestic market alone. Many Indian firms are becoming and have to become global players, and they should be able to meet global competition. Our search for identifying new competitive advantages must begin earnestly.

The revolution in telecommunications and information technology (IT) is simultaneously creating a huge single-market economy, while making the parts smaller and more powerful. What we need today is a road map for the Indian industry delineating the path different industries must take to achieve productivity and efficiency levels comparable to the best in the world. The key to India's growth lies in improving productivity and efficiency in all sectors. This has to permeate all walks of our life. In fact, from the point of view of long-range sustainability, the need for greater efficiency in the management of natural resources like land, water, and minerals has become urgent. In a capital-scarce economy like India's, efficient utilisation of our capacity becomes even more critical. For all this to happen, India badly needs well-trained and highly skilled manpower in different sectors.

The Indian situation

Our primary purpose in this discussion has been to examine the interactions of the twin forces of globalisation and localisation in the Indian context. Since the 1990s, India has embarked upon a neo-liberal development path by offering more space to the market and the private sector as compared to the state. Also, encouragement is being given to other non-state actors such as the NGOs. It needs to be examined how this so-called 'paradigm shift' in governance, with its inherent centralist tone, affects both India's earlier and more recent institutional public policy measures to execute a development agenda through the instrumentality of decentralised and participative local governance.

Everywhere today the central governments are increasingly being squeezed from both above (internationally) and below (internally). The greater mobility of persons and goods, and the ease of communication and information flows have brought a number of public activities within effective reach of local government. A stronger civil society and a more assertive population have been pressurising the centre to 'download' authority and resources to lower levels of governance. The overall trend is that internal decentralisation seems as unstoppable as globalisation.

At the same time, paradoxically, decentralisation of certain functions generates the need for greater 'centralisation' of other functions (or for stronger central supervision). And the need to meet the challenges of globalisation is itself a centralising factor. The vector resulting from the contrasting forces of centralisation and decentralisation will, of course, vary in different countries.

In this context, instead of arguing about decentralisation or centralisation, it is more useful to review the overall geographic assignment of state functions in the light of the new context. The questions that need to be raised are (1) which functions are suitable for greater decentralisation (and which are not); (2) what is needed to make such decentralisation effective; and (3) what modifications in the central government role are necessary to protect the country from the risks and costs of decentralisation?

In supplementation of earlier discussions on this theme, it can be pointed out that the recent interest in different countries in decentralising authority for planning and administration to regional agencies, special-purpose bodies, and in particular representative (elective) local governments can be traced to a number of converging forces. These pressures on the central government to steadily move from the conventional centralised planning and administrative model toward a relatively decentralised administrative format, gave rise to a number of socio-political issues. First, there had been increasing disillusionment with the results of central planning and control of development activities.

Second, during the 1970s, pressures were mounting for the pursuit of a growth-with-equity policy which dictated more decentralised ways of managing development programs and projects, keeping in view the 'felt needs' of the people at the grassroots level.

Third, many authentic field-level studies (Bardhan and Mookherjee, 2006; Baviskar and Mathew, 2009) by eminent national and international experts helped reveal a gross mismatch between the centrally planned projects and the genuine needs of the people at the local level.

Fourth, widespread popular movements at the grassroots level (Narmada Bachhao Andolan, Chipko Movement, etc.) started voicing legitimate demands for participative local planning and implementation – a movement to replace the prevailing system of 'planning for the people' with one of 'planning by the people'.

Fifth, during the 1980s and 1990s there was a growing awareness about mounting social complexities in the domestic sphere and increasing international trade and economic interconnections in a much more globalised world.

Under these circumstances, it becomes increasingly difficult to plan and administer all development activities effectively and efficiently from the central government level. Also, the international agencies like the World Bank and the United Nations Development Programme (UNDP) and many international donor agencies have in recent years been ardent advocates of decentralisation and participative development management, which has been generally characterised as 'engaged governance'. Currently, developing countries like India and African and Latin American nations have been actively engaged in the experimentations of 'decentralised' grassroots governance with local people – men and women – actively taking part in planning, implementation, and evaluation.

Effective governance in an era of globalisation will likely require a regime of intergovernmental relations that allows sub-national governments the autonomy that they need to innovate while finding measures such as the development of efficient labor markets to promote better inter-regional integration. Given the likely population shift to urban areas, the reforms will also increase pressures on already abysmally inadequate infrastructure in most municipal areas in India.

With more and more integration of India's economy with the global economy, India has to compete with other nations for the global market share. From this perspective, the urban centres, particularly the large metropolises in India, have to considerably upgrade their urban infrastructure and improve urban living conditions generally, both for more upscaled skill formation and to attract investments for industry and employment. Urbanisation in India, as elsewhere, is considered an important determinant of national economic growth and poverty reduction. It is characterised by the most dramatic increase in the number of large cities. As per the 2001 population census, 285.35 million people reside in urban areas. This constitutes 27.8 percent of the total population of the country. In the post-independence era, although the population of India has grown three times since the end of colonial rule, the urban population has grown five times. At the current rate of growth, the urban population in India will reach a staggering total of 575 million persons by 2030 CE. As per 2001 estimates, the slum population is estimated to be 61.8 million. The ever-increasing number of slum dwellers causes tremendous pressure on urban basic services and infrastructure. The supply of land for housing has failed to keep pace with the increase in the urban population, resulting in a large number of households without access to basic services, poor housing and proliferation of slums, and widespread poverty.

As part of India's economic liberalisation, in particular the Common Minimum Programme (CMP)[6] of the former United Progressive Alliance (UPA) government at the Centre, the Jawaharlal Nehru National Urban Renewal Mission (JNNURM), the most massive programme on India's planned urban renewal, was launched in 2005. It "aims at improving the living conditions by planned infrastructure development and capacity building of the Urban Local Bodies (ULBs) through a series of reforms at the State and city level". JNNURM is a central government programme that seeks to regenerate sixty-three Indian cities by initiating planned governance reforms and infrastructure development. Planned Central investment of over Rs.500 billion, along with additional State- and city-level funding is expected to inflate the total programme budget to Rs.1,500 billion. This is the single largest government effort so far to rebuild India's sprawling and most complex urban space; it is still too early though to discern its full impact on India's urbanisation.

Much would depend on a successful and speedy implementation of the JNNURM programme with its emphasis on (1) infrastructure upgrade and (b) slums improvement, particularly improving the low-cost housing situation in the interest of the urban poor. Alongside this, local government management capacity needs to be substantially enhanced to plan and effectively utilise the funds that would be made available under the programme. In a competitive situation when India has to expand her market share vis-à-vis China, for instance, the large urban centres need to be developed as potential engines of growth and development.

For their part, local governments – particularly large municipal corporations like Mumbai, Chennai, Kolkata, Delhi, and others – have to strengthen their managerial and resource mobilisation capacity in order to be able to raise funds to meet rising demands for facilities and services and to administer the resources efficiently to achieve time-bound targets. In this context, mention should be made of the local government training institutions that have been set up in many States for municipal- and *panchayat*-level capacity building. In reality, however, due to a variety of reasons, such as a positive State policy for local capacity building, requisite faculty, and other modern up-to-date resources, these institutions have, in general, not been able to live up to their expectations. What has been missing is the kind of dynamism and forward-looking stance that would have made these institutions vibrant forums of 'good local governance' training.

Decentralisation: a futuristic vision

Theoretically, by devolving the provision of government services to 'local' administrative levels whose jurisdiction coincides with the scope of their benefits, decentralisation is supposed to enhance the allocative efficiency of government by improving the match between the levels and mixes of services and local preferences. Successful decentralisation requires striking the proper balance between providing local governments with the autonomy and discretion necessary to accommodate local preferences and ensuring local government accountability to policy objectives.

With the passage of the 73rd and 74th Constitutional Amendments (1992), India took important steps to restructure the incentives of its municipal and rural *panchayat* governments. The amendments required that elections be held every five years to constitute these bodies. There is now a constitutional provision for the establishment of State Finance Commissions (SFCs), along the lines of the Finance Commission of India to make recommendations concerning the distribution of resources between State and local governments. The amendments also added a list of recommended functions for local government in the Eleventh Schedule. Also, the Constitutional Amendment provides for the constitution of District Planning Committees to coordinate planned developmental activities among local governments – both urban and rural.

Despite such laudable national-level efforts though, there has not been a conscious policy reorientation in India toward realigning local government institutions, both urban and rural, with the contemporary globalising trends. In other words, the large issue of strengthening of local government generally and bigger municipal institutions particularly (in view of their special importance in meeting the challenges of globalisation) has not really been posed or firmly grappled with in India at any level of government. On top of it, India's general track record in terms of developing and strengthening the urban and rural local governments has not been very encouraging.

Talking about rural local government – *panchayati raj* – a veteran observer of the field situation has lamented:

> Not only was there an absence of any determined policy to decentralize functions to the *panchayats*, for each new function, the state governments continued to expand their own bureaucracy. Thus, the dream of the votaries

of decentralization of establishing autonomous and self-reliant *panchayats* remained unfulfilled. On the other hand, a bloated bureaucracy, controlled from the State capitals, occupied the administrative space which should have been left to the elected democratic bodies.

(Ghosh, 2000: 36)

An important reason has been the States' poor financial status and consequent refusal or reluctance of State governments to provide the local government institutions with adequate finance. Intergovernmental relations at the level of state-local relationships need to be understood more from the political angle rather than the economic or administrative angle. In situations where different political parties would be in power at the State and the local government (municipal/*panchayat*) levels, State governments have in general been reluctant to effectively 'decentralise' powers and resources. It is common for States to deliberately delay the process of holding local elections, and even supersede municipalities and rural *panchayats* and keep them in suspended animation for political reasons.

In essence, the 73rd and 74th Amendments were designed to rejuvenate the municipalities and *panchayats*, and make them more planning- and development-oriented. To ensure 'social inclusion', special provisions have been made for a substantial representation of women (as high as 50 percent in many States) and the Scheduled Castes and Scheduled Tribes (Baviskar and Mathews, 2009). The recommendations of the SFCs were intended to infuse the local governing institutions with the resources and responsibilities necessary to play an active role in local affairs. In reality, however, the States have often not been very regular in appointing SFCs, nor have the States been very eager to implement the recommendations of the SFCs within a definite time frame.

Politically, the fragmented and clientelistic (Manor, 2012: 13–26)[7] nature of partisan competition has impeded the empowerment of Indian municipalities and *panchayats*. However, the fragmentation of India's party system and the increasing power of regional parties have been contributing to the development of norms that will likely limit the dissolution of State governments by the centre. By increasing the terms and time horizons of States, this will increase their developmental role. However, much depends on the extent of devolution the States are to concede to the sub-State-level governing institutions. Hopefully, this should in turn help develop the local government institutions, assuming the States would be willing to part with their powers and resources.

The incentives shaping the role of Indian sub-national governments have been quite different. State governments, under political compulsions, have been experimenting with 'soft budget' constraints that have inevitably encouraged financial irresponsibility. India's economic reforms have only begun to promote competition that is expected to create a reform dynamic. The personalistic fragmentation of the party system has contributed to a populism that has taken advantage of the soft budget constraints of State governments to promote populist rather than developmental competition. Short-term partisan considerations rather than long-term genuine people's needs fulfillment have often governed local distributive policies with regard to services and benefits. The phenomenon of 'elite capture' of powers and resources has not been uncommon in view of lax and irregular audits, a weak sense of public accountability, and the general absence of any effective local 'ombudsman' type institution (Kerala being an exception).

To cut the long story short, the close interactions between globalisation and decentralisation in India have had their objective manifestations in the economy and the society. But these manifestations have not found adequate response from the top- and middle-level policy framers. As a consequence, decentralisation lives its own limited life under conditions and traditions of a highly centralised polity and the responses to globalisation are to be found, at best, at the higher echelons of governance without much consciously contrived involvement of the decentralised units of governance.

The fact remains that the contemporary manifestation of globalisation and liberalisation represents a certain tendency towards centralisation of economic decision-making This tendency is manifested in multiple ways: in the widening control of a technocracy in economic decision-making, the increasing inaccessibility of the language in which economic policies are made and presented, and the greater space and powers being accorded to multinationals. At the ideological level also there seems to exist a serious contradiction. At both national and international governance levels, a 'marketization economic philosophy' is being propounded and propagated.

> Within this discourse, the tendencies towards centralizing of economic power and decision making are implicitly, if not explicitly, acknowledged. The defined emphasis on decentralization has emerged at the same time, and from the same institutions, which advocate marketization. Thus decentralization – both as an ideology and a set of institutions – distracts attention from the centralizing tendencies of marketization.

It is within this context of an interactive practical-ideological field that any meaningful 'decentralising' policy needs to be worked out.[8]

Conclusion

The contemporary concern about decentralisation in the context of globalisation also has to be viewed in light of the historical trajectories of decentralisation in India. India's track record on the decentralisation experiment has been a mixed one. Urban (municipal) decentralisation goes back to the colonial era when the British colonialists decided to create municipal institutions for a variety of reasons, such as enlisting local people's support for tax raising, politically accommodating the new educated class, and ensuring a modicum of essential civic services in the municipal areas. Because of its relatively long existence, municipal administration, despite all its faults and foibles, has evolved a fairly stable administrative and financial structure. With the growing urbanisation trend – especially the larger 'metro' cities attracting more and more people and creating in the process a large slum population – relatively more attention has been paid by central and state policy planners to their improvement in terms of financial and administrative strengthening. By contrast, the decentralised rural local government is a late starter: the impulse came from the national level, with the inauguration of planned development in the 1950s, to bring about institutional innovation to the aid of 'rural development'. Although the concept of 'democratic decentralisation' was coined at this juncture, 'democracy' was at that time a more ritualistic pronouncement, the real objective being to successfully push through development projects on the ground with people's participation.

In India, decentralisation has to be considered in the context of a multi-level governmental system with the centre occupying, for historical reasons, the most dominant position. As the federal political life process started rolling out, more and more conflicting relationships between the centre and the States developed over the years due to uneven political configurations. This process facilitated the evolution of a more 'shared' federal life, with States receiving relatively more administrative and financial autonomy.

By way of contrast, decentralisation in terms of growth and development of local government – both urban and rural – relied more on central decisions than on the States' 'power-sharing' mood. In fact, the aggressive and assertive State posture vis-à-vis the centre has been impermissible by the States when it came to conceding more and more administrative and financial autonomy to the local government institutions. The latest central move – in terms of the 73rd and 74th Constitutional Amendments – to further 'democratise' and strengthen local government has not been reciprocated equally forcefully by the States. To illustrate this, the constitutional provisions for the formation of three important institutions – Metropolitan Planning Committees, District Planning Committees, and SFCs – have been either side-stepped altogether or casually adopted. In most States, the first two committees are yet to be formed and made operational. The SFCs are not regularly constituted in many States, nor are their recommendations taken seriously enough to implement the constitutional intention of intergovernmental fiscal and financial transfers.

Against this background, relatively poor performance of decentralisation efforts in India needs to be looked at more holistically. The usual trend has been to telescope the multiple arguments into one of two camps.[9] One argument has been that the devolution of fiscal, political, and administrative powers from State to local government has been insufficient. Thus, lack of substantive decentralisation due to the State's reluctance explains the modest impact of decentralisation on the ground. From this perspective, decentralisation is viewed as being at odds with the interests of central (State) agencies and officials whose control of the State apparatus disfavours strengthening of local government.

The second argument has been that decentralisation reforms have been largely of cosmetic value. Real distribution of power and resources in urban and rural areas is dependent on ground-level political realities and the pre-existing pattern of social inequalities created by caste, religion, class, gender, and other forms of social groupings. India's decentralisation efforts, propelled more by central policy drives than States' willing abdication of power in favour of local government, have tended so far to empower the local elites who have been consistently capturing a larger share of public resources, often at the expense of the poor and the socially marginalised.

Where do we go from here? There is no easy answer to this question. As it has been aptly remarked:

> We believe that a number of important issues linking globalization and the movement of authority between central, sub-national, and even super-national governments remain unresolved. We believe that the most important work on the horizon will emphasize the role of political goals and institutions.
>
> (Garrett and Rodden, 2000)

Considered in the Indian context, at a time when the central-level political configurations increasingly point towards messy coalitions, and the centre itself is struggling against heavy odds vis-à-vis the international interests and institutions, as well as the powerful domestic forces, it seems the most unpropitious time for the framing of well-designed decentralisation policies to bolster up local democratic governance which could face up to the challenges of globalisation. From a scholarly point of view, more pointed attention needs to be paid in terms of field-level empirical studies to clearly unravel the global-local interactions in real-life situations.

Notes

1 This point has been ably argued in Sharma (2009).
2 See, in this connection, Khondker (2004).
3 See in this context the *World Public Sector Report: Globalization and the State*, United Nations, New York, 2001.
4 For instance, in the Asian context, see Sung-Bok Kee, 'Administrative Reform in Decentralization and Globalization for the Twenty-first Century', Paper under the auspices of Kon-Kuk University, Thailand.
5 'Responding to Globalization: India's Answer', 4th Ramanbhai Patel Memorial Lecture by Dr. C. Rangarajan, Chairman, Economic Advisory Council to the Prime Minister, Ahmedabad, February 25, 2006.
6 The CMP emphasises the building of infrastructure throughout India for facilitating investment and movement of goods and services. For further details, see Sáez and Singh (2012).
7 See for further details, Manor (2012).
8 The quotations and the broad ideas in this paragraph I owe to the imaginative write-up 'Decentralization and Globalization' (unpublished) by one of my bright students, Supriya Roy Chowdhury, currently on the faculty of ISEC, Bangalore.
9 See in this context Johnson, Deshingkar, and Start (2005).

2 Changes in Indian politics until the 1990s
Issues and trends

T. R. Sharma

Introduction

Analysing the contours of Indian politics until the 1990s in its entirety is a challenging task. Obviously, such an analysis must address numerous issues, including the evolving nature of coalition politics on a national, regional, and local level; co-operative and competitive aspects of federal governance (Bhattacharyya, 2010; Singh and Saxena, 2013; Lobo, Sahu, and Shah, 2014); the rise of the forces of communalism; the reaction of the right, on the one hand, and that of varieties of left extremism (Guha, 2012), on the other. Further crucial aspects to be considered include the nature of the emerging political economy in the era of globalisation; the role of the judiciary, particularly the phenomenon of judicial activism (Krishnaswamy, 2009) where the higher courts have started overseeing *suo motu* the functioning of the executive and, in some cases, even of the legislature, along with the rising incidence of Public Interest Litigations (PILs); the issue of Good Governance; the changing role of institutions of grassroots democracy; and the persistent demands for participative, decentralised strategies of development entailing devolution of powers to rural and urban local bodies (de Souza, 2008: 79–92; Jain, 2005; Baviskar and Mathew, 2009). This enumeration is only illustrative, not exhaustive. These issues will have to be put in broad historical perspective by providing an overview of some of the major structural and operational dynamics of Indian politics witnessed during the last sixty years.

This chapter seeks to provide a prelude to the far-reaching changes, economically and politically, in India since the early 1990s without which the post-1991 scenario will not be intelligible. The overview that is offered here will direct our attention to the setting within which India's globalisation as a multifaceted process had to take shape and work, if at all. The chapter will show that the route the political system, the state, and the economy had been taking since the mid-1960s was already preparing the foundation for the Indian government to make the momentous decision to embrace globalisation in 1991.

A concept of politics

First of all, it must be considered that politics is not autonomous. One may view it as a reflection of social reality. It is possible also to view it as transformative in nature, insofar as it is an interventionist activity of conscious human actors to change the given social, economic, and political reality. It is not a passive force; rather, it is interactive in nature. It reflects social reality even while it is trying to transform that reality. Any analysis must understand this dialectical relationship between politics and society. If we analyse Indian social and political reality, we find a powerful interaction between the positive and negative features of Indian democracy. The colonial rulers à la Kipling and Churchill and the prophets of doom like Selig Harrison (1960) were always sceptical about the capability of poor and illiterate Indians to successfully operate the complex parliamentary democratic institutions of governance. They were of the view that the objective conditions for the functioning of universal franchise and elected and accountable government were not given factors in India. The answer already given by India's remarkable records of democratic governance over the last half-century is that although the political decision making of the high order has remained in the hands of the political elite of sorts, political power has also percolated down the social scale so that mass citizenry takes part in the political process and in decision-making at the lower tiers of the system below the state level. The existing research on the *panchayats*, for example, testifies to that (Baviskar and Mathew, 2009).

Polity, politics, and economic performance

The interrelationships between Indian polity, politics, and her economic performance since independence have been unique. While examining the structures and processes of Indian politics, Rudolph and Rudolph (1987) in their seminal work on India's political economy analysed Indian politics along two axes: the nature of regime, whether democratic or authoritarian, and the nature of polity, which they categorised as 'command polity' or 'demand polity'. According to this four-fold classification, they characterised the Nehruvian era as a democratic regime and a command polity, which implies that the ruling elite was fully committed to the observance of democratic norms and the regime enjoyed full legitimacy and confidence of the ruled. However, as Rudolph and Rudolph observed, this political economic system has had serious flaws too, especially on the economic front:

> When we related periods of command and demand politics and of authoritarian and democratic regimes to investment taken as a summary indicator of economic performance, we found that economic performance was at best marginally and contingently affected by type of politics and type of regime.
> (Rudolph and Rudolph, 1987: 14)

In their subsequent writings, they drew attention to India experiencing bold political changes and yet surviving as a pluralist state, when in the Cold War era, the predication of the country's 'balkanization' and collapse was very much in the air:

> India's pluralist state is not a panacea for living with difference. Civil wars in the Punjab, Assam, and the tribal states in the North-East make that clear.

But the existence of domestic violence in India should not blind us to how successful its federalism has been. The roots of this success lie in the decision taken by India's founders in 1953 and 1960 to reorganize states along linguistic lines, recognizing and legitimizing cultural difference. The result refuted predictions about that cultural nationalism would lead to balkanization or dictatorship.

(Rudolph and Rudolph, 2008: 412)

In sharp contrast to this, the period 1965–75 could be described as demand polity and democratic regime because even though the regime remained committed to democracy, the polity was under serious strain because of rising demands which the system could not cope with, leading to a chaos-like situation in some parts of the country. Political changes since the mid-1960s became very serious and grave, and paved the way for the near cancellation of the democratic façade during 1975–77, that is, the Emergency rule. Because the political changes and their implications are well documented (Bhattacharyya, 1992: 64–85), I will only point out the most fundamental ones here. To begin with, the economic performance of the state was abysmal, with rising prices, rising unemployment, devaluation of the Indian rupee, and a nearly stalled growth process; the situation was so alarming that the fourth Five-Year Plan was stopped ('Plan Holiday'). During 1965–66 and 1972–73, the Gross Domestic Product (GDP) growth rate went down to 2.54 percent from 4.99 percent from the earlier decades (Tendulkar and Bhavani, 2007: 47). At the point of the declaration of the Emergency under Article 352 of the Indian Constitution, the average growth rate since the mid-1960s was around 3 percent (Tendulkar and Bhavani, 2007: 70). In short, Tendulkar and Bhavani (2007) characterised the period in the Indian economy as 'the slow-growth phase'. Although there was employment, most of it was in the white-collar public sectors and not, arguably, very productive. The "overcrowded bureaucracy" co-existed with an economy of "persistent shortages" (Tendulkar and Bhavani, 2007: 48–49). Since the assumption of power at the highest level in the party and in the government in 1966 by Indira Gandhi (Prime Minister of India from 1966 to 1977 and from 1980 to 1984), the polity was experiencing what Morris-Jones called 'creeping authoritarianism'; India experienced a weakening of political institutions as a result of Gandhi's personalisation of powers, both in the Congress party and in the government. The resultant volatility of the political process was evident, among other things, in cancelling out duly elected State governments without any constitutional basis. Zins (1989: 150–189), who did a detailed study of the Emergency, argued that the crisis precipitating the declaration was three-dimensional: "a crisis of hegemony; a crisis of the political system and a crisis of leadership". As he said, "the Emergency was the culmination of a long and deep erosion of this system, a process which had started in the second half of the sixties" (Zins, 1989: 150). In this framework the 1975–77 period would eminently qualify to be called a phase of command polity and an authoritarian regime. As Zins has documented, it was a totalitarian regime that was prohibitive of civil and democratic rights that the Indian Constitution provides for. Although the Emergency was lifted in 1977 and the fresh elections that were held saw a big defeat of the Congress and rise to power of the anti-Congress Janata (1977–80), with the fall of the Janata regime in 1980 and Indira Gandhi coming to power again, the political system became, in fact, more authoritarian, although not totalitarian. She became more reckless in dealing with the opposition, politically and personally.

Post-Emergency, overall, the regime remains democratic and authoritarian. Thus, one way to analyse Indian politics since the 1990s can be in terms of how democratic or authoritarian the institutions of governance are and whether or not the masses consider these institutions to be legitimate. Do citizens feel alienated from the system? Do they tend to fall in line or not? Do they, by and large, abide by the decisions of the state, or do they agitate against them? What is the degree of consent in the political system?

One can look at the changing political canvas over the last sixty years in many different ways. Bhambhri (1996), for example, refers to the 1947–67 period of Indian politics as 'the foundational phase' which had its own opportunities and achievements, as well as its own problems and challenges. The most prominent feature of this phase was that the political leadership at all levels – national, regional, and local – enjoyed a fair amount of legitimacy. However, this was a phase of democracy from above. The voter turnout at the successive elections did not go beyond 55 percent, except for 1984. In fact, there was some element of political apathy and the voters' immediate reference points were caste, community, and region. In that era of 'vote-bank politics', traditional social and cultural hierarchies were considered somewhat legitimate. However, economic development with a focus on basic and heavy industries, coupled with radical land legislation entailing a ceiling on the size of land holdings, abolition of intermediaries, consolidation of holdings, and some progressive social legislation such as the Hindu Marriage Act (1955) and the Hindu Succession Act (1956), although highly contentious, accorded legitimacy to the political system.

In the first phase of Republican India, economic development was the primary concern of the democratic polity. Large dams and steel mills, which Nehru referred to as the 'temples of modern India', as well as the 'Green Revolution' (Frankel, 2005), were some of the flagship programmes of this phase, which was a very challenging period for democratic nation-building and modern state formation. It needs to be noted and appreciated that India was following an uncharted and untested path of development where the main challenge was to reconcile the apparently irreconcilable: a mixed economy, a traditional society, and a modern democratic polity. It was a phase when the contradictions had to be tackled and resolved and where the resolution of one contradiction gave rise to another (Bhambri, 1989: 73–87).

1967–1990: Trends

The period between 1967 and 1990 can be categorised as the 'consolidation phase'. It was a period of crises and challenges to Indian democracy. During this phase, Indian democracy became increasingly assertive, which changed the quality of the Indian voter. All this posed new challenges to political institutions, political leadership, and the political parties. The Indian voter abandoned political apathy and voter turnout ranged between 60 and 75 percent, figures which mark the successful operation of universal adult franchise.

Table 2.1, adapted from Mitra and Singh (2009), shows that since 1952 not only has the total number of voters in India increased, but voting turnout has also increased.

In that second phase of post-colonial Indian politics, democracy from above became a thing of the past. Instead, democracy now marched into the very essentials of social life of India, and politics became volatile with all sorts of challenges to leadership. Social structures, values, and ways of life got increasingly disturbed and destabilised. The authority of caste leaders and clan elders came under strain, and a new political and social discourse emerged. In the economic sphere, the thrust was on self-reliance, export promotion, and import substitution. The phase between 1967 and 1990 was also a period when the working class became increasingly restless, assertive, and demanding. They were searching for solutions which the system failed to provide. Overall, this was a phase of democracy from below (Alam, 2013); but democratic politics also reached a new low due to an increasing nexus between politicians, criminals, and big business. Democracy was defiled by the increasing role of money and muscle power in (electoral) politics. Also, voters began to feel electoral fatigue, with politicians becoming more self-centred. Rajni Kothari (1989) has provided a very apt analysis of this peculiar sickness of the Indian polity. He rightly argues that there was a decline of democratic temper and an erosion of institutional space. The Westminster model had by then lost its

Table 2.1 Popular participation in the Indian parliamentary elections (1952–2004)

Year	Votes Polled (in millions)	Turnout (in percent)
1952	79.1	45.7
1957	92.4	47.7
1962	120.6	55.4
1967	153.6	61.3
1971	151.6	55.3
1977	194.3	60.5
1980	202.7	56.9
1984	256.5	64.1
1989	309.1	62.0
1991	285.9	55.9
1996	343.3	57.9
1998	373.7	62.0
1999	371.7	60.0
2004	389.9	58.1

Source: Adapted from Mitra and Singh, 2009: 296.

relevance because it was based on an atomistic view of the individual which is out of sync with the deeper and perennial synthesis of Indian life rooted in the caste system (Kothari, 1989). A similar view is expressed by A. S. Narang (1996), in whose view political mobilisation in India is taking place under the impact of universal franchise, and state planning entails the transformation of an agrarian society. It involves building a new state in an old society, a process which impinges on the traditional value system, religious beliefs, the structure of social groupings, economic arrangement, and political institutions. In India, democratic development is not a function of economic modernisation. While in the West, industrialisation led to the development of democracy, in India, the development of democracy (mass political participation) arguably led to economic modernisation.

This has led to rising expectations which the system has not been able to meet. Consequently, there are heightened social tensions, increasing ethnic assertions, and protest movements. The phase from 1967 to 1990 also witnessed a spate of new social movements which were gender-based or oriented towards marginal groups, human rights, or environmental issues (Shah, 2004; Mohanty and Mukherji, 1998; Jayaram, 2005; Shiva, 2005; Guha, 2000).

Party system changes

Yet another way of analysing changes in Indian politics can be in terms of the nature of the party system. Rajni Kothari has termed the 1952–67 phase the 'one party dominance phase' (Kothari, 1964; 1974). It was a phase when the Congress party clearly outdistanced all other political parties, singly and jointly. The 1967–77 decade witnessed the rise of numerous State-level political outfits organised, more often than not, along cast-, communal, or regional lines. The 1977–80 period indicated that the polity was moving towards a two-party system. However, the disintegration of the Janata Party in 1980 and the emergence of the Bharatiya Janata Party (BJP), the Janata Dal, and other splinter groups amply demonstrated that the party system in India was still in flux. Sridharan (2011) has labelled the 1952–67 phase the period of 'Congress hegemony'; the 1967–85 phase saw polarisation of State party systems, whereas the phase from 1989–2009 witnessed the fragmentation of party systems.

This fragmentation occurred when certain individuals who failed to get their 'due place' in the party hierarchy, or failed to get a party ticket for elections to the State legislature or the Union parliament joined the rival party or set up a new political party. In the face of this fragmentation were the rapid rise of the BJP in the 1990s and the steady decline of other non-Congress parties, including the Left, which seemed to show that a two-party system was still a distant possibility. However, the developments of the last ten years leave no doubt that the regional parties have not only come to stay, but have also acquired the strength to significantly determine the contours of national politics. One can clearly see that during the last decade the forces of communalism, regionalism, right reaction, and left extremism have consolidated their base in different parts of the country. How does one explain this phenomenon? Today, we do not have the one-party dominance of the 1950–67 phase, nor do we see the embryonic two-party system of the later decades; rather, we witness the emergence of two broad alliances: the United Progressive Alliance (UPA) and the National Democratic Alliance (NDA), coalition governments consisting of a cluster of several political parties of different hues and colours. Each alliance is led by one dominant partner, the Indian National Congress (INC) and the BJP, respectively, who clearly outweighs all its other constituents put together. Repeated desperate attempts to forge a non-Congress and non-BJP third alternative have hit roadblocks, primarily because there are several constituents ready to join but none is in a dominant position to legitimately claim leadership; rather, each of them aspires to be the leader of the alliance, a claim which the other constituents are not ready to concede. In fact, every such attempt becomes a battle of wits where each contender tries to outmanoeuvre the other, thus creating a trust deficit, with the effect of the alliance falling apart even before it is born. Evidently, the underlying reason is that there is not even a semblance of ideological affinity among them (Saez and Adeney, 2005; Saez and Singh, 2012).

Political changes since the 1990s

The 1990s witnessed two major developments on the international plane which have posed new challenges for Indian politics on ideological grounds as well as on the politico-economy plane. One was the disintegration of the socialist camp followed by the break-up of the mighty Soviet Union, thus putting an end to bipolar world order; the other was heightened globalisation. As a consequence, the Indian polity underwent an ideological swing to the right. In addition, the rising threat of terrorism and the compulsion to meet the increasing energy demands of the country precipitated the process of the Indian polity gravitating to the right, despite vociferous opposition from the Indian Left.

On a domestic level, there has been a gradual withdrawal from welfare policies and disinvestment in the public sector. However, the political system has to periodically buy legitimacy for itself and consequently it hesitates to fully embrace full-scale privatisation. In order to soften the rising dissent and tackle social unrest which inevitably arises due to widening disparities in different spheres, the system is trying to ensure inclusive growth, but due to contradictory pressures and the logic of capitalism, the economy is caught in a quagmire. Several disadvantaged groups are agitating, sometimes in a violent manner, for affirmative action (Mitra, 1999; Mitra and Lewis, 1998). There is no doubt that the forces of globalisation have changed the face of the Indian polity, but due to democratic pressures from below and the compulsions of electoral democracy, the state does not have the required autonomy to pursue the path of reforms smoothly. Taking note of these developments Rudolph and Rudolph (2008: 108–119) have reworked their earlier formulation. The Indian state is no longer an interventionist state, as it was until the 1980s; now it is much more of a merely regulatory state.

The second major challenge to the polity with long-term implications emerged in the wake of the demolition of the Babri Masjid on 6 December 1992 by the forces of Hindutva which have polarised the country along a secular/communal binary. In short, during the 1990s the basic issues of Indian democracy became ideology-centred. The ruling elite gradually compromised its commitment to socialism, equity, and distributive justice. Caste, religion, and regional chauvinism, along with social exclusion (Thorat, 2007; Bhattacharyya et al., 2010), emerged as the new strategies of winning elections and holding on to political power. The vulnerable strata of society began to organise and articulate their interests to have its share of the political cake, by democratic means if possible, and by other means, if necessary. This amply manifested itself in the rise of the Bahujan Samaj Party[1] (Pai, 2002), on the one hand, and that of the Maoists, on the other. Newer challenges have surfaced due to widening inequalities which are manifesting themselves today in the opulence of the few, the rise of a new class of billionaires, and the structurally visible skyscrapers and shopping malls, on the one hand, and the slums and 'slum dogs', on the other.

Here it seems relevant to ask the question of what the overall balance sheet of the recent phase is. Probably, one can say that the Indian polity has achieved one important goal: it has made India a politically conscious society. There is a general tendency to bemoan political apathy, but the fact remains that the Indian voter has become more discriminating, and consequently the vicious circle of incumbency does not operate with predictable patterns as it used to earlier. Today, performance – real or perceived – features significantly, and factors like accountability and transparency and the issues of development have started weighing with the electorate. Now it is also being realised that corruption in high places is bound to lead to a loss of faith in the governing institutions and to create serious crises of legitimacy. Measures like RTI[2], RTE,[3] and food security have found their place in a system which is struggling to sustain legitimacy. There is a growing demand from below for comprehensive human security, and several human rights organisations are demanding more public space for citizens. The political system is also under pressure to protect and promote the collective rights of communities, particularly the rights of the tribals, *dalits*, women, and physically and mentally challenged, as well as homosexual people. There is now also pressure for greater power sharing between the centre and the States, and between State governments and the grassroots institutions of governance.

Among the achievements of the last two decades, one can refer to the deepening of democracy which is evident in the greater representation of the marginalised and the disadvantaged. At the same time, one can easily notice several negative features that have emerged in recent decades. Increasing incidences of social violence, institutionalised caste hatred, communal violence (Kohli, 1990), foreign-sponsored terrorism, and rural indebtedness leading to farmer suicides (Patnaik, 2004; Vaidyanathan, 2006) are some of these features, among many others. The benefits of economic growth remain concentrated in urban centres and have not reached the rural areas in sufficient measure. Whatever benefits have reached the rural areas have not reached the target groups for which these were intended. Even the 'trickle-down effect' and 'percolation theory' have not accrued the expected dividends.

However, one can also notice that the representative character of Indian democracy is becoming more diverse and wide-ranging. Several socially disadvantaged groups, which had previously only been peripheral, are becoming more and more assertive, which is indeed an encouraging sign for the Indian democracy. However, despite this deepening of democracy and the democratic upsurge from below, the gap between what the political parties, be they national or regional, and political alliances, be it NDA or UPA, promise and what they actually deliver is widening. Because of several measures like the Right to Information (since 2005); growing transparency in governance; and the role of the media, particularly the electronic media, sting operations, and investigative journalism, the involvement of politicians and top bureaucrats in corrupt and unethical practices entailing scams of massive proportions have come to light. The incidence of corruption in the elected urban and rural local bodies is no less, even though the amount siphoned off may be much less. All these developments have prompted some non-governmental organisations (NGOs) and individuals, such as civil society leader Anna Hazare, to resort to mass agitations and hunger strikes, demanding post-haste creation of appropriate statutory mechanisms to cleanse politics of corruption and scams and to retrieve the huge sums of black money clandestinely deposited in foreign banks. This has also resulted in engendering a widespread feeling of dismay and anger among the people in general and the educated unemployed youth in particular. However, one needs to discern the target of this anger and dismay. Does it amount to a loss of faith in democracy as a form of government? This seems rather unlikely. After all, during the Vidhan Sabha (State Assembly) elections in five States in early 2012, there was a far greater turnout of voters than earlier. Thus, people's trust in democracy does not seem to have declined. Is this anger and dismay directed at the political parties and the institutions of governance? Apparently, the people's anger is directed at corrupt politicians, irrespective of their party affiliation. One notices, though, some dissatisfaction with political parties and politicians as vehicles of representation and governance. Paradoxically, voters feel that parties are essential for the functioning of democracy, but do not seem to trust them to make democracy work ('State of Democracy in Asia: A Report', 2008). In a nutshell, one can say that democracy as a form of government enjoys considerable legitimacy in India and so do the political parties and the institutions of governance: the legislature, the executive, and the judiciary. Of course, masses feel deceived due to non-delivery or late delivery of various public utility services and, to some extent, due to the non-fulfilment of promises made to them by the political parties in their election manifestos and election speeches.

In fact, democracy in India is more vibrant today than ever before. Given the present-day scenario, one can say that the evaluation of Indian democracy and its major institutions by the Western (mainly the British and the US) prophets of doom during the 1960s and 1970s seems out of place today. As Yogendra Yadav has argued, this negative view of Indian democracy emanated because of some of the reigning superstitions of our times: the idea that there is a universally valid institutional design of liberal democracy, the suggestion that a set of best political practices can and should be replicated all over the world, the theory that the idea of democracy can be reduced to a standard 'checklist'. Once it is recognised that there is no universally applicable and valid package of political reforms or a model of democracy, it follows that a reasonable starting point for thinking about political reforms has been reached. We can thus take the next step of working towards an agenda that is anchored in time and space, is context-sensitive, takes the logic of politics as integral to thinking about institutional design, and is conscious of the differential consequences for different social groups (Yadav, 2011).

Writing in the same vein, Zoya Hasan (2011) has argued that "the most striking feature of India's party politics is that it does not fit neatly into any of the theories of liberal democratic politics or the conventional categories of party systems known to the West" (Hasan, 2011: 241). It may be pointed out here that thirty years ago, the present author had forcefully asserted that Indian politics could only be understood in the context of the country's unique social structure, colonial heritage, the type and nature of the freedom struggle, aspiration and expectations of individuals and groups, the nature of the elite that came to power after independence, and the availability of resources to satisfy the needs of the people (Sharma, 1984). It was further argued that India's political institutions, structures, and processes could not be understood simply in the context of theoretical stereotypes borrowed from the West. Attempts to compare the performance of the nascent political institutions of independent India with their century-old counterparts in the Western liberal democracies were seen as methodologically questionable. Even while agreeing with Morris-Jones that India was not Uganda, not even Ghana, and that its political experience distinguishes it quite clearly from Bangladesh and from its own twin Pakistan, I had joined issue with him by pointing out that by the same logic, India was not Great Britain or the United States. The point is that if most of the new states of Asia and Africa have had a history of illiberal regimes and India is different from them as Morris-Jones' argument implies, then India also does not have a very rich experience of a liberal regime as the Western societies do, nor does its experience stretch over several centuries as does that of the United States or Britain. Hence, India's experience of democratic governance cannot be measured by the yard stick that applies to institutions of democratic governance in the West. Thus, the question arises as to what the reference point is in terms of which the political institutions and their performance ought to be measured? The point to be made here is that history bears testimony to the fact that each component institution of the liberal democratic model of the West had to struggle hard to strike roots and gain acceptance and legitimacy in Western societies. In Britain, the Magna Carta, the civil war which put an end to absolutism, the Glorious Revolution of 1688, and the various Reform Acts of the nineteenth and twentieth centuries are some of the major milestones in the evolution of the Westminster model. The United States had to fight a civil war to ensure the survival of the republic and its liberal emancipatory agenda. Democratic institutions in India, however, are still trying to come out of their initial teething troubles.

Conclusion

It needs to be noted that the negative evaluation of Indian democracy during the 1960s and 1970s has gradually given way to a more realistic and matter-of-fact evaluation in recent years. For example, there has been a marked shift in the assessment of Indian democracy by Atul Kohli, who, in 1990, lamented the growing crisis of governability in India (Kohli, 1990), to a more moderate one some time later when he ascribed the success of India's democracy to the twin processes of institutionalisation and accommodation. Recently, Kohli has given a still more favourable assessment of Indian democracy, which is very aptly summed up in the title of his edited work, *The Success of India's Democracy* (Kohli, 2001). In this volume, Kohli holds the view that the success of democracy in India defies many prevailing theories that stipulate preconditions for the success of democracy anywhere and everywhere. He argues, and rightly so, that even if one concedes the feeble capacity of India's democratic state to alleviate mass poverty, its poor governance, and its failure to ensure universal primary education, one still needs to celebrate its success in institution-building. Kohli argues that among the poor countries of the world, India stands out as the most significant country that has successfully harnessed its urge towards self-government into a functional democracy. Explaining the success of democracy in India, James Manor argues that it hinges on the crucial fact that relations between the centre and the States have usually remained within manageable limits (Manor, 2011). He further argues that if the balance of power has gradually shifted from the legislature and executive to the judiciary in recent years, it is mainly because the Union government did not have a two-thirds majority in both Houses of Parliament to override the Supreme Court's judgements, nor did it have the assured support of half of the State legislatures, which is a necessary stipulation to carry out major constitutional amendments to ensure the supremacy of the legislature over the judiciary. Here one also needs to remember that the system of checks and balances which is built in the very design of the Constitution is a way of ensuring that acts of omission and commission and excesses and infirmities of one organ of government can be complemented and negated, as the case may be, by another. As such, the check that the Supreme Court exercises on the Parliament and the Cabinet should not be a subject of concern; rather, it needs to be welcomed, at least so long as its objective is to safeguard the basic structure of the Constitution. Scholars ought to remember that it is often said that the Supreme Court of the United States has become the third chamber of Congress with more power than the other two. Moreover, the onerous duty of the Supreme Court, more implied than express, is to safeguard the lives and liberties of the people, as well as the constitutionally guaranteed powers of the States.

Notes

1 Founded in 1984 by Kanshi Ram, the Bahujan Samaj Party is the most important *dalit*-based party in Uttar Pradesh. During the 2007 elections to the Uttar Pradesh State legislature, it won an absolute majority and came to power in the biggest State in the country. However, in 2012, it lost to the Samajvadi Party.

2 The Right to Information Act, 2005, was enacted on 15 June 2005, and its preamble states that its objective to "provide for setting out the practical regime of right to information for citizens to secure access to information under the control of public authorities in order to promote transparency and accountability in the working of every public authority" (Mukhopadhyay, 2007: 99).
3 The Right of Children to Free and Compulsory Education Act was enacted on 1 April 2010 by the Indian Parliament. This has been given the force of the same legal status as the right to life provided by Article 21A of the Indian Constitution. Every child in the age group of six to fourteen years will be provided eight years of elementary education, the cost of which shall be borne by the state.

3 Cultural globalisation in India
Towards a 'third space'

Lion König

Introduction

Globalisation is the spectre that has been haunting the self-proclaimed saviours of 'indigenous culture' and the defenders of 'original and authentic ways of life' for the past decades. The term 'globalisation' has become synonymous with 'Westernisation', and more precisely 'Americanisation', connoting the alleged economic and cultural domination of the United States and the ensuing forcible coordination of lifestyles along a monolithic US model. Brand names like Coca-Cola and McDonald's have become the omnipresent spearheads of globalisation, so much so that terms like 'Coca-colonization', used in Latin America in the 1970s to refer to the policies of multinational corporations, which were seen as harbingers of US modernisation (Pieterse, 2010: 342), and 'McDonaldization' (Ritzer, 2010) have been coined to illustrate the widely held belief that globalisation is essentially a culturally imperialist undertaking marked by predictability, uniformity, and standardisation,[1] whereas the "Disneyfication of culture" (Lieber and Weisberg, 2002: 281) denotes the replacement of culturally diverse and vibrant spheres with an infantile, one-size-fits-all culture.

In this chapter, however, an attempt is made to debunk the myth of an economic globalisation that originates from the United States, as it is argued that globalisation is not a phenomenon that emerged in the late twentieth century, but a process which has been ongoing for millennia.[2] Between 500 BCE and 200 CE, some two millennia ago, the Roman Empire was the first military and political power that was global within the boundaries of the world as the Romans knew it, Hellenic culture reached India, and the Han Empire established contact with India (Modelski, 2003: 55). However, because these interactions between countries and peoples remained for a long time "intermittent, indirect, nonpolitical, and not yet truly global" (Modelski, 2003: 55), the beginning of the period of globalisation is dated to about 1000 CE, with the worldwide political order of the Muslim world, which ranged from Spain and Morocco, through Damascus, Cairo, and Baghdad, to Persia and the north of India (Modelski, 2003: 55). The information revolution, satellite television, and other additions to the audio-visual media arsenal of countries all over the world are only the latest, and therefore the most visible, additions to our age of heightened, increased, or, in Douglas Kellner's terms "accelerating" globalisation (Kellner, 2012: 3). Globalisation thus should not be seen as an instrument to achieve cultural domination of the West over the East or the developed over the developing world through economic-political homogenisation; rather, it is a process which has to allow for diversification and adaptation to local circumstances in order to be successful. It is not a one-way development, but a multi-polar phenomenon, which can only be fully comprehended if the analysis takes into account multi-directional flows of actors, goods, ideas, and institutions.

Generally, 'cultural globalisation' is discussed in terms of three major paradigms: cultural differentialism, cultural convergence, and cultural hybridisation. The first paradigm entails lasting differences between cultures and these differences explain why even though on the surface changes occur, at their core, cultures remain largely unaffected by globalisation. The second paradigm is based on the idea that because of the various processes of globalisation, cultures are converging, that is, changing towards increasing sameness; and the third one, cultural hybridisation, emphasises the mixing of cultures as a result of globalisation and the production of new and unique hybrid cultures that are not reducible to either the local or the global culture. Rather, new and distinctive hybrid forms are produced that indicate continued heterogenisation rather than homogenisation (Ritzer, 2010: 340).

Cultural globalisation as an analytical unit is discussed here against the background of India, which has seen vehement protests against global cultural influence and thus serves as a case study to explore the ways in which the form and content of global cultural artefacts are negotiated between global producers and local consumers. Indian modernity as the result of an encounter with the West is an established notion. P. C. Joshi (1989) starts his analysis of culture, communication, and social change in India with a discussion of D. P. Mukherji's *Modern Indian Culture* (1947) wherein he outlines that "what is called modern Indian culture was shaped by historical forces and processes, the most important being the economic, political and cultural impact of the West" (Joshi, 1989: 1). India, which is itself a producer of global culture, illustrates the blurring of boundaries in a globalised world and thus holds explanatory value for larger questions of identity formation and -assertion in the age of increased globalisation.

Globalisation: a multi-dimensional concept

Globalisation is an umbrella term which, strictly speaking, defies definition. It is used to describe the increased economic, political, social, and cultural processes of exchange between corporations, states, civil society organisations, and individuals which enforce greater interdependence and can lead to adaptation of economic, social, political, and cultural practices. It is a continuously dynamic process of increasing interaction among these agents of change. The metaphor of the 'global village' (McLuhan and Fiore, 1968) is but one way to describe the outcome of this interaction: supra-national organisations, multi-lateral trade agreements, and fast and cheap modes of transport which make even the most distant places easily accessible, combined with an information technology so sophisticated that the need to embark on actual journeys to these places has, in many cases, been replaced by digital voyages. All these factors have given rise to the notion of the world as a village where people can see each other, talk to each other, and send and receive information within seconds at any given point in time.[3]

The digital generation of information and its virtual exchange is a phenomenon of the late twentieth and early twenty-first centuries, and because it is a strong component of what is commonly understood by globalisation, there are tendencies to equate the advent of globalisation with the 'information revolution'. This, however, is misleading because globalisation is a process which is almost as old as the globe itself. Even prior to the formation of nation-states, people have crossed borders and continents in an effort to explore, discover, trade, and learn.[4] These efforts have led to the exchange of goods, people, and information, all of which in turn have acted as motors of innovation and change. Media have always been a substantial part of this change, and media development has triggered broad changes with long-lasting effects. Elaborate networks of communication existed at the time of the Roman Empire, in Renaissance Europe after the invention of the printing press, and increasingly in the nineteenth century, when underwater cable systems were established, international news agencies and international organisations were founded, and communication networks were systematically organised on a global scale, including a telegraph link between India and Britain which was completed in 1865 (Thompson, 2003: 247–248).

A watershed in media development and ensuing global communication was the invention of the printing press with moveable type by Johannes Gutenberg in 1457. From Germany, the technique spread to various places in Europe, until it reached India on 6 September 1556. Jesuit missionaries brought the printing press first to Goa, from where it was taken to various other parts of the country as an important tool to accelerate the process of proselytisation.[5] Gutenberg, however, would not have been able to invent his world-changing mechanism without paper, for which credit goes to ancient China.[6] The example of the printing press in India thus provides insights into two very significant features of globalisation. First, it emphasises the fact that globalisation is circular rather than linear and multi-dimensional rather than one-dimensional. Globalisation is a cultural phenomenon, and hence comprises a mosaic of diverse and seemingly contradictory elements that contribute to an inherent dynamic. It can therefore only be conceptualised as an interaction which neither has a clearly locatable origin nor a definite endpoint. Second, the example shows that globalisation requires agency and this agency can lead to significant twists, turns, and setbacks in the non-linear process of globalisation. In 1780 the printing press enabled the Irishman James A. Hicky to publish India's first newspaper, the *Bengal Gazette*, which he used to criticise and personally attack the first Governor-General of India, Warren Hastings (1773–85). Hicky was arrested in 1781, prosecuted and imprisoned for 19 months in 1782; his printing press was confiscated and the *Bengal Gazette* ceased publication (Priolkar, 1958: 105). One hundred fifty years later, the Indian independence movement used the press very efficiently to express discontent with the status quo, propagate a vision for the future, and garner support for the ultimate aim of independence from Britain. Mahatma Gandhi and Jawaharlal Nehru, the leaders of the movement, who were both educated in England and thus products of a globalised education, were also gifted journalists and prolific writers who edited their own newspapers as effective instruments in their common cause. In this light, globalisation, with its flow of goods, people, and ideas, can be seen as leading to rupture and change of world politics rather than to a continuation of dominance, a process which Douglas Kellner has described as "globalisation from below", with marginalised individuals and social movements using the institutions and instruments of globalisation to further democratisation and social justice (Kellner, 2012: 16).

Throughout world history, the media did and do play a crucial role in the process of globalisation. Ever-changing forms of media, from cave paintings to the Internet, have accelerated the speed in which we exchange information, but more importantly, they are the determining carriers of meaning through which we perceive globalisation and its effects on our daily lives. The extent to which globalisation with its more recent phenomena, such as truly 'global' media and consumer items, has affected India's cultural sphere is subject to analysis in the following section.

The Indian media in a globalised world: risks, opportunities, and strategies

At the beginning of the twenty-first century, India's media sphere is one of the most diverse and vibrant ones in the world. Newspapers, television channels, radio stations, and movies are constantly proliferating in umpteen languages and with ever-growing audience support. Indian and foreign companies are competing in a media market which already is one of the largest in the world, but still holds vast potential. The market, which is so attractive now to media entrepreneurs from all over the world, only emerged in the 1990s when satellite television came to India and the hegemony of the state-owned public broadcaster Doordarshan ended. Until 1991, and in legal terms until as late as 1995,[7] Indian viewers could only watch one television channel, Doordarshan. Between 1995 and 2007, India experienced the rise of more than 300 satellite networks,[8] more than 50 of which were 24-hour satellite news channels, broadcasting news in eleven different languages (Mehta, 2008a: 6).[9]

These satellite channels are carriers of media globalisation in the form of a one-to-one export of entertainment formats from the West to India. TV shows like *Kaun Banega Crorepati?*, an adaptation of the UK game show *Who Wants to Be a Millionaire?*, aired in India in 2000 and since then, the rest of the world learnt about its existence in India through the award-winning film *Slumdog Millionaire* (2008). In 2004, the UK show *Pop Idol*, after having inspired *American Idol* in the United States and variants of the show in forty-two other countries, found its Indian avatar, *Indian Idol*. *The Bachelor*, a dating show which was first broadcast in India in 2009, and the cooking show *Master Chef* are other examples of media imports to India. Contrary to the argument of critics of the globalisation process, these shows have not abolished cultural particulars, but have been used by the Indian recipients as a forum for identity articulation. Mehta (2008a) shows how the casting show *Indian Idol* acted as a catalyst for bridging cultural divides. In 2007, two young men, Prashant Tamang and Amit Paul, from Darjeeling and Meghalaya, respectively, entered the final round of the show. In Paul's case, this led to a massive, state-wide campaign for his victory, which was led by the Chief Minister and in which State legislators competed with each other to donate public telephone booths to facilitate voting (Mehta, 2008a: 3). The Bengali Paul was seen as the perfect medium to connect the predominant Khasi tribes of the State with the non-tribals after two decades of ethnic conflict since 1979 (Mazumdar, 2007, cited in Mehta, 2008a). A UK-designed entertainment programme broadcast in India thus not only had an impact on identity assertion and political mobilisation, but also through its country-wide appeal made a northeasterner for the first time "a national figure in popular culture" (Mehta, 2008a: 3), thus bridging the divide between the northeast and the 'mainland'.

Another instance of global media as a liberating device is given by Shahani (2008) who in an ethnographic study of a website, a newsgroup, and physical events around a homosexual community in Mumbai shows that

> . . . all the respondents felt that globalisation [. . .] had had some impact on their lives and on the larger gay scene at large within India. Many respondents praised the international media that were available in India post 1991, as the harbinger of a liberal worldview towards homosexuality.
> (Shahani, 2008: 234–235)

For at least two of the respondents, globalisation presented an opportunity for the young Indian gay movement to learn from the legal, media, and social battles already fought in the West. Thus, with globalisation, the determination to find one's identity and express it also rises (Shahani, 2008: 235).

Although identity articulation by means of the "localized appropriation of globalized media products" can help individuals to take a distance, to imagine alternatives to dominant narratives, and to question traditional practices (Thompson, 2010: 257), these global media influences are more often than not a source of tension and potential conflict. The agitations against cultural imports like Valentine's Day, the Miss India and Miss World Pageants, and the infamous burning of chickens in front of the first Indian outlet of the fast food chain Kentucky Fried Chicken (KFC) are expressions of anxiety and resistance against a perceived global danger which has set out to destroy indigenous ways of life. However, as the ongoing controversy over allowing foreign direct investment (FDI) in retail in India shows, partisan politics is often the driving force behind such agitation. Bharatiya Janata Party (BJP) politician Uma Bharti's threat to "set fire to the first Wal-Mart store whenever it opens here, regardless of the consequences" (Times of India, 2011), which was voiced during the debate over permitting big retailers to enter the Indian market, and Shiv Sena founder Bal Thackeray's statement that he will not allow KFC food to be served in Maharashtra (Aiyar, n.d.), show that the resistance against processes of economic and cultural globalisation is often orchestrated by Hindu nationalist groups for whom anti-Westernism in general, and anti-Americanism in particular, is an identity-constituting factor and part of the political repertoire. Contrary to the fears invoked by the Indian Right, American products do not necessarily mark the end of Indian (food) culture:

> The chicken that is served in the restaurants of the fast food chain is bred by Venky's, a desi breeder. Only the batter is a special formula of the US company. Once the batter is spread over the chicken and fried, what you will get is a chicken pakora.[10] So, far from being an alien invention, Kentucky Fried Chicken is merely a chicken pakora. It is a belated American discovery of an ancient Indian delight.
>
> (Aiyer, n.d.)

By jokingly claiming that Americans have only rediscovered a dish known in India for centuries, the common argument is turned around: it was then Indians who globalised Americans. Despite its polemics, there is a true core to the statement. Critics of globalisation often fail to see that the forces of globalisation work in many different directions at the same time, and they often do not notice that there is a difference between political strategy and mobilisation and genuine concern for the consumer. When we look at how globalisation manifests itself and which reactions this manifestation provokes, we also need to carefully differentiate between different actors and their aims.

An investigation into the media sphere of India shows that many of the claims made by globalisation critics are factually incorrect. There is, for example, neither any evidence that "American movies and soap operas replace local movies and productions" (Guven, 2006: 60), nor that the film industry in many developing countries is now "concerned at the prospect of a free market that would lead to the disintegration of national culture from cheap American films" (Guven, 2006: 62). The frequently made argument that globalisation is essentially standardisation because it strives towards creating a uniform global culture or imposing a Western cultural hegemony and is "neo-liberal, not democratic and against any form of religious ideals or traditional culture" (Guven, 2006: 62) can hardly be upheld. For a product to become globally successful, it has to adapt to local conditions. Two important prerequisites for globalisation are therefore marketing and appropriation. Products have to be marketed in such a way that they can be associated with modernity (Galeota, 2004: 22) and, more importantly, they have to appeal to the tastes of local consumers. It is through the localised process of appropriation that products are embedded in sets of practices which shape and alter their significance (Thompson, 2010: 256).

Although McDonald's, the largest global provider of fast food, offers beef burgers all around the world, it does not do so in India, the country with the world's largest Hindu population. Beef is replaced by either chicken or *paneer* to cater to the tastes of the not insignificant number of vegetarians in the country, thus providing an answer to Ritzer's question of whether vegetarianism could be

'McDonaldized' (Ritzer, 2010: 75)[11]. The fast food franchise has also succeeded in localising content and taste: a burger in India is prepared with different spices than in the United States or in Europe.[12] In addition, the names of the products are not uniform, but context dependent: ever since Quentin Tarantino's *Pulp Fiction* (1994), Americans are aware that their 'Quarter Pounder with Cheese' is only known as 'Royal with Cheese' in Europe, due to the metric system which prevails in that part of the world. Similarly, the ubiquitous 'Big Mac' becomes the 'Maharaja Mac' in India.[13] Although labelling is undeniably a marketing strategy to prevent alienation on the part of the customers, it has the positive side effect of working against uniformity. In the competition between Coca-Cola and Pepsi over the Indian consumer market, the latter won the race because it

> ... deployed local as opposed to global forms, images, and ideas, and in particular, because it understood a deeply rooted Indian penchant for tamasha[14] – or put simply, because it had acquired more instrumentally useful knowledge about South Asian consumer preferences.
>
> (Pollock, 2014: 2)

That itself is not a new mechanism devised by cunning market forces: in his account of historical economics, Angus Maddison shows how the Romans were "pragmatic polytheists", who were, in the course of the expansion of the empire, "generally willing to respect the gods and temples of the peoples they conquered, as well as introducing them to their own gods", thus minimising ideological conflict (Maddison, 2007: 14).

These empirical examples illustrate a central feature of globalisation: the hybridisation of cultures leading to a new and unique cultural form that is not reducible to either the local or the global culture (Ritzer, 2010: 340). The cases also provide a good example to illustrate the idea of an 'alternative modernity', also drawing on A. K. Ramanujan, who writes that

> ... cultural borrowings from India to the West, or vice versa, also show interesting accommodation to the prevailing system [. . .] the new ways of thought and behaviour do not replace, but live along with older 'religious' ways. Computers and typewriters receive *ayudhapuja* ('worship of weapons') as weapons of war did once. The 'modern', the context-free, becomes one more context [. . .].
>
> (Ramanujan, 1990: 57)[15]

The largest Indian commercial film industry, popularly known as Bollywood, either in imitation of or in opposition to Hollywood (Tyrrell, 2008: 327), is a case in point. Bollywood is "a wild card in the globalisation process", with a constantly shifting position, influenced by its diasporic audiences, new technology, and a constantly changing relationship with the West (Tyrrell, 2008: 333).

The US film studio Twentieth Century Fox has been hugely successful in India with *My Name Is Khan*, a film about an Indian Muslim struggling in the post-9/11 world. The film grossed $23 million in India, thus rendering a Hindi film without special effects almost as successful as James Cameron's *Avatar*, which earned $26 million in India (Chatterjee, 2010). *My Name Is Khan* was produced in collaboration with India's Dharma Productions and Red Chilli Entertainment, with the result that more film studios are setting up bases in India and are "using local talent to produce Indian-language films as they try to crack a market that sold more than 3.2 billion tickets [in 2009]" (Chatterjee, 2010). Localisation, the process of adapting a product to a specific country or region – for example, by weaving foreign elements into local narratives – thus increasingly becomes a strategy of global producers to sell a cultural product. After 1992, when the US film industry tried to attract the Indian audience by dubbing major films that were commercial hits in the United States into Hindi, it was only moderately successful: in 1994, when *Jurassic Park* grossed $6 million, the Indian production *Hum Aapke Hain Koun. . .!* grossed $60 million (Tyrrell, 2008: 331),[16] which is why the way for American films to make an entry into the Indian market is to "become localized" (Chatterjee, 2010).

The actions of global players are motivated by a maximisation of economic interest. Although it would be naïve to assume anything else, it is equally wrong to accuse them of doing exactly that. Instead, the question to ask is what the profit-maximising intentions of global corporations have for an understanding of globalisation and its effects on life. If American films are only successful in India in Indian languages, with an Indian cast and Indian film songs, this is a strong argument against a view of globalisation as cultural convergence. As in the case of foreign films, foreign television networks were also only successful in collaboration with Indian companies. Global media tycoon Rupert Murdoch's Star Network, which featured Western programmes, could only attract a minority audience in India. The Hindi satellite channel Zee TV, on the other hand, attracted a much larger market, which marked the beginning of a whole industry of Indian satellite and cable channels, which Star then bought into (Tyrrell, 2008: 332). Star TV thus saw a metamorphosis from a "pan-Asian broadcaster to one that was more regional" (Thomas, 2006: 44).[17] The case underlines the potential of hybridisation as a political and economic strategy: transnational media providers have not bullied their way in, but instead successfully "engaged [Asian media], not only economically [. . .], but also culturally as buyers, providers and users of 'glocalized' programming" (Thomas, 2006: 182).*

However, a discussion of cultural globalisation cannot merely be restricted to processes of adaptation of Western products to the Indian consumer market, but also has to take into account the increasing flow of media products from India which are equally modified and hybridised in the process: the flamenco song 'Senorita' from the 2011 Bollywood film *Zindagi Na Milegi Dobara* is a mix of Spanish and Hindi featuring Spanish singer Maria del Mar Fernández,[18] and the song 'Darling' from the movie *7 Khoon Maaf* (2011) is an example of the musical fusion of the melody of the Russian folk song 'Kalinka' with Hindi lyrics.[19]

---

* 'Glocalisation' emphasises the hybrid results of the multi-directional flows through which ideas, images, and languages travel and often become parts of new third entities.

50 Lion König

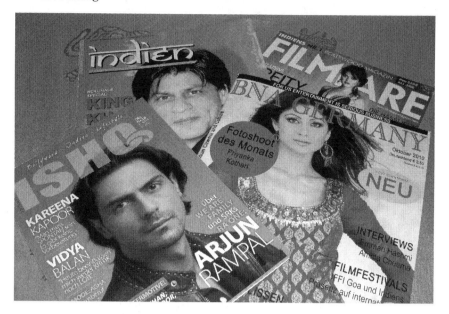

Figure 3.1 Covers of the German editions of international magazines on Indian film
Source: Courtesy Kati Brauchmann-Saeed

The Hindi film is tremendously popular in the West, with Bollywood films being dubbed in European languages and broadcast on television. Shah Rukh Khan, whose film *Don—The King Is Back* (2011), was partly filmed in the German capital of Berlin, is a regular at the film festival Berlinale, and the Berlin tourist office has published a city map indicating the locales where Khan's film was shot. Bollywood has made a successful entry into Western popular culture and is seemingly there to stay. Magazines in German supply their readers with the latest information about newly released films and updates on their favourite celebrities. The range of magazines – both in print and online – which cover the world of Indian cinema and the lives of its actors and actresses (Figure 3.1) illustrate the fact that globalisation is not a one-way process; that is, it is not 'the West' modifying 'the East' (which are both, in any case, non-existent as cultural entities) along its lines, but both are entering into a creative discourse, which is not necessarily always a harmonious one, but which leads to the exchange of ideas and ways of life, and can therefore serve to enrich the respective cultural spheres.[20]

Conclusion

At the outset of this chapter, it was argued that globalisation is an umbrella term which entails economic, social, political, and cultural aspects, all of which are interlinked. Hence, closer economic cooperation between countries will also trigger cultural (ex)changes. However, it would be wrong to assume that in the process of globalisation cultures become indistinguishable from each other.

Culture is inherently dynamic and subject to constant change, but at the same time it also has a non-negotiable, identity-providing core.[21] The successful Indian film *Shree 420* produced in 1955, almost four decades before India's economic liberalisation, and even longer before American film studios set out to participate in the Indian film business, features a well-known Hindi song, the chorus of which can be seen as symptomatic of the self-understanding of India in a globalised world:

> *Mera joota hai Japani*
> *Yeh patloon Inglistani*
> *Sar pe lal topi Rusi*
> *Phir bhi dil hai Hindustani.*[22]

Written at a time when India celebrated its newly gained status as an independent, sovereign nation, when industrial modernity and its symbols were embraced by India's leaders, and when Nehru famously proclaimed that 'dams and steel mills are the temples of modern India', the song tells us that global goods themselves do not transform an individual into a foreigner who is unrecognisable to his or her peers. Rather, it shows that globalisation can be embraced without giving up one's identity and the emotional and cultural ties to a specific place of origin.

It has often been argued that the West is the sole benefactor of globalisation, understood as "a process of incorporating external parts into the ongoing fabric of Western-centred world politics" (Modelski, 2003: 59). However, as the chapter has shown, there is no 'homogenous modernity' (Nayar, 2006: 64), and an asymmetrical flow of culture as one-way traffic from the West to the rest of the world (cf. Thompson, 2010: 254) can be observed less and less. Instead, what we are witnessing is not a Westernisation of the East or an 'Easternisation' of the West (cf. Pieterse, 2010: 345), but an increasing hybridisation in the course of which new elements arise out of the contact of East and West, and a "third space" (Bhabha, 2007) comes into existence.

Homi Bhabha argues that with the idea of the "third space" in mind, observers and actors alike may be in a position to conceptualise an

> ... *inter*national culture, based not on the exoticism of multiculturalism or the diversity of cultures, but on the inscription and articulation of culture's *hybridity*. To that end we should remember that it is the 'inter' – the cutting edge of translation and negotiation, the in-between space – that carries the burden of the meaning of culture. It makes it possible to begin envisaging national, anti-nationalist histories of the 'people'. And by exploring this Third Space, we may elude the politics of polarity and emerge as the others of our selves.
> (Bhabha, 1994: 38–39, emphasis in original)

Thus, the third space,

> ... though unrepresentable in itself, [. . .] constitutes the discursive conditions of enunciation that ensure that the meaning and symbols of culture have

no primordial unity or fixity; that even the same signs can be appropriated, translated, rehistoricized and read anew.

(Bhabha, 1994: 37)

This chapter has shown that hybridisation is more than a romantic idea. It is increasingly taking place not only in the cultural sphere, but in many other contexts in India and elsewhere.[23] Like globalisation, of which it is an outcome, hybridity is not a top-down process; it involves (trans)national and local agents for the enterprise to be successful. A renewed *swadeshi* movement along the lines of the earlier boycott of foreign goods (and ideas) in favour of Indian enterprise is thus the wrong way forward. Critics of the current phase of globalisation (which for many is the only 'true' globalisation) ought to bear in mind that the resilience of India's political system lies in its successful exploration of the 'third space' between the local and the global.

The controversy around the framing of the Indian Constitution is a case in point: Mahavir Tyagi, a member of the Constituent Assembly, was "very much disappointed [to] see nothing Gandhian in this Constitution", and K. Hanumanthaiya complained that whereas freedom fighters like himself had wanted "the music of *Veena* or *Sitar*, what they had got instead was 'the music of an English band'" (cited in Guha, 2007a: 121). The problem generally, as Granville Austin points out, is that it was never defined what 'Indian' in this socio-political context means, which is why the proponents were on thin ice. "To declare that the Constitution is un-Indian or anti-Indian", Austin writes, "is to use the undefined – if not the undefinable – as a measuring stick" (Austin, 1966: 326).

This chapter has argued that equating globalisation with homogenisation overlooks the potential of this phenomenon to facilitate an articulation of hitherto silent voices and act as a motor for the promotion of identities. More than anything else, the concept of cultural globalisation draws attention to the fact that cultures are constantly in motion. In the twenty-first century, boundaries might only have become increasingly blurred due to the speedier exchange of information, values, and ideas. But clearly demarcating where one culture ends and another one starts, what one entails and another excludes, has always been next to impossible, precisely because we have lived in a globalised world all along.

Notes

1 George Ritzer uses the term 'McDonaldization' to refer to a wide-ranging process "by which the principles of the fast-food restaurant are coming to dominate more and more sectors of American society as well as of the rest of the world" (Ritzer, 2010: 4). The success of the fast food chain and more generally of what it stands for is attributed to four factors: efficiency, calculability, predictability, and control (see Ritzer, 2010: 16–18). 'McDonaldization' thus is a study in the line of Weberian sociology as it describes processes of rationalisation of contemporary society (Turner, 2010: 77).
2 Emphasising the historical dimension of globalisation, Modelski (2003: 55) defines it as "the process by which a number of historical world societies were brought together into one global system".

3 Lechner and Boli (2008) stress the fuzzy nature of the concept and define it as "the set of processes by which more people become connected in more and different ways across even greater distances". In this vein, they equate globalisation with 'deterritorialization', "the process in which the constraints of physical space lose their hold on social relations" (Lechner and Boli, 2008: 4). Subscribing to the convergence paradigm, Lieber and Weisberg describe globalisation as "the increasing global integration of our economies, information technology, the spread of global popular culture, and other forms of human interaction" (Lieber and Weisberg, 2002: 274).
4 See, for example, Rao (2005) on the role of early Indian traders in a global trade network.
5 For a comprehensive account of the history of the printing press in India, see Priolkar (1958).
6 Interestingly, early forms of printing can be traced back to China, where it was used for the same purposes as the Christian missionaries employed it in India much later: block printing is believed to have been used to print portraits of the Buddha in an effort to propagate Buddhism in 650 CE (Priolkar, 1958: 1).
7 Until 1995, the Indian state retained a monopoly over broadcasting through the Indian Telegraph Act, 1885 (Mehta, 2008a: 10).
8 The Union Ministry of Information and Broadcasting has a master list of 303 channels, 26 of which are licensed Indian private channels, 60 are foreign-owned channels, and 27 are run by the Doordarshan network (data updated until 30 June 2007, Ministry of Information and Broadcasting (2005/06), cited in Mehta, 2008a: 10). Mehta (2008a: 10) claims that the actual number of channels is much higher because a large number of both foreign and local channels are not registered and hence do not figure in the official record.
9 For a discussion of Indian television from its beginnings in 1959 via the change in broadcast policy in 1991, which led to increasing plurality, see, for example, Mehta (2008b).
10 A *pakora* is a traditional fried snack that is served across South Asia.
11 See also Waters (2010: 353) who notes that 'McDonaldization' promotes demands for authenticity, even to the extent of the "fundamentalism of vegetarianism".
12 The situation, however, is quite different in China, where a menu in English and Chinese is the only concession McDonald's makes to the local consumers. The Hong Kong franchise, for example, promotes McDonald's basic menu and does not offer items that would be more recognisable to Chinese consumers (Watson, 2008: 128). Yet, Watson holds that this does not mean that people have been stripped of their cultural heritage, nor that they have become the "uncomprehending dupes of transnational corporations" (Watson, 2008: 134).
13 Kellner (2012) cautions the observer that such examples as these, drawing on the various cultural meanings in diverse local contexts, as well as different products, organisation, and effects, go "too far towards stressing heterogeneity, downplaying the cultural power of McDonald's as a force of homogenizing globalisation and Western corporate logic and system" (Kellner, 2012: 31).
14 *Tamasha* is a traditional form of Marathi theatre.
15 A. K. Ramanujan is here taking up the idea of 'compartmentalising', which he gets from Milton Singer (1972: 320 ff).
16 Chatterjee (2010) uses cultural reasons to explain this phenomenon. He attributes the failure of Hollywood's attempt to enter the Indian market with American films dubbed in vernacular languages to a difficulty on the part of the audience to understand American culture, humour, or slang.
17 The Star TV network started with a Hong Kong family-owned satellite broadcasting one signal across Asia; subsequently, with the purchase by Rupert Murdoch, it became regional, with a strategy of regionally diverse programming (Thomas, 2006: 49). A quasi-domestic, thoroughly hybridised, transnational phase started when domestic

programming in India became diverse in order to reach the multiple cultures and languages of Asia: Star TV entered into joint ventures with Zee TV to broadcast in Tamil, Hindi, and Arabic. For a thorough analysis of the wider cultural impact of Star TV on India, see Butcher (2003).

18 *Zindagi Na Milegi Dobara* (*You Don't Get Life a Second Time*) is a road movie, which itself is an American film category, thus exemplifying how Indian cinema increasingly steps out of its familiar settings and explores new modes of narration. *Zindagi* tells the story of three friends, Arjun, (Hrithik Roshan), Kabir (Abhay Deol), and Imraan (Farhan Akhtar), who meet for a holiday in Spain. As a reference to increased global mobility, one of them has left India to work as an investment banker in London. In the course of their road trip through Spain, the trio discovers a range of Spanish attractions, like the bull chase in the streets of Pamplona and flamenco. The friends join in a flamenco performance and take turns with the Spanish singer, thus making the song 'Senorita' a fusion of Spanish and Hindi lyrics.

19 The film, the title of which can be translated as *Seven Murders Forgiven*, revolves around the Anglo-Indian Susanna Anna-Marie Johannes (Priyanka Chopra) who is in search of love but does not find it in any of the six men she marries in the course of her life. She murders all of them because of a flaw she sees in each one. The Russian actor Aleksandr Dyachenko plays Nicolai Vronsky, Susanna's fourth husband, a Russian secret agent. During their marriage celebrations in India, Susanna dresses in a Russian folk costume and performs the song 'Darling' with Hindi lyrics and the well-known Russian melody in reference to her husband and his native land.

20 Indian film and lifestyle magazines published for the German market also illustrate the claim that marketing and appropriation of the product to local tastes are the points that render globalisation a successful venture. The attempt to publish a German version of the Indian film magazine *Filmfare* failed because the Indian edition, which was merely translated into German without any change to its content, was not tailored to the needs of the German readership.

21 The concept of identity is here understood in Sudhir Kakar's terms as a "sense of the self" (Kakar, 1979: IX).

22 The lines can be translated as "My shoes are Japanese, these trousers are English, the red hat on my head is Russian, but even then my heart is Indian".

23 For hybrid elements in independent India's political set-up, see, for example, Mitra (2011).

4 Challenges to democratic governance in India since the 1990s
An 'unfinished symphony'

Asok Kumar Mukhopadhyay

Introduction

Economic 'reforms' in India have, since their introduction in the early 1990s, remained a matter of debate among scholars (Nayar, 2007; Corbridge and Harriss, 2000: 143–231; Frankel, 2005; Sen, 2006), opinion makers, and the general public alike. Although officially embraced in 1991, India had begun to liberalise at least a decade earlier. Some scholars argue that the first attempt to liberalise certain items was made in the late 1960s (Hardgrave, 2000: 367–408). Hardgrave shows that India's industrial growth dropped down to only 1.6 percent during 1966–69, but during the early phase of liberalisation from 1974–79, industrial growth increased to 5.9 percent and then accelerated in the 1980s (Hardgrave and Kochanek, 2000: 399). During Rajiv Gandhi's administration, industrial growth plummeted to 8.5 percent (Hardgrave and Kochanek, 2000: 399). Subsequently, 'growth' in terms of the Gross Domestic Product (GDP) fluctuated: from as high as 10.47 percent during 1989–90 to as low as 1.30 percent during 1991–92 (Tendulkar and Bhavani, 2007: 210). Due to a whole variety of factors, such as social contexts, poor state of agriculture, mass illiteracy, and the extremes of social and economic inequalities, India's 'reforms' have not been as sweeping as elsewhere, and the process has remained embedded in the labyrinth of a vast society with multiple challenges (Hardgrave and Kochanek, 2000: 1–13). Whereas the proponents of reform would defend the phenomenon on the grounds of a free market (with state protection) and abolition of the 'license permit raj' and the social welfare state of the 'Indian brand' (Bhagawati, 2007: 149–161; Harriss-White, 1997), others have pointed out many pitfalls of the same on the ground that the phenomenon could not produce equal effects and that some people will have to pay the penalties of globalisation (Sen, 2007: 117–133; Kohli, 2009: 164–186).

This chapter seeks to provide a critique of India's ongoing reforms with respect to democratic governance in the country. After achieving some successes (Kohli, 2001) and considerable failures (Kohli, 1991), Indian democracy is now witnessing three basic trends which desperately need a successful reconciliation: aspiration for quick economic gain among the upper classes, strong demand for inclusive growth, and the rising power of the people's voice. At the end of the first decade of the twenty-first century, India's politics and economy are seen to be achieving economic growth in terms of GDP without achieving meaningful inclusive growth and genuine equity of the nation (Bardhan, 1984; Rudolph and Rudolph, 1987; Frankel, 2005: Kohli, 2009: 140–186).

Socio-political developments since India's 'Tryst with Destiny'

India gained independence through a process of intense political bargaining between the leaders of the Indian National Congress and the Muslim League on the one hand, and the departing British imperialist authorities, on the other (Sarkar, 1983). Simultaneously, the Indian capitalist business class and the feudal class contributed to the transfer of power (Menon, 1957) by protecting their class interests through their successful lobbying with the powers that be.

Quite rhetorically, India began her tryst with democratic governance by declaring the highest sentiments and ideas of liberty, equality, fraternity, and justice to protect the unity of the nation and the dignity of the individual in the preamble to the Constitution. The Constitution, which was drafted by the Constituent Assembly during 1946–49 and inaugurated on 26 January 1950, contains a host of fundamental rights (Part III) and a set of social and economic rights (Part IV); the latter are not justiciable in a court of law, but since the 1980s, in the wake of various Social Action Litigation judgments of the Supreme Court, they have assumed the status of 'basic rights' (Baxi, 1998: 342–343). However, after six eventful decades since the enforcement of the Republican Constitution, India now appears to be functioning as a successful case as far as genuine democratic governance is concerned. Although the uncritical approach to India's democracy that only looks at the formal institutional dynamics of democracy would overlook this aspect. It would be incorrect to say that India has not made any progress in the last six decades, but the kinds of achievements made have failed to satisfy the economic needs and political aspirations of the majority of the people. There has been very fast development of the symptoms of national disunity, mal-development, and heavy dependence on foreign support in economic and military affairs, thus reducing politics to an unprincipled scrambling for political power, and to making politico-administrative corruption almost a part of the national culture. Right now, the challenges of poverty, development, and identity confront India as a nation (Drèze and Sen, 2002; Sen, 2006; Bhattacharyya, Sarkar, and Kar, 2010).

Even after the completion of many Five-Year Plans, today 40 percent of Indians still live below the poverty line. The seven priority States outlined by the United Nations Development Assistance Framework (UNDAF) that are home to India's poorest are Bihar, Chhattisgarh, Jharkhand, Madhya Pradesh, Odisha, Rajasthan, and Uttar Pradesh. Along with Uttarakhand, these States account for 64 percent of the population living below the poverty line. Across India, multi-dimensional poverty continues to rise. Recent government data on poverty based on new methodologies of estimation has revised the figure upwards, and rural poverty has also risen significantly. Further, poverty continues to remain concentrated in specific regions and social groups. Poverty levels are also much higher among people belonging to Scheduled Castes (SCs), Scheduled Tribes (STs) and Other Backward Classes (OBCs) who comprise half of the poor and deprived households.[1] All-India estimates for the headcount ratio of poverty have been revised from 27.5 percent to 37.2 percent, and rural poverty estimates have been revised from 28.3 percent to 41.8 percent as per the 'Report of the Expert Group to Review Methodology for Estimation of Poverty' (Planning Commission, Government of India, 2009). India's position in the world development index is very low with respect to supply of potable water, production of power and energy, spread of elementary and primary education, and ensuring a global standard of public health. India's position, as the World Development Report of 2011 reveals, is even below some sub-Saharan countries, ranking 134 among 187 countries. Ruefully enough, India ranks below countries such as Sri Lanka, Mongolia, Philippines, Botswana, Vietnam, Guatemala, and Nicaragua. Second, the countries that lag behind India are Ghana (135), Congo (137), Bhutan (141), and Nepal (157).[2] Although the maximisation of public welfare should have been the real goal of planned development – that is, the greatest benefits should have been ensured for the least privileged sections of the population – the truth is that the rich have become richer and the poor poorer in the course of India's development efforts. Prepared by the Institute of Applied Manpower Research (IAMR), an autonomous body affiliated with the Planning Commission, the Human Development Report (HDR) released by Planning Commission Deputy Chairman Montek Singh Ahluwalia reveals the overall well-being of the population based on three indicators: consumption expenditure, education, and health. The findings of the report are significant because they are used to formulate the twelfth Five-Year Plan. The report states:

> In India, the distribution of assets is extremely unequal, with the top 5 per cent of the households possessing 38 per cent of the total assets and the bottom 60 per cent of households owning a mere 13 per cent.

The disparity is more glaring in the urban areas, where 60 per cent of the households at the bottom own just 10 percent of the assets. Predictably, asset accumulation is minimal among the agricultural labour households in rural areas and casual labour households in urban areas. It is not just the gaping income inequality that is alarming. The difference in the consumption expenditure between the rich and poor households has also increased, both in rural and urban areas, between 1993–94 and 2004–05. The report paints a grim picture on the poverty front. It clearly states that despite the economy growing at 6 percent, this is not enough to reduce poverty in the country. In fact, the rate of decline in poverty in India is not in sync with the high rate of economic growth, which is evident from the fact that the number of poor people in the country has barely fallen over a thirty-year period. In 1973–74, the number of poor in India stood at 332 million. The figure remained the same in the next decade, registering a marginal decline in 1993–94 (320 million) and becoming stagnant again in 2004–05. The report also highlights the fact that despite affirmative action on the part of the government, a high incidence of poverty persists among the SCs and STs, as well as the Muslims. One-third of the Muslim population, the report states, continues to live below the poverty line.[3]

Reforms and their effects

India embraced neo-liberal reforms of its economy and the governing structures starting in 1991 under certain 'constants', although the economy was not doing that bad in the 1980s, and the country had its own method of liberalisation starting as early as the late 1960s. The other important issue to mention here is that India's adoption of the reforms coincided with a major change in the political system, that is, with the onset of a coalition government at the Union level. A coalition government may suggest a relative absence of strong political will (understood as the inability to resist externally propelled reforms), and hence an advantage for the reformers, or 'globalisers', both indigenous and foreign. In actual practice, however, this may not be the case given the federal compulsions and unwillingness and reluctance of many State governments to swallow the 'bitter pill' (Bhattacharyya, 2009a: 99–112). This growth-centric and free market–oriented model of development has already produced many surprises.

The Indian economy has recently entered the exclusive elite club of a trillion-dollar GDP, and the trend is still growing phenomenally. Corbridge and Harriss (2000) have termed it "an elite revolt" and questioned also the "partiality of the Reforms" (Corbridge and Harriss, 2000: 159–160). If the account of why India embraced reforms in 1991 is to be believed, then it is seen that India in the 1980s was actually not doing badly in terms of the economy due to what is called the "Rajiv effect" (Corbridge and Harriss, 2000: 150–151). Corbridge and Harriss have looked for a balanced understanding of the reforms in India:

> If some of India's urban, industrial and financial elites have been in revolt against an earlier mode of economic development which served some of their interests very well [. . .] we need to recognise that this revolt was being staged in part against the model that had run its course and which needed to be reformed. We should also acknowledge that the sequencing of the reforms process in India has been dictated by political consideration as much as economic imperatives, with the result that structural adjustment has not always corresponded to the desires of particular class groupings or business elites.
>
> (Corbridge and Harriss, 2000: 166)

It has been estimated that in 2010 India's economy was the ninth largest in the world and the fourth largest by purchasing power parity (PPP). The country is one of the G-20 major economies and a member of Brazil, Russia, India, China, and South Africa (BRICS) group. The country's GDP per capita PPP was $3,408, according to the International Monetary Fund (IMF) – the 129th in the world in 2010 – making it a lower-middle income economy.[4] Whereas in 2004 only four Indians were US-dollar billionaires, the number had risen to twenty-one in 2010. As of now, India has fifty-five US-dollar billionaires (individuals with a total net worth of one billion dollars and above), which accounts for roughly 4.5 percent of the global total of 1,210 billionaires.[5] The Indian corporate sector, an eager partner in global capitalism, is constantly pressing the government to reform labour laws in order to curtail trade union rights of the organised working class (Sridharan, 2014: 4–8).[6] From one recent estimate, it is revealed that India during 2011–12 had a huge reserve army of labour of 226.9 million, which was 10 percent more than the size of the active army of labour (D'Mello, 2014: 36). On the basis of further calculations, D'Mello has shown that 720.6 million (59.5 percent) of the total population of India who are at the bottom of the class system (D'Mello, 2014: 39) fall under the category of the reserve army of labour, broadly speaking. Needless to say, this provides ample opportunity for the capitalists, both indigenous and foreign, to further curb labourers' rights. The term 'casualisation' is one form of this new exploitation.[7]

India's GDP growth rate during 2010–11 was 8 to 10 percent, although the signs of slowdown are already visible, as Figure 4.1 shows.[8]

These growth figures, which have not been steady in any way, as we have seen earlier, stand in relation to a nearly collapsing 'social security' system where only 2 to 3 percent of GDP is spent on social security, whereas it is around 30 percent in the countries of the European Union. In a vast country such as India with massive illiteracy, and where most of the world's hungry people also 'live', this 'growth-centric' development model does not seem well grounded.

India's reforms policy is not connected to empowerment of the poor who are the vast majority in the country. According to Amartya Sen, such a policy can empower the poor "only if the prices of goods and services they sell rise in

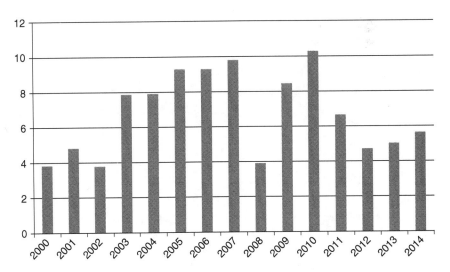

Figure 4.1 India's GDP growth rate, 2007–11
Source: Orbis Economics

line with the rise in price of food which makes up most of consumption basket" (quoted in Corbridge and Harriss, 2000: 165). Corbridge and Harriss do not see any optimism here, for such a scenario is unlikely to arise. Consider their pertinent remarks in this context:

> Projected cutback in government spending on employment guarantees schemes, together with the rising unemployment and more brutal conditions in the non-agricultural markets in which the rural poor participate so heavily, are just as likely to ensure a rise in rural poverty level as a fall.
>
> (Corbridge and Harriss, 2000: 165)

Politics in India since the 1990s has hardly produced any optimism in the minds of India's present generation either. Dishonest motivation is palpably apparent in the behaviour patterns of most politicians, from the national to the village level. The inflation rate, especially in terms of food prices, is allowed to climb with impunity as the ruling or political class goes on advancing the stock reply that there is no magic wand to control inflationary pressures. Even the responsible politicians have occasionally frowned upon the Reserve Bank's anti-inflationary monetary measures based on the specious argument that such policies would impede the economy's growth. The government also does not seem to be serious about controlling public expenditures. The warehouses of the Food Corporation of India (FCI)[9] are overflowing with food stocks, but there is no assurance that these will be used to bring down food prices.[10]

Also, there are no serious government efforts so far to reduce the number of people living in poverty and suffering from hunger by the year 2015, as envisaged in the UN Millennium Development Goals.

In vast tracts of rural India, the dominating socio-economic features include shortage of potable water and serious deficits in irrigation facilities, the vicious circle of loans, and political and administrative indifference accompanied by pious but ineffective resolutions and vote-catching rhetoric. According to National Family Health Survey data (2005–06), only 45 percent of households in the country had access to improved sanitation in that year. India has over 35 percent of the world's total illiterate population (UNESCO Education for All Report 2008) – only 66 percent of the country is literate (76 percent men and 54 percent women).

Regional discontent

One typical example of this state of affairs is the situation in the Vidarbha region in the State of Maharashtra. At the initiative of multinational corporations and with consent of the government of India, Bt. cotton farming[11] was introduced in 2002–03. About 75 percent of the cotton growers there were allured to take up Bt. cotton farming, with decent profits for the initial two years. Thereafter, however, they incurred huge losses because the land had lost its fertility. The burden of agricultural credit simply proved too back-breaking. About 69 percent of these cotton growers could not repay their loans and they had to take fresh loans to repay the old ones. The officially available data for the period 1993–2010 show that throughout India 1.20 lakh farmers committed suicide and about 90 percent of such suicide cases occurred in the Vidarbha region. The People's Movement Samiti, the mass organisation developed to fight against the onslaught of reforms, calculated that, on average in Vidarbha, one farmer committed suicide every eight hours, with the average age of these victims ranging between twenty and forty-five years. The government's development policy has been found to be insensitive to the people's miseries, with the government responding to the cases of farmer suicide by only giving the widows a one-time compensation of Rs. 2 lakh (100,000) each.[12] Similar regional discontent can be cited from other areas of India (see Chapters 2 and 9 in this volume). The profound class consciousness in those regional assertions must not be lost sight of. In the areas 'infested' with Maoist violence, tribal ethnicity and class exploitation have combined against the neo-liberal reforms.

The state responses

Since independence, the Indian state has generally been insincere in addressing the grievances of the *aam admi*, the 'common man' (and woman), and indifferent to increased administrative inefficiency in implementing development projects. In recent years, the Union government (United Progressive Alliance [UPA] I and II) has launched a number of flagship development projects, like the Mahatma Gandhi National Rural Employment Guarantee Scheme (MGNREGS), the Bharat Nirman development projects, the Integrated Child Development Scheme, the Sarba Siksha Abhiyana, and the National Rural Health Mission, to name but a few (Saez and Singh, 2012). Significant public funds have been spent, but the common experience of the *aam admi* is not at all encouraging because of a tardy and inefficient implementation, as well as due to substantial political corruption. One example of corruption in implementing the MGNREGS has come from the Tonk district of Rajasthan, where those who were employed under this scheme were paid wages varying between Rs. 1 and Rs. 11 per day, considering only those days on which they actually worked.[13] The families refused to take payment and appealed to the higher authorities.

In a situation of rising food prices, wages of less than Rs. 100.00 per day pose a problem for a poor family, and the lower-level administration does not provide sufficient information to the poor about their entitlements under the law. Sometimes, providing information on a government website amounts to a cruel joke at the expense of the illiterate rural poor.

If the deprived and marginalised *aam admi*'s bitterness leads to widespread suspicion about the sincerity of the government, neither bureaucratic planning, nor promises of attractive development packages, nor police/military action would be the adequate answer to restore social peace and establish law and order. Political leadership must not avoid coming to terms with the real issues of popular disaffection, especially among the youth, raising its ugly head in an environment of distrust and violence generated by failed democratic governance.

Malfunctioning governance cannot be cured without whistle-blowers. The Right to Information (RTI) Act (2005),[14] a piece of legislation intended to achieve transparent governance, is supposed to be a credible anti-corruption whistle. Although functioning somewhat credibly at the central level, this legislation has been implemented in a tardy manner in some States of India, including West Bengal. The major point of concern, however, is that recently, RTI activists have died under mysterious circumstances after exposing corruption in the public administration. Both Ramdas Ghadegavkar, an RTI activist in Mumbai who was active in uncovering corruption in the public distribution system of food and fuel in the Marathawala region, and Amit Jethava, an RTI activist in Gujarat responsible for exposing illegal mining activities surrounding the Gir wildlife sanctuary, were murdered.[15]

Another aspect of the government's development efforts relates to forest areas spread over five States with vast mineral resources like iron ore, bauxite, coal, limestone, tin, granite, and dolomite. The Union government has committed itself to allowing Indian and foreign multinational corporations to gain control over these mineral resources, which has led to fierce reactions on the part of the landowners. Under the Forest Protection Act (1980), the tribal forest dwellers lost their age-old traditional rights to the forest. The Forest Rights Act (2006) has recognised their rights in terms of minor and marginal forest production, but many of the State governments have not implemented this legislation.

Much of the violence in major parts of Indian society during the last two decades has arisen out of a situation where at least 5 percent of the lowest strata of society are compelled to live in conditions of abject poverty, even after sixty years of planned democratic governance.

Democratic governance under severe challenges

The time has come to realise that development is a greater challenge and a bigger movement than gaining independence from British rule. The mere injection of cash money into rural life through various development projects, formulated by the bureaucracy and poorly implemented by power-hungry politicians, is not a satisfactory development policy. Both Rabindranath Tagore and M.K. Gandhi quite appropriately underlined the essence of 'development' as building a new relation between the government and the people. In that understanding, development aims at instilling a sense of self-dependence and self-respect in the minds of the people, who should never be treated as the mere beneficiaries of government projects.

In the actual process of governance and politics in India, however, a vicious circle of victory and defeat seems to operate: 'victory' creates hate towards the vanquished, and 'defeat' produces misery, anger, and vengeance. The prudent democratic policy would be to overcome the defeat–victory syndrome and to adopt an attitude of empathy and a policy of genuine sharing of the miseries of the people.

Reviewing the trend of Indian politics since the 1990s, it becomes clear that the poor in India are convinced of the limits of opposing the combined power and influence of the political and economic establishment. The development paradigm adopted by Indian policymakers, where planned development is increasingly sidelined in favour of a market economy, has led to an eviction of the poor from their land and economic exploitation of the marginalised section in society. The economic reformers claim that globalisation enhances welfare, but the pertinent question is: for whom is welfare basically meant? Increased foreign investment in Special Economic Zones (SEZs) giving fiscal and other concessions to capitalist investors, both foreign and Indian, never translates into greater economic welfare for the people at large, but benefits the political and techno-industrial elites only.

The economic reforms introduced in India over the last two decades have not benefited the majority of the people – a scenario which Amartya Sen has aptly described as the "penalties of globalisation" (Sen, 2006: 120–122). The development policy creates mass unemployment in a country where employment opportunities are scarce. Under the influence of the globalisation-liberalisation-privatisation mode, India's current overall economic system is quite different from what it used to be in the 1950s when the Indian Left formally opted for electoral politics but kept talking of proletarian revolution, which is one of the factors that led to the decline of Left politics in the first decade of the twenty-first century.

Economic Progress, Governance, and Alienation

In the mid-1970s, however, the Indian Left stopped talking of revolution by workers, peasants, and landless labourers, and instead started indulging in the petite bourgeois politics of the traditional middle-class professionals. Recently, socio-economic circumstances compelled the Left to learn how to cohabit with the neo-liberal philosophy and rhetoric, but at a heavy cost to their original cause. At the beginning of the second decade of the twenty-first century, there is a strong possibility of realignment within India's political class (D'Mello, 2014: 36–50). With a more aggressive posture of this neo-liberal reform under way now, D'Mello has suggested for uniting under 'united and popular fronts', an idea critically worth taking on.

As has been argued at the outset of this chapter, India's tryst with democratic governance over the last six decades has failed to line up with the people's expectation and to integrate the citizens. Three sections of the Indian population, for different circumstantial reasons, have come to feel a strong sense of alienation. These are the Kashmiri Muslims (Ganguly and Bajpai, 1998); the Maoists, active in seven central and eastern States (Banerjee, 2010); and the tribals in the northeastern region of the country (Bhaumik, 1998; Baruah, 1999, 2005, 2009, 2010), especially in Manipur, Nagaland, and parts of Assam and Meghalaya. The Kashmiris agitate over the issue of their right to self-determination; the Maoists protest against economic exploitation and the issue of ownership of forest and agricultural lands; and the indigenous people of Odisha, Jharkhand, Chhattisgarh, and the northeast uncompromisingly complain against the Union government's neglect of their separate ethnic cultures and systems of governance. Multinational corporations like Vedanta Resources and Cairn India have launched development projects which not only displace the tribals from their forestlands, but also endanger the environment. What all these groups have in common is that they are not treated as equal stakeholders in India's democratic system. The (mis)use of the Armed Forces Special Powers Act (AFSPA) (1958)[16] has in effect provided impetus to the paramilitary forces to further alienate the aboriginal peoples of the northeast, who remain indifferent to various special economic packages intermittently announced by the government of India. Democratic governance and nation-building have been conducted after independence, mostly in a majoritarian language, often without consideration for the specific requirements of various minorities, including ethnic communities, which is at variance with what India stood for until the 1990s. Earlier approaches are now called into question, and the militant ethno-nationalist upsurges are a constant reminder of failures in the political and economic strategies pursued by the state.

Conclusion

This critique of India's political economy since the 1990s has shown that in the changed circumstances of globalised capitalism and market-oriented neo-liberalism, India's political economy seems to be inclined to equate 'development' with shining multiplexes and shopping malls. Poverty in India has until now been estimated in various ways by the Union government and the Planning Commission, with the Supreme Court questioning the methodology of defining poverty. The internationally accepted definition of poverty as $1.25 (that is, Rs. 79) per day income is at variance with India's official definition of the poverty line, which itself has recently lost its relevance in view of the fact that food prices in India have more than doubled between 2007–08 and 2010–11. The poor and marginal in India have become the victims of state-sponsored deviousness, violence, and statistical juggling. The juxtaposition of a high GDP growth rate and abject poverty and deprivation on a mass scale has given rise to the paradoxical view of India being 'a rich country inhabited by poor people'.

There is no road map of where India is going today, and, as has been argued in this chapter, a rising GDP is not always a correct indicator of a country's economic progress. A national economy can develop with most individuals in a society being worse off, as was the case in the United States in the first decade of the twenty-first century. What started with protesters occupying Wall Street in New York has spread to other cities in European countries, such as Greece, Spain, Italy, and Portugal, but also to Japan. These protest movements are, however, inchoate and sometimes contradictory in their priorities. The shared feature in these agitations is the anger against the inequalities of capitalism, whose two main pillars, a market economy and a liberal democratic polity, are tilted in favour of the rich. Ironically enough, since the global economic slowdown of 2008, it is no longer the Left, but the mainstream of civil society, that has started questioning the legitimacy of the capitalist development policy. From the Indian perspective, the abysmal diversion of corruption in India since the 1990s shows the vulnerability of the democratic polity.

A section of Indian politicians has been arguing for further capital market liberalisation, but such liberalisation does not lead to faster economic growth; rather, it creates social tensions and political instability. In 2012, Economics Nobel laureate and former senior vice-president of the World Bank Joseph Stiglitz forewarned that Indian democracy would cease to be meaningful if inequalities were not properly addressed (*The Times of India*, Kolkata edition, 13 January 2012). Similar claims had been heard before from the Chief Justice of India, S. H. Kapadia, who was reported to have said in his Law Day speech that growing economic disparity in India was unacceptable and that he did not want 300 million to prosper at the cost of 700 million (*The Sunday Times*, New Delhi edition, 27 November 2011).

A pressing requirement, therefore, is to achieve fiscal discipline in the midst of avoidable economic profligacy and rampant political-administrative corruption, and to adopt a consensual democratic attitude to conflict resolution. In the international arena, the guiding principle should be to make an abiding commitment to India's national integrity, the protection of civil liberties, and the dignity of the individual.

India launched its tryst with democratic governance with some high principles proclaimed in the Constitution's preamble and the Directive Principles of State Policy. The real danger today is the political displacement of these goals. In interviews with the freedom fighters in the districts of West Bengal in the 1930s and 1940s, acute disillusionment with India after independence was noted by historians. One such response was "This is not the country we had dreamed and fought for" (quoted in Chatterjee, 1998: 1). Consider the response of Sabita Debi, resident of Bankura:

> When the country became free, it would bring good to people. We were in servitude. They were ruling us, oppressing us ... All we wanted was enough coarse rice and coarse cloth to live in comfort. But we have never got those satisfaction of freedom ... We freed ourselves from the hands of foreigners. But now we can't free ourselves from our own brothers in our country.
> (Quoted in Chatterjee, 1998: 2–3)

Such cases of disillusionment could be multiplied. The point that is driven home is that the dream that the sacrifices made to free India from the British remains unfulfilled – comparable to an 'unfinished symphony' of the Austrian composer Schubert, the melody of which was relegated to posterity.

Notes

1 www.undp.org.in/sites/default/files/reports_publication/UNDP_Annual_Report_2011.pdf, retrieved on 9/1/2012. With less than Rs. 20.00 as daily income, India's per capita income (nominal) is $1,219, ranked 142nd in the world, whereas its per capita PPP of US$3,608 is ranked 129th ("Report for Selected Countries and Subjects" Imf.org. 2006–09–14).
2 HDR_2011_Statistical_Tables.xls (http://hdr.undp.org/en/statistics/hdi/, retrieved on 10/1/2012.

3 *India Today*, New Delhi, 23 October 2011, http://indiatoday.intoday.in/story/rich-and-poor-division-penury-hdr-planning-commission/1/157212.html.
4 International Monetary Fund. www.imf.org/external/pubs/ft/weo/2011/01/weodata/weorept.aspx?sy=2008&ey=2011&scsm=1&ssd=1&sort=country&ds=.&br=1&c=534&s=NGDPD%2CNGDPDPC%2CPPPGDP%2CPPPPC%2CLP&grp=0&a=&pr.x=49&pr.y=13, retrieved 26 May 2011.
5 *Forbes Magazine*, 10 March 2011.
6 Sridharan (2014) rightly argues that the Bharatiya Janata Party (BJP)–led Modi government at the centre (National Democratic Alliance [NDA]) (2014–present), elected on a massive majority, has taken an aggressive path of privatisation that resulted in the sale of valuable public assets. This, he argues, defies economic logic and threatens labour rights by enriching the corporate sector, and seeks to undermine a social compact that has endured since independence (Sridharan, 2014: 4–6).
7 This has been happening globally as well. Tilly's argument is that globalisation threatens labour rights by undermining state capacity to guarantee those rights (for further details, see Tilly, 1995: 346–356).
8 The GDP in India expanded 6.9 percent in the third quarter of 2011 over the previous quarter. Historically, from 2000 until 2011, India's average quarterly GDP growth was 7.45 percent, reaching an historic high of 11.80 percent in December 2003 and a record low of 1.60 percent in December 2002 (www.tradingeconomics.com/india/gdp-growth, retrieved 22 January 2012).
9 The Food Corporation of India was set up under the Food Corporation Act (1964) in order to fulfill the following objectives of the Food Policy:

- Effective price support operations for safeguarding the interests of the farmers;
- Distribution of food grains throughout the country for public distribution system;
- Maintaining satisfactory level of operational and buffer stocks of food grains to ensure National Food Security.

Since its inception, the FCI has played a significant role in India's success in transforming the crisis management–oriented food security system into a stable security system (http://fciweb.nic.in, retrieved 22 January 2012).
10 Incidentally, Sen (2006) has shown in his study that the most important reason for the Great Famine of 1943 was not the underproduction or absence of food grains, but illegal hoardings. Although production of food grains was quite satisfactory in this period, there was crisis due to a weak distribution system, illegal hoarding, and black markets.
11 *Bacillus thuringiensis*, or Bt., is a naturally occurring soil bacterium used by farmers to control Lepidopteron insects by means of a toxin it produces. Through genetic engineering, scientists have introduced the gene responsible for making the toxin into a range of crops, including cotton. In India, although cotton is grown on 5 percent of the total crop area, it uses 55 percent of all pesticides. Intensified chemical use has led to a dramatic rise in pest infestation as, over time, they have become resistant to insecticides. Increasing chemical costs and falling cotton prices have pushed thousands of cotton farmers in India, where the majority of the 17 million cotton-cultivating families subsist on less than two hectares, into a vortex of debt. Unable to face the consequences of crop failures and mounting debts, thousands of farmers across the country ended their lives in the last years (*Frontline*, April 13, 2001; www.frontlineonnet.com/fl2011/stories/20030606006012600.htm, retrieved 22 January 2012).
12 *The Hindu* 1 July 2010; *The Statesman* 11 January 2010; *The Hindu* 17 January 2010; *Deccan Herald* 21 January 2010; *The Times of India* 2 February 2010; *Hindustan Times* 26 February 2010.
13 Aruna Roy of Mazdoor Kishan Shakti Sangathan called this payment "shockingly unconstitutional". For details, see *The Indian Express* (Kolkata edition), 24 August 2010.

14 The Right to Information Act (2005) was enacted on 15 June 2005, and its preamble proclaims to "provide for setting out the practical regime of right to information for citizens to secure access to information under the control of public authorities in order to promote transparency and accountability in the working of every public authority" (Mukhopadhyay, 2007: 99).
15 For details, see *Indian Express* (New Delhi edition), 30 August 2010.
16 The AFSPA empowers the officials of the armed forces to fire upon or use any kind of force, even if it results in death; the power to arrest without a warrant, if necessary, by using force, even on the basis of suspicion; and to enter or search any premises for making such arrests. There is legal immunity for the army officials for all such actions when acting in areas where the law is in force; they cannot be prosecuted or placed under any other legal proceedings. This has undoubtedly resulted in serious human rights violations in the northeast and other areas where the law is in force.

5 The new political economy of judicial review in India

Mahendra Pal Singh

Judicial review and the Constitution

Judicial review, in the sense that the courts of a country can examine whether the actions of the other two branches of the state – the legislature and the executive – are consistent with the constitution of that country, had long been recognised in the countries of the Euro-American tradition well before the constitution-making process started in India in 1946. It was very much part of the Indian law to the extent that the courts could examine if the laws and the executive actions of the government of India or of the provinces were consistent with the provisions of the constitutional acts of British Parliament, such as the Government of India Act, 1935, and similar acts before that. The Constitution makers were, therefore, fully familiar with the exercise of the power of judicial review and its pros and cons. They were also familiar with other countries and their constitutions, such as that of the then-Soviet Union and other socialist countries, where this kind of power could not be exercised by the courts. Because, after due deliberations, the Constitution makers decided to have a constitution based on the Euro-American model, it was presumed from the very beginning that the courts would have the power of judicial review. It was a conscious decision on their part which did not require the kind of justifications Chief Justice Marshall had to develop one and a half centuries before in *Marbury v. Madison*[1] in the United States. Such a model of the constitution is based on a philosophy that supports limited powers of the state vis-à-vis its own citizens. Citizens are attributed certain rights which are considered to be natural and which they are never supposed to have surrendered to the state when, through the so-called social contract, they agreed to establish it. The recognition of rights, however, was not enough unless suitable arrangements were made for their protection from the state. Among those arrangements, the doctrine of separation of powers, along with its accompaniment of checks and balances, emerged as an instrument of statecraft which was meticulously incorporated into the Constitution of the United States by vesting the legislative, executive, and judicial powers in three different bodies whose personnel and functions were different and separate from one another. It is under this arrangement that the doctrine of judicial review acquired its legitimacy in the Constitution of the United States.

Although a constitution which establishes a parliamentary form of government, as the Constitution of India does, cannot incorporate the doctrine of separation of powers exactly the same way it has been done in the Constitution of the United States which establishes a presidential form of government, the constitutions establishing the parliamentary form of government along the lines of the United Kingdom have ensured the protection of the rights of the individual by separating the judiciary from the legislature and the executive. In this regard, the makers of the Indian Constitution did everything possible to make the judiciary separate from and independent of the legislature.[2] In the words of Granville Austin:

> The subjects that loomed largest in the minds of the Assembly members when framing the judicial provisions were the independence of the courts and two closely related issues, the powers of the Supreme Court and judicial review. The Assembly went to great lengths to ensure that the courts would be independent, devoting more hours of debate to this subject than to almost any other aspects of the provisions. If the beacon of the judiciary was to remain bright, the courts must be above reproach, free from coercion and from political influence.
>
> (Austin, 1966: 164–165)

In light of the experience of the working of the constitutions whose model they were following, as well as their own experience with the working of the colonial constitutions, the Constitution makers assumed judicial review as a natural attribute of the Constitution. "Judicial review, Assembly members believed, was an essential power for the courts of a free India, and an India with a federal constitution" (Austin, 1966: 165). Therefore, as the first case came before the Supreme Court challenging legislative and executive measures against the rights of the individual, the Court, without entertaining any doubts about whether those measures were consistent with the Constitution, invalidated at least one of the provisions of law (see *A. K. Gopalan v. State of Madras*, AIR 1950 SC 27). However, as was pointed out by some of the members of the Constituent Assembly, the courts were not expected to be super-legislative or super-executive (Austin, 1966: 174); the Supreme Court also warned itself and other reviewing courts quite early in a matter of judging the reasonableness of restrictions on certain fundamental rights in the Constitution. Speaking for the Court, Chief Justice Patanjali Sastri said:

> In evaluating such elusive factors and forming their own conception of what is reasonable, in all the circumstances of a given case, it is inevitable that the social philosophy and the scale of values of the judges participating in the decision should play an important part, and the limit to their interference with legislative judgment in such cases can only be dictated by their sense of responsibility and self-restraint and the sobering reflection that the Constitution is meant not only for people of their own way of thinking but for all and that the majority of the elected representatives of the people have, in authorising the imposition of restrictions, considered them to be reasonable.
>
> (*State of Madras v. V. G. Row*, AIR 1952 SC 196, 200)

Judicial review in practice

Even though the Constitution makers expected the judges not to act as a super-legislature or super-executive and the judges also instructed themselves that they must honour the wishes of the representatives of the people, by its very nature, the task of judicial review brings the judiciary and the other two branches of government into conflict. It does not happen normally when the three branches of the state are performing their respective functions in the administration of the state, but it happens when the legislature or the executive or both are dealing with the affairs of the individual. Whereas in the United States it took some time before such an issue arose in *Marbury v. Madison*, in India, such issues started arising soon after the commencement of the Constitution on 26 January 1950. Interestingly, however, although in matters of civil liberty the courts were slow in interfering with legislative or executive action, they did not show similar reluctance in matters of property or business or affirmative action for the weaker sections of society designated as Scheduled Castes or Scheduled Tribes, or socially and educationally backward classes. Consequently, within a year of the commencement of the Constitution, major changes had to be made to it concerning these areas. Even these changes failed to bring the desired understanding of the Constitution between the courts and the legislature and, therefore, the Constitution had to be amended time and again until the Court, in early 1967, held that the fundamental rights, including the right to property, could not be abridged even by an amendment of the Constitution (*Golak Nath v. State of Punjab*, AIR 1967 SC 1643). In such a situation, some other socio-economic measures affecting business or property were also invalidated (see, e.g., *R. C. Cooper v. Union of India*, AIR 1970, SC 564 and *Madhav Rao Scindia v. Union of India*, (1971), 1 SCC 85). In 1969, the rift between the political elements that stood for property and individual rights and those that stood for social welfare rights reached the stage which led to the vertical division of the main and, until then, the sole ruling political party at the centre. Judges were also suspected of bias towards the propertied class of society. In a situation that appeared to be leading to a constitutional breakdown, mid-term elections to Parliament in early 1971 gave the supporters of social welfare measures a vast majority.[3]

Emboldened by the support of the people, the government initiated major changes in the Constitution, removing first fetters on the power of amendment of the Constitution and then making it clear by another amendment that social welfare had to have priority over individual right to property.[4] Barring a minor part of these amendments relating to the power of judicial review, these amendments were upheld in the famous *Kesavananda Bharati* case[5] with the rider that the power of amendment did not include the power to amend the basic structure of the Constitution. The decision led to the supersession of those judges who supported a limitation on the power of amendment, ultimately leading to an open conflict between the judiciary and the other two powers. This in turn finally led to the infamous internal Emergency from 25 June 1975 to 21 March 1977, when the powers of the superior courts were drastically cut by the equally infamous 42nd Constitutional Amendment (1976), which also unsuccessfully tried to remove the basic structure limitation on the power of amendment. The limitations on the basic structure doctrine were invalidated by the Supreme Court which has since been invalidating amendments that directly or indirectly curtail the power of judicial review, but not the ones that promote social welfare or relate to socio-economic reforms; however, it did invalidate primacy of all the Directive Principles of State policy over certain fundamental rights and held that harmony between the fundamental rights and the directive principles of State policy is part of the basic structure of the Constitution.[6]

Much of the conflict between the Court and the other two branches of the state could be attributed to the supposed basis of the Constitution in the Euro-American tradition and pursuance of socialist policies by the government in the regulation and control of economic resources and means of production. Because the lawyers and judges trained in the Euro-American tradition of constitutionalism carried a perspective of the Constitution that did not match the socialist policies of the government, they could not reconcile the latter with the former. Consequently, a constant mismatch continued in terms of the understanding of the Constitution by the courts and the government. This mismatch also led to frequent and sometimes major Constitutional Amendments on the part of the government and consciousness on the part of the courts to preserve the Constitution as its guardians or custodians. Although in line with the socialist policies pursued by Jawaharlal Nehru, India's first prime minister, and after him by Mrs. Indira Gandhi, a persistent difference of understanding of the Constitution between the courts and the government continued until the beginning of 1977, when a change of regime at the Centre took place for the first time and led to a different understanding of the Constitution on the part of the government and the courts. Although the government removed many aberrations in the Constitution through its amendments, including the deletion of the fundamental right to property which had been a bone of contention from the very beginning between the courts and the government, the courts also started supporting the cause of those sections of society in whose name the government had been making policies and laws which the courts found inconsistent with the Constitution. It opened a new jurisprudence of the right to life which required assurance of dignified life to everyone in the country.[7] Even though Mrs. Gandhi was re-elected in 1980, she did not take any major policy initiatives on the previous lines. Initiative was taken with respect to transfer and appointment of judges of the High Courts, which was settled in favour of the government; the Court also established independence of the judiciary as part of the basic structure of the Constitution and laid the foundation for public interest litigation by relaxing the requirement of *locus standi*.[8] After the assassination of Mrs. Gandhi in 1984, Rajiv Gandhi, her son and new prime minister, started pursuing liberal policies, but without making an open statement to that effect. The same approach continued during the short administrations of the next two non-Congress prime ministers. It was only after the 1991 elections, in the course of which Rajiv Gandhi was assassinated and Narasimha Rao became the prime minister and Manmohan Singh became his finance minister, that the New Economic Policy (NEP) was openly announced in mid-1991. The process of globalisation and fall of the East European bloc were the prime factors in the adoption of this policy (Fraenkel, 2005; Nayar, 2007; Rudolph and Rudolph, 2008).

The New Economic Policy: its constitutionality and judicial review

Briefly speaking, through its budgetary, industrial, trading, and financial provisions the New Economic Policy (NEP) relaxes many restrictions on private investment, inflow and investment of foreign capital, international trade, and foreign exchange. It opens up the Indian market for free competition as part of the global economy. It reduces the so-called state or public sector and widens and encourages the sphere of private enterprise. In a way, it is an attempt to bring the Indian economy in line with the economy of the Euro-American countries which in Marxist language is called a capitalist economy. The economic policy which India was pursuing was not a fully Marxist economy, but it definitely was highly influenced by countries such as the Soviet Union, which were pursuing a Marxist economy. Many economists in the West predicted the doom of the Marxist economy, and in fact, it finally came in 1989–90, exposing all its drawbacks and weaknesses. Although until then two competitive ideologies of political economy existed in the world, with the fall and rejection of the Marxist governments, only one ideology of liberalism was left, albeit with some variations. The prevalent dominant paradigm of liberalism is composed of a fourfold political economy: (1) maximum play of market forces by privatisation, (2) representative democracy, (3) free trade, and (4) welfare state. This paradigm has been forced or produced by many national and international considerations, but at the moment it is expanding from the nation-states to the global economy. In lay terms, it represents a free market as opposed to state planning. The NEP has also been a movement in the direction of that paradigm.

Sharp differences have existed among economists and political thinkers about the wisdom of NEP with respect to its adequacy and desirability. These differences are inevitable and cannot be wished away. But my concern, as a legal scholar, is whether this also conflicts with the Constitution? Some scholars and constitutionalists have argued that the NEP is inconsistent with several provisions of the Constitution, such as the Preamble and Articles 19, 38, 39, 43-A, 305, etc., and is not legally sustainable unless India goes through a similar exercise of constitutional revision as some of the former socialist countries in Europe did after the fall of socialism.[9] In my view, these arguments are not consistent with the background and the nature of the Indian Constitution. The Constitution of India, as we have noted, is based, subject to its peculiarities, on the Euro-American model of liberal constitutions, which does not incorporate any specific economic policy within it that cannot be changed by the elected representatives of the people either in Parliament or State legislatures. Such a conception of the US Constitution was stoutly rejected by Justice Holmes well before in his memorable dissent in *Lochner v. New York*[10] stating:

> The Fourteenth Amendment does not enact Mr. Herbert Spencer's Social Statics. . . . [A] constitution is not intended to embody a particular economic

theory, whether of paternalism and the organic relation of the citizen to the State or of laissez faire. It is made for people of fundamentally differing views and the accident of our finding certain opinions natural and familiar or novel and even shocking ought not to conclude our judgment upon the question whether statues embodying them conflict with the Constitution of the United States.[11]

His dissent later became the law of the land, and all misconceptions about the nature and interpretation of the Constitution on this account were removed without any constitutional amendment. Although, of course, it took some time before Justice Holmes' dissent became the law, it has created an unforgettable precedent on the nature and interpretation of a constitution. Drawing lessons from that precedent, we can say that the Constitution of India also does not propound any particular economic theory. It does not incorporate any of the Marxist maxims of political economy that could be noticed in the socialist constitutions. The Constitution talks of social, economic, and political justice and of the welfare of the people. It also talks of distribution and control of material resources in such a way that they subserve the common good of the economic system in a way that does not result in the concentration of wealth and means of production to the common detriment. But it does not tell precisely how these goals will be served, except by leaving it to the determination of the elected representatives of the people. The elected representatives of the people pursued a particular kind of economic policy for over forty years to achieve these goals. Having failed in achieving them through that policy, they have decided to pursue a different policy. If they still fail, they may try a third alternative, and so on. This is what is expected from a durable constitution, and this is what the Indian Constitution does. There is no question of its coming into conflict with any economic policy – liberal, socialist, or any other. The following statement of the chairman of the Drafting Committee of the Constitution, Dr. B.R. Ambedkar, is instructive in this regard:

> [S]ocial and economic side are matters which must be decided by the people themselves according to time and circumstances. It cannot be laid down in the Constitution itself, because that is destroying democracy altogether. If you state in the Constitution that the social organization of the State shall take a particular form, you are, in my judgment, taking away the liberty of the people to decide what should be the social organization in which they wish to live. It is perfectly possible today, for the majority people to hold that the socialist organization of society is better than the capitalist organization of society. But it would be perfectly possible for thinking people to devise some other form of social organization which might be better than the socialist organization of today or of tomorrow. I do not see therefore why the Constitution should tie down the people to live in a particular form and not leave it to the people themselves to decide it for themselves.
>
> (Ambedkar, 1994: 326)[12]

These propositions apply equally to the provisions mentioned here and are relied upon by some scholars to establish conflict between the Constitution and the NEP. The Constitution sets the goal of social justice in a number of provisions, but it does not set the economic policies by which they alone will be achieved. The NEP is expected to pursue those goals as much as any policies, both in the past and in the future. Even the inclusion of "socialist", added to the preamble of the Constitution in 1976 does not change the position in light of doubts expressed about the constitutionality of its inclusion, as well as the vagueness of the notion.[13]

When the issue came before it in *Delhi Science Forum v. Union of India*,[14] the Supreme Court, rejecting the challenge to privatisation of telecommunications, observed:

> ... [t]he national policies in respect of economy, finance, communications, trade, telecommunications and others have to be decided by the Parliament and the representatives of the people on the floor of the Parliament can challenge and question any such policy adopted by the ruling Government.

Thus, national policies cannot be tested in a court of law. The courts cannot express their opinion as to whether at a particular juncture or under a particular situation, any such national policy should have been adopted or not. There may be views and opinions which may be shared and believed by citizens of the country, including the representatives of the people in the Parliament. But that has to be sorted out in the Parliament, which has to approve such policies. Privatisation is a fundamental concept underlying the questions about the power to make economic decisions. What should the role of the State be in the economic development of the nation? How shall the resources of the country be used? How shall fixed goals be attained? What are the safeguards to prevent the abuse of the economic power? What is the mechanism of accountability to ensure that the decision regarding privatisation is in the public interest? All these questions have to be answered by a vigilant Parliament. Courts have their limitations because these issues rest with the policymakers for the nation. No direction can be given, nor is it expected from the Courts, unless while implementing such policies, there is violation or infringement of any of the constitutional or statutory provisions.[15]

Again in *BALCO Employees Union v. Union of India*,[16] the Court observed:

> In matters relating to economic issues, the Government has, while taking a decision, right to 'trial and error' as long as both trial and error are bona fide and within limits of authority. There is no case made out by the petitioner that the decision to disinvest in BALCO is in any way capricious, arbitrary, illegal or uninformed. Even though the workers may have interest in the manner in which the Company is conducting its business, inasmuch as its policy decision may have an impact on the workers rights, nevertheless it is an incidence of service for an employee to accept a decision of the employer which has been honestly taken and which is not contrary to law.

The Court has reiterated the same position in a number of cases subsequently.[17] Thus, the constitutional position in this regard is well established. The NEP as such cannot be challenged on the plea that it is against the Constitution. Its specific implementation may, however, be questioned on a case-to-case basis on the ground that such implementation conflicts with any express provision of the Constitution that limits the powers of the legislature or of the executive. In the last few years, the Court has, however, held that policy decisions should not be outright irrational or unfair so as to transgress the fundamental or other constitutional rights of the individual.[18]

Federalism, the New Economic Policy and judicial review

Even though the Constitution of India creates federal arrangements between the Centre and the States with distribution of powers and resources and an independent government machinery for the performance of their respective functions, the federal arrangements are quite flexible, ensuring cooperation between the Centre and the States. Although in some matters the Centre and the States have exclusive legislative and executive powers, the Centre can override the State powers, either with or in some cases even without, the consent of the States. International affairs and international treaties are exclusively within the domain of the Centre. Not only can the Centre exercise these powers without consulting the States, it can also make any laws for the implementation of any international treaty, agreement, or convention irrespective of the fact that the subject matter of that law falls within the exclusive domain of the States.[19] In the exercise of such powers, in addition to making laws in several other matters, the Centre has been able to make several laws implementing its obligations in the process of globalisation. Some of the examples of such laws that followed the adoption of the NEP and membership of Trade-Related Aspects of Intellectual Property Rights (TRIPS) agreements and the World Trade Organization (WTO) are the Competition Act of 2002 that prohibits anti-competitive agreements in the interest of a free market economy, ensuring allocation of resources solely on supply and demand; making of or changing the intellectual property–related laws such as the Patent Act (2005), Trade Mark Act (1999), Geographical Indications Act (2000), and the Designs Act (2000); the Special Economic Zone Act of 2005, whose main objectives are generation of additional economic activity, promotion of exports of goods and services, promotion of investment from domestic and foreign sources, creation of employment opportunities, and development of infrastructure facilities, ensuring 'Single Window Clearance' of different projects in order to attract foreign direct investment; and the Foreign Exchange Management Act (FEMA) of 1999 which replaced the Foreign Exchange and Regulation Act (FERA) of 1973, with the objective of facilitating international trade and payments and promoting orderly development and maintenance of a foreign exchange market.

These and similar laws, either amending or replacing the existing laws or enacted for the first time, have been possible because the Constitution facilitates the making of such laws, irrespective of federal arrangements. Such arrangements also ensure unity of the nation, which Granville Austin refers to as one of the three strands of the seamless web of the Indian Constitution. Therefore, when it comes to internationalisation of trade or economy or monetary regulation or any other matter, the Constitution of India ensures quick realisation and regulation without the fear of hindrance by federal arrangements.

Back to the political economy of judicial review

The foregoing discussion in some ways establishes a connection between the political economy and the judicial review of legislative and executive actions. A socialist economy, founded on unification and concentration of ultimate power of the people in one organ of the state, or, ultimately in one person, does not align itself with the idea of independent judges reviewing the judgments of that organ or person. Therefore, the socialist constitutions did not and do not have provision for effective judicial review. Even if the courts have been created in such constitutions, their interpretation of the constitution is respected only so long as it is consistent with the ideology and decisions of that organ in which ultimate power is concentrated. If a judicial decision goes against the ideology or decision of that organ, it shall be set aside or ignored by that organ and necessary instructions will be issued to that effect. Perhaps one could argue that was the reason for the constant conflict between the courts on the one hand and the legislature and the executive on the other so long as the political power in the state pursued socialist policies, even though this power acknowledged that the Indian Constitution was not a socialist constitution, but was rather based on the liberal model of the West. It could be one of the reasons that quite often Court decisions were not found to be in sync with the political decisions and the Constitution had to be amended time and again to bring it in sync with political aspirations. Several judges could successfully reconcile the Constitution and its amendments with political aspirations, but not all of them could do that all the time. This could be for ideological reasons or for reasons based on their training and understanding of the Constitution. It could also be for reasons based on political leanings of judges, as was occasionally alleged. But, as we have seen, it happened and allegations and counter-allegations flowed.

The NEP has removed that dissonance between the political ideology of socialism and the liberal foundations of the Constitution. Therefore, much of the cause of the clash between the Constitution and political action presumably stands removed. This does not mean – and could never be expected to mean – that under the doctrine of separation of powers associated with checks and balances that no differences have existed or ever will exist between the courts and the political branches because of the change brought by the NEP. Serious differences have occasionally cropped up between the courts and the political institutions on several issues, particularly with respect to the rights of socio-economically disadvantaged sections of society. In certain instances, either the courts have failed to provide the expected judicial frameworks for the affirmative programmes of the state, or they have invalidated political decisions in favour of the industry or trade in disregard of vulnerable sections of the society, such as Scheduled Tribes.

A matter of concern in the exercise of power of judicial review is the fact that, unlike in the past, when the Court, as required by the Constitution, decided important questions of constitutional interpretation by means of a bench of five or more judges, during the last few years, it has been deciding several such questions in smaller benches of two or three. Apart from creating conflicting interpretations, this undermines the sanctity of the Constitution itself. If the Court fails to attend to this issue, it loses its claim to be the custodian of the Constitution and to question the decisions of the other two powers of the state.

Notes

1. 2 L.Ed. 60 (1803).
2. For details see M. P. Singh, Securing the Independence of the Judiciary – the Indian Experience. 10 *Indiana Int'l & Comp. L. Rev.* 245 (2000).
3. For details, see Austin, 1999, 171 ff.
4. Introduction of Art. 31-C.
5. *Kesavananda Bharati v. Union of India*, (1973) 4 SCC 225.
6. See, *Minerva Mills v. Union of India*, AIR 1980 SC 1789.
7. See, *Maneka Gandhi v. Union of India*, (1978) 1 SCC 248 and *Francis Coralie v. Union Territory of Delhi*, (1981) 1 SCC 608.
8. *S. P. Gupta v. Union of India*, 1981 Supp SCC 87.
9. See, for example, U. Baxi, Constitutional Perspectives on Privatization, *Mainstream* (6 July 1991) and S. S. Singh and S. Mishra, Public Law Issues in Privatisation Process, 40 *Indian Journal of Public Administration*, 396 (1994); also infra p. 11.
10. 198 US 45 at 75–76 (1905).
11. *Lochner v New York*, 198 U.S. 45 (1905).
12. B.R. Ambedkar. 1994. *Writings and Speeches*, vol. 13 (Bombay: Government of Maharashtra), p. 326.
13. For the application of the expression 'Socialist' see, e.g., *Excel Wear v. Union of India*, AIR 1979 SC 25; *National Textiles Worker's Union v. P.R. Ramakrishnan*, AIR 1983 SC 75; *D. S. Nakara v. Union of India*, AIR 1983 SC 130; *Kerala Hotel and Restaurant Assn. v. State of Kerala*, AIR 1990 SC 913.
14. *Delhi Science Forum v. Union of India*, 1996 AIR 1356.
15. Id. at 1359.
16. (2002) 2 SCC 333.
17. See, e.g., *Narmada Bachao Andolan v. Union of India*, (2000) 10 SCC 664; *Ashoka Smokeless v. Union of India*, (2007) 2 SCC 640; *ITDC Worker's Union v. ITDC Ltd*, AIR 2007 SC 301; *Centre for Public Interest Litigation v. Union of India*, AIR 2003 SC 3277; *APPSC v. BalojoBhadvath*, (2009) 5 SCC 1; *Dilip Kumar Garg v. State of UP*, (2009) 4 SCC 753; *Kusumam Hotel Pvt. Ltd. v. Kerala SEB*, (2008) 13 SCC 213.
18. See, e.g., *CSIR v. Ramesh Chandra Agarwal*, (2009) 3 SCC 35 – Policy matters are subject to judicial review and can be interfered on the ground of irrationality; *Mohd. Abdul Kadir v. DGP*, (2009) 6 SCC 611 – Though Courts avoid framing of policies, it is the duty of the court to draw attention of the authority concerned wherein issue involving public interest has not received attention; *Union of India v. Asian Food Industries*, (2006) 13 SCC 542 – A vested or acquired right cannot be taken away by reason of policy/amendment of policy; *Reliance Energy v. Maharashtra State Road Development Corporation*, (2007) 8 SCC 1.
19. Art. 253 of the Constitution of India.

6 Globalisation, extremist violence, and the Indian Left

A critical appraisal

Sobhanlal Datta Gupta

Although it is an established fact that the story of the Indian Left has been one of fragmentation, the advent of globalisation, at least apparently in the closing decade of the last century, has closed its ranks. Globalisation, with its focus on neo-liberal economic reforms and unbridled market forces, together with its rejection of state-centric welfarism, has been the Left's *bête noire* all over the world, and the Indian Left is no exception. Consequently, all shades of the Left in India, ranging from mainstream to non-mainstream, with the former represented by the parliamentary Left and the latter by the extremists, dubbed today Naxalites/Maoists, share the idea that globalisation is a force to be resisted, as it is the main engine of international finance capital. However, at the operational level, in the actual struggle against globalisation, there is hardly any sign of these two streams coming together. The difference centres on basically two issues. First, while critiquing globalisation because of its neo-liberal implications, the mainstream Left, however, differentiates, theoretically speaking, between its modernist thrusts and their appropriation by the proponents of neo-liberalism. The Left extremists are not inclined towards recognising this differentiation, since in their understanding, modernity, capitalism and globalisation are the three components of a single chain. Second, there are serious differences between these two streams of the Indian Left on the question of the alternative path of development vis-à-vis globalisation. In the mainstream Left, understanding globalisation is to be encountered by radicalising and democratising the state, whereas in the Left extremist perception, development is people-centric rather than state-centric, since the Indian state per se is a structure of violence to be dumped – lock, stock and barrel – by use of force. Globalisation, then, has superficially united and effectively fragmented the Left in India. This is truly an enigmatic issue, since, whereas the *adivasis* and the *dalits*, who are the worst victims of poverty in Indian society and of the kind of corporatism that globalisation has unleashed in the rivers, jungles, and mines which characterise the regions inhabited by them, making them the natural allies of the Left, it is the Naxalites/Maoists rather than the mainstream Left parties who have established a definite foothold in these areas. The situation, however, has assumed a more complex turn since 2004, when two Left extremist groups, namely, the People's War Group and the Maoist Communist Centre of India (MCC), joined hands and the Communist Party of India (CPI) (Maoist) was born. Since then, the Maoists have been involved in a protracted war against the Indian state as well as the mainstream Indian Left, notably the Communist Party of India (Marxist), as evident in its activities in West Bengal until 2011 when the Left Front was in power.

With globalisation-induced development being the heart of the problem, the question needs to be examined on multiple levels. First, how has globalisation impacted the rise of extremist violence in the area commonly now known as the red corridor, and what has the response of the Indian state been? Second, how does the CPI (M) view the phenomenon of Maoist violence and its bid for power, as the relations between the CPI (M) and the Maoists have worsened over the years? Third, how should the differences within the mainstream Left in regard to the Maoists be understood?

Concerning the first issue, it is now an established fact that globalisation in the name of corporate development and with the full backing of the neo-liberal state poses a very real threat to the local population in the areas inhabited by the *adivasis*, and the *dalits*, who have been the worst sufferers. Given that their livelihood is totally dependent on local resources like rivers and forests, the kind of development triggered by globalisation leads to their displacement and alienation from the development process itself. The affected zones in India are large belts of Odisha, Madhya Pradesh, Bihar, Jharkhand, Chhattisgarh, Andhra Pradesh, parts of Maharashtra, and West Bengal. The grinding poverty of these people, coupled with the threat to their very life and existence, explains the growing resentment among the people in these areas. The politics of Left extremism, which has thrived in these areas, to a large extent under the aegis of the Maoists, gives expression to these concerns. This has been admitted in at least two reports, one prepared by an expert committee formed by the government of India and the other by a task force formed by the Federation of Indian Chambers of Commerce and Industry (FICCI). Although the thrusts of the two reports are quite different, both have admitted that the major causes underlying extremist violence are poverty and backwardness – that is, lack of development, the primary victims of which are the local people who have been residing in these areas for ages. In the expert committee report prepared under the aegis of the government of India, the following States were identified as the hubs of Naxalism: Andhra Pradesh, Bihar, Chhattisgarh, Jharkhand, and Odisha. The following elements have been held as explanatory factors contributing to extremist violence in these areas: (1) large Scheduled Castes/Scheduled Tribes (SC/ST) population; (2) low levels of literacy; (3) high level of infant mortality; (4) low level of urbanisation; (5) high share of forest cover; (6) high share of agricultural labour; (7) low per capita food grain production; (8) low level of road length per 100 km^2; (9) high share of rural households which have no bank account; and (10) high share of rural households without specified assets (Government of India, 2008 : 20). That it is poverty and backwardness of the *adivasis* which constitute the breeding ground of Left extremism, commonly labeled Naxalism, was also admitted by the FICCI in its own task force report, which emerged out of a conference,

"Terrorism and National Security", held in 2008 in New Delhi. It admitted, "It is our long neglect of development in tribal areas, which has created large pockets of alienation against the government and these pockets have become the spawning grounds of Maoist insurgency" (FICCI, n.d.: 42). Thus, that the spurt in extremist violence in recent times is largely a consequence of the neo-liberal model of corporate development, which is globalisation's agenda in India, is admitted in both reports in two altogether different styles. In the expert committee report, alienation from land, destruction of community life, the stranglehold of contractors and the land mafia on the indigenous population in the forests and the mining zones, and the formation of Special Economic Zones (SEZs) have been held responsible for the wrong development strategy that is being pursued. The government of India's report stated the following:

> The development paradigm pursued since independence has aggravated the prevailing discontent among marginalized sections of society. This is because the development paradigm as conceived by the policy makers has always been imposed on these communities, and therefore it has remained insensitive to their needs and concerns, causing irreparable damage to these sections. The benefits of this paradigm of development have been disproportionately cornered by the dominant sections at the expense of the poor, who have borne most of the costs. Development which is insensitive to the needs of these communities has invariably caused displacement and reduced them to a sub-human existence. In the case of tribes in particular it has ended up in destroying their social organisation, cultural identity, and resource base and generated multiple conflicts, undermining their communal solidarity, which cumulatively makes them increasingly vulnerable to exploitation.
>
> (Government of India, 2008: 29)

That extremist violence is a direct challenge to the corporate model of development, the gift of globalisation, is made unambiguously clear in the FICCI report. There, it is noted that:

> . . . [t]he Naxalites may be the sleeper threat to India's economic power, potentially more damaging to foreign Indian companies, foreign investors, and the state than pollution, crumbling infrastructure, or political gridlock. The growing Maoist insurgency over large swatches of the mineral-rich countryside could soon hurt some industrial investment plans. Just when India needs to ramp up its industrial machine to lock in growth and just when foreign companies are joining the party – the Naxalites are clashing with the mining and steel companies essential to India's long-term success. The threat doesn't stop there. The Naxalites may move next on India's cities, where outsourcing, finance, and retailing are thriving. Officials at the highest levels of government are starting to acknowledge the scale of the Naxal problem.
>
> (FICCI, n.d: 36)

The dominant strategy that the Indian state has adopted for countering Naxalite/Maoist violence may broadly be described as one of counter-violence, resulting in repression of the local people, that is, the *dalits* and the *adivasis*, the social base of the extremists, as the police operation to hunt down the Maoists fails to differentiate between the activists and their social mainstay. This has unleashed a process which on one level widens the divide between the state and the poverty-stricken masses in the areas controlled by the Maoists, and on another level deepens the bond between the Maoists and the local people. Consequently, the Indian state in these regions appears in the eyes of the local people as a rogue state, and they consider the Maoists as their ally, as it is they who promise to protect them and fight for their cause against the assault of the state machinery on their habitat. It is not without reason that Himanshu Kumar, a noted Gandhian activist, has raised the question that viewed in this perspective, the problem lies not with the Maoists but with the Indian state which has created its own problem, since it is the latter which to them is the incarnation of violence and repression (Kumar, 2009: 8–12). But it is also a truism that the Maoist dream of coming to power in India through armed struggle is an illusion, at least in the immediately foreseeable future. Consequently, tribal India, as one commentator has pointed out, is the victim of a double tragedy: first, the Indian state treats the *adivasi* citizens with contempt and condescension; second, no long-term protection can be provided by the Maoists, who are supposedly their protectors (Guha, 2007: 3311).

Several interconnected issues are at play here. First, the development strategy that is at work under the aegis of globalisation is a threat to the identity and livelihood of the local people. Second, the Maoists are capitalising on this anger and discontent and have launched their crusade against the Indian state, the alleged purveyor of violence and repression. Third, the state retaliates with full fury against the Maoists and the local population, resulting in a kind of war of attrition. Fourth, in this cycle of violence the ultimate victims are the indigenous people, as well as the cause of development itself.

It is in this context that the second issue, namely, the CPI (M)'s position on the issue of Maoist violence, needs to be addressed, since for the CPI (M), a major constituent of the mainstream Left in India, globalisation, which is reflective of the spirit of neo-liberalism, has always been a target of scathing criticism. Historically speaking, the relations between the Left extremists and the CPI (M) have been quite unsavoury because the birth of the CPI (M-L) – Communist Party of India (Marxist–Leninist) – the parent organisation of today's Maoists, emerged out of an ideological and organisational split of the CPI (M) in 1969. Since then it has dubbed the CPI (M) a 'revisionist' party treading the path of parliamentary democracy by indulging in revolutionary rhetoric. In recent times, Naxalite groups of various shades and the Maoists stepped up their campaign against the CPI (M) when the Left Front Government in West Bengal, overwhelmingly dominated by the CPI (M), adopted a programme of hasty industrialisation in the name of development, allowing the setting up of SEZs and soft-pedalling of multinational corporations, while in many areas of the State the poor were left behind as victims of grinding poverty, underdevelopment, maladministration and show of muscle power by local CPI (M) leaders. It is these terrains which became the breeding ground of Naxalite/Maoist activities, with their proximity to Odisha and Jharkhand, the hotbed of Left extremism, being a contributory factor. The rise of the Maoists in West Bengal resulted in a violent show of strength by the Maoists as they virtually declared a war on the CPI (M) in a bid to decimate their strongholds, resulting in the killings of a number of CPI (M) activists. By using sophisticated devices, together with the local support extended to them by the Trinamool Congress, until the time of the Assembly elections in West Bengal in 2011, the Maoists succeeded in transforming large tracts of the districts of West Midnapur, Bankura, and Purulia into zones where administration virtually came to a standstill.

It is against this background that the CPI (M)'s estimation of Naxalism/Maoism has to be viewed. In the political resolution adopted at the 20th Congress of the Party in 2012, the Maoists were described as 'self-styled' revolutionaries indulging in a 'degenerated form of ultra-Left adventurism'. They were labelled 'anti-Left', working 'under the cover of revolutionary rhetoric', and it was alleged that by pitting the tribal people against the state through armed actions, the state was being provoked to resort to repressive measures against the tribals, with the latter being thus used as cannon fodder. The resolution read:

> They are pitting the tribal people against the State through armed actions by which they invite the full brunt of State repression on the tribal people. The Maoists do not attack only the security forces. They target a wide range of people, including political parties, and those who refuse to cooperate with them.
>
> 2.49 The startling fact is that the Maoists have killed 210 cadres and supporters of the CPI(M) in West Bengal in the last three years. This exposes their true character – under the cover of revolutionary rhetoric they act as an instrument of the anti-Left forces. The Maoists have killed more persons belonging to the CPI(M) than all the other political parties in the entire country.
>
> 2.52 The Maoists are thus a degenerated form of ultra-adventurism. They have to be fought by exposing their retrograde ideology and disruptive politics. Some sections of the petty bourgeois intelligentsia which claim to be Left, continue to support the Maoists. Their dubious positions should be ideologically combated and exposed.
>
> 2.53 The Party should fight the Maoists politically and ideologically and mobilise democratic opinion against the incessant violence of the Maoists, their fascist-like intolerance of political opponents, and their targeting of CPI(M) cadres and supporters in West Bengal.
>
> [CPI (M), 2012]

This criticism of the Maoists notwithstanding, the CPI (M), like any other Left political party, considers globalisation a menace to India. That globalisation in the guise of neo-liberalism is the other name for imperialism was made unambiguously clear by Prakash Karat and Sitaram Yechury, two key figures in the CPI (M) leadership. As early as 1998, in an article 'The Communist Manifesto: Globalisations, Nation-State and Class Struggle', Karat explained how Marx had already anticipated as early as 1848 the phenomenon of globalisation as a manifestation of expansion of capital across the world (Karat, 1998), and Yechury in 2001 in a seminar presentation entitled 'Globalisations and Impact on Indian Society' highlighted how globalisation posed a threat to India by its strategy of homogenisation, which was authored by Western finance capital (Yechury, 2001).

The appropriate question that becomes significant in this context is the theoretical underpinning of the Maoist and the CPI (M) position on globalisation. In critiquing globalisation, the Left extremist understanding is grounded in the post-modern/post-colonial viewpoint that the homogenising force of globalisation needs to be countered by the assertion of identity politics, which espouses the cause of pluralism and contests the very notion of the modernist state, with the latter being considered the agent of globalisation. The Naxalites' defence of the cause of the tribals and the *dalits* and their declaration of war against the Indian state has to be explained in this light. This post-colonial focus on micro-identities to the exclusion of the macro-concept of the Marxist notion of class struggle is anathema to the CPI (M), which is made abundantly clear in its ideological document adopted at its 20th Congress in 2012. The implication is that it is a methodological difference between post-colonialism and Marxism vis-à-vis globalisation, with the latter being the manifestation of Western modernity. The document reads:

> 10.9 In the current situation, Maoism as an expression of Left adventurist deviation continues to pose ideological challenges to the advance of the revolutionary class struggles of the Indian people. Despite its understanding being proved wrong, it continues to characterize the Indian ruling classes as comprador/bureaucratic and continues to adhere to a strategy of immediate armed struggle against the State. [. . .]. It collaborates with bourgeois reactionary political parties and forces to mount physical and murderous attacks against CPI (M) cadres and sympathisers. It is necessary to strengthen the ideological struggles against such a Left adventurist trend and combat it both politically and organizationally. [. . .]
>
> 10.17 The anti-Marxist ideological construct, post-modernism, argues that politics can only be 'micro' or local, that politics can be based on only 'differences' and 'identity'. Thus it provides a new basis for identity politics in the current situation.
>
> 10.18 In identity politics, as practiced by proponents of post-modernism, in today's conditions, identity based on ethnicity, religion, caste, tribe or gender increasingly becomes the basis for politics and political mobilisation. Class is considered to be only one fragment of identity. Identity politics thus negates the concept of the working class. By its very nature, identity politics excludes and demarcates those of one identity from others. Wherever identity politics takes hold, it divides the people into separate and disparate groups often in conflicting and competing terms.
>
> [CPI (M), 2012a]

The position of the CPI on Naxalism/Maoism is, however, altogether different from that of the CPI (M). Although there is no disagreement on the question that it is the neo-liberal state's protection of corporate interests which lies at the root of the misery of the *adivasis* and the *dalits* (Salwa Judum in Chhattisgarh being one classic instance of state-sponsored terrorism), it blames the state for trying to settle the problem by using violence instead of implementing its own programme of development work in these regions. Consequently, the strong-arm tactics of the Indian state employed in the affected areas are not endorsed by the CPI. Besides, the CPI is in favour of initiating a dialogue with the Left extremists instead of branding them terrorists. In the Draft Political Resolution of the CPI's 21st Congress held in 2012, it was stated:

> 135. Despite claims of three pronged policy to fight Maoism – law and order, development work and political fight – in most of the states police excesses, non-implementation of the development programme, corruption and state-sponsored drive for domination of ruling party are the main features.
>
> 136. Apart from that, the Union government too is having an agenda. It is trying to create an impression that Left extremism is more dangerous than terrorism. It wants to create an impression that Communists as such are dangerous. This is a very sinister move and need to be countered effectively. . . . We should insist that the rise of Left extremism is a socio-economic problem. While opposing the violence by Maoists, we should also condemn the brutal repression by the police under the garb of fighting Maoists. [. . .].
>
> 137. While rebuffing the government's move to discredit and marginalize the Communist movement as a whole by claiming that Left extremism is more dangerous than terrorism, we must initiate a dialogue and ideological campaign to refute the wrong interpretation of Marxism-Leninism by the Left extremists.
>
> (CPI, 2012: 34–35)

Notwithstanding the admission that the sufferings of the *adivasis* and the local poor, together with the rise of the Maoists, are to be attributed to the policies of the neo-liberal state, the Maoist line of violence and its strategy of seizure of power by use of armed violence are not endorsed by the CPI (ML, Liberation) either, which is now a constituent of the mainstream Left. This also is significant in the sense that it is a departure from the line that it has followed in the past, namely, the path of violent seizure of state power. Dipankar Chakrabarti, one of its top-ranking leaders and ideologues, in an article written in 2010 critiqued the Maoist position on two counts. First, in a country like India, the clandestine war launched by the Maoists against the Indian state would be ultimately of no avail, since its social base is extremely narrow. The vast majority of India's working people, with its most important segment being the working class, remains outside their purview. Second, in today's world, the credibility of a political party among the masses would largely be decided by its democratic credentials. There is no evidence so far that the Maoists are guided by the spirit of democracy; neither their organisational set-up nor their idea of an alternative state structure suggests that (Chakrabarti, 2010).

This debate within the mainstream Indian Left on the politics of Left extremism has two major theoretical implications for globalisation. One: Anti-statism, the core of globalisation, ironically is endorsed by Maoism, whereas the agenda of the mainstream Left is not to negate or oppose the state, but to democratise it and to pressurise it to carry out its own welfarist agenda in the regions which constitute the stronghold of the Maoists. Two: The Maoist position is essentially anti-modernist, which explains its post-modern/post-colonial outlook, resulting in its valorisation of identity politics and romanticisation of violence. Whereas for the Maoists, the onslaught of globalisation is to be countered by assertion of micro-level identities and pluralism, the mainstream Left strategy is to link these micro-level struggles to the larger macro-level battle for democracy involving the masses. Ultimately, then, it is a debate between anti-statism and statism, micro-identities like community, ethnicity, tribalism, etc., vis-à-vis class. For the Naxalites/Maoists who have waged a war against the state, the latter is nothing but a structure of violence, bereft of any democratic potential, while the mainstream Left contests this position, the argument being that by building up a strong mass movement, every effort has to be made to compel the state to work out the various welfare programmes it has already announced, since these have good potential to generate development in the areas affected by Maoist violence. In other words, whereas the Indian state's developmental strategy is marked by its two faces – namely, neo-liberal and welfarist – the Maoists' vision is coloured by a kind of one-dimensionality, the presumption being that the welfarist agenda is non-existent or simply irrelevant, guided as it is by a state that plays second fiddle to the interests of corporate global capitalism.

One commentator has explained that, although on one level, the government policy of encouraging private investment and ownership in mining, forestry, and SEZ has alienated the tribals by displacing them from their homeland and prepared the ground for the rise of Maoism, on another level, the various welfarist programmes of the government of India, like the National Rural Employment Guarantee Act (NREGA), the Right to Food, etc., if properly utilised, would be quite effective in combating Naxalism (Chenoy, 2007). Sumanta Banerjee, a leading commentator on Maoism, also decries the extremist defence of violence against the state, while declaring that it is the Indian state which has to come forward with a welfarist agenda and simultaneously take appropriate measures for controlling the unbridled activities of the police and the paramilitary forces which severely affect the livelihood of the local people (Banerjee, 2010).

The debate provides an interesting lead to the understanding of a larger question, namely, the nexus between modernity and democracy in the context of globalisation. In the Naxalite/Maoist understanding, since the dismantling of the Indian state is the principal task, the group does not hesitate to obtain finance and weapons from all kinds of sources, including local contractors, drug dealers, and various terrorist groups. This is indicative of the fact that the Left extremist vision is blinded by the understanding that for seizure of state power, any kind of unprincipled alliance rather than mass mobilisation is acceptable, since their vision is not informed by the idea of democracy. Consequently, an overarching centralism is the hallmark of the Maoists, which raises a couple of inter-related questions. First, adherence to centralism, with a focus on secrecy and armed struggle, may facilitate the idea of sticking to a power centre for a brief period, but in the long run it alienates the leadership from those who are at the receiving end, resulting in the erasure of the distinction between the allies and the enemies. Second, their organisational setup, being bereft of democratic values, and their idea of seizure of power in India fail to take into account the fact that the Indian state, despite all its shortcomings, until now has had to operate within the normative structure of a constitutional democracy, the marker of which is the practice of electoral politics. In other words, to use the Gramscian idiom, the Indian state today is closer to the 'West' rather than to the 'East' and it rules, unlike many other states in South Asia, not simply by force, but by a mixture of coercion and consent, with the latter being a key component. This explains their isolation and the political line of annihilation of anyone, who is a suspect in the eyes of the central leadership, irrespective of class moorings. Consequently, a number of victims of the Maoist violence have been the members of the oppressed classes. One commentator has graphically identified the features of their party as (1) no history of struggles outside jungles; (2) no history of participation in broad resistance movements; (3) clear complicity with mafia and reactionary forces; (4) little concern about abject conditions of health and poverty in control areas; and (5) enforced large-scale use of children for welfare (Mukherji, 2012: 25). Consequently, he raises a thoughtful question, namely, if the Maoists, devoid of any idea of democracy hypothetically speaking,

> . . . are able to improve on their dismal record on welfare and human rights in their areas of control, stop the use of children, use arms only to defend themselves strictly in accordance with international conventions, avoid contacts with the mafia, develop a friendly attitude towards other radical groups etc. *without giving up on the programmes of secret organisation, armed struggle and protracted war* . . .

then they would cease to be a party of the Maoists (Mukherji 2012: 26, original emphasis). Third, there is a crucial epistemic issue raised by Virginius Xaxa in an article written in 2005 which has an important bearing on the claim of the Maoists that they are supposedly the true representatives of the tribal interests, this being the ground for justifying their acts of violence. There is, the author points out, a necessary hiatus between the consciousness of the tribals themselves and the consciousness that is attributed to them by others, including scholars and administrators, for the reason that their primordial consciousness is not coterminous with the way it is articulated through their co-option by the state on its own terms (Xaxa, 2005: 1369). This difference between the consciousness of the incorporated tribals and their true consciousness cannot be bridged by the Maoists either, despite their tall claim. The clue to this understanding can be traced back to the argument advanced by Gayatri Chakravorty Spivak in her path-breaking essay "Can the Subaltern Speak?" that ontologically, the authentic subaltern is not the same as the constructed subaltern, with the latter being a product of the cultural flows of modernity (Spivak, 2000: 1427–1477).

In the Left extremist understanding, democracy becomes a casualty due to more than its emphasis on overt centralism. In its bid for anti-statism, with the latter being treated as the villain to be destroyed, it objectively also opens up spaces precisely for those players, namely, non-governmental organisations (NGOs), civil society, and the network of private institutions which are projected by the strategists of globalisation as the agents of development vis-à-vis the all-pervasive authority of the state. The implication is that the Left extremist position on the state accomplishes precisely what globalisation aims to achieve. As the citizen is taken out of the control of government and put into the clutches of the market and various non-state actors in the name of governance, the most essential component of citizenship, namely, politics, faces erasure (Chandhoke, 2003: 2964). It relocates the citizen in an identity discourse whereby the latter is concerned with the framing and guarding of his or her own space in a group or community, away from the political space controlled by the state. It is this astatist, apolitical orientation which is taken advantage of by the private players, ranging from civil society to various agencies, resulting ultimately in the shrinkage of the very idea of democracy itself. Ironically, the Maoist agenda thus works in tandem with that of globalisation, as the state is anchored off the project of development and the non-state private players step in, and this precisely is what the mainstream Left has opposed. In a perceptive article written quite recently, Andre Béteille has examined the prospects of a so-called "stateless society" in the wake of liberalisation and globalisation and shown the complete futility of the argument that development for the common man can be engineered by NGOs, markets, or any other private player as substitutes of the state in a country like India, since this involves investment that would not generate profit, that is, primary schools, basic health care and sanitation facilities for millions, and a supply of drinking water (Béteille, 2011).

That the Left-extremist position cannot provide any credible model of development is largely explained by its flawed understanding of modernity. Initially, the mainstream Left also failed to negotiate this issue, as manifest in their dogged opposition to information technology, with the latter being viewed as a mechanism which would promote the cause of capitalism, since its global dissemination is controlled by the Silicon Valley in the United States and its operation is monopolised by giant multinational corporations like Microsoft. Eventually, as the Indian state embraced, generally speaking, a neo-liberal path with an emphasis on reforms and liberalisation and entered the global network, acceptance of this new technology became a historical imperative, with the agenda of industrialisation following therefrom. However, the mainstream Left in India, unlike the Naxalites/Maoists, are faced with a complex question, namely, how to project the idea of modernity, with the adoption of new technology and industrialisation being its major offshoot and the entry of private players being unstoppable, in a direction which would serve the interests of the working people and not those of the private players who control the market. For the mainstream Left in India, this involves the adoption of a strategy which would usher in an alternative construction of modernity whereby the society at large would be its beneficiary. This touches upon the question of making a distinction between the agenda of good and that of bad modernity, between modernity which would be conducive to the interests of the common man and the kind of modernity which would cater to the interests of the market.

This is precisely where the question of democracy comes in. This alternative perception of modernity was worked out by Lenin in the form of a highly ingenuous formulation, namely, communism = soviets + electrification (Lenin, 1966). While speaking at a conference of the Russian Communist Party (Bolshevik) in 1920, Lenin said:

> There can be no question of rehabilitating the national economy or of communism unless Russia is put on a different and higher technical basis than that which has existed up to now. Communism is Soviet power plus the electrification of the whole country, since industry cannot be developed without electrification.
>
> (Lenin, 1920: 419)

Its implication was quite deep and far-reaching. It meant a strategy which would combine democracy from below and the accomplishments of modernity in a backward country, predominated by the peasantry. But in doing this exercise, he scrupulously refrained from romanticising the peasantry, which was most strongly evident in his critique of the Narodniks. Simultaneously, he underscored the importance of learning from American efficiency, while recognising at the same time the importance of tradition. This was apparent in his critique of the Proletcult, an outlook represented by militant young radicals who ridiculed tradition in their quest to establish the post-revolutionary social order in Russia. For Lenin, therefore, the issue was not to provide a critique of modernity per se, but to distinguish between good and bad modernity and to combine good modernity with democracy. What he contested was bad modernity that impaired democracy (Datta Gupta, 2012: 19–20). To a large extent, this is also the challenge before the mainstream Left in India today in times of globalisation. The Maoists, thanks to their views on democracy and modernity, can afford to ignore this challenge, engrossed as they are in their utopian vision of an agrarian revolution through a violent seizure of state power. In this agenda, modernity is a taboo and their love for democracy being minimal, they are spared the problem of combining democracy and modernity. For the mainstream Left, the challenge is far more complex, as in today's globalised world, while accepting new technology and the compulsions of the market, it has to work out an appropriate strategy of channelising the positive fruits of globalisation to the lowest levels of society, the zones of darkness, which have acted as the nurseries of Left extremism in India in recent times.

7 Policing in India
A failed case of institutional reform?

Surajit C. Mukhopadhyay

Policing under any circumstances at any point in time is a complex phenomenon that is determined by a multitude of factors, critical among which are the political and the historical dimensions. The structure of the Indian police has largely remained unchanged since colonial times, although its functions and expectations have changed radically since independence and the democratisation of the polity. On a global scale, shifts have occurred from a predominantly statist perspective where the raison d'être of the police was seen as serving the government of the day, to modern policing increasingly being viewed from a citizen's point of view. As with all other aspects of governance, this citizen-centric perspective makes policing a service – one that is measured with reference to the expectations of a rights-bearing individual. This stands in sharp contrast to the more entrenched understanding of policing as part of the coercive apparatus of the state only.

The emergence of this perspective in police studies (Ahire, 1991; Anderson, 1994; Aydin, 1995) has created a new discursive field for the practice of policing variously called 'community policing' or 'community-oriented policing'. This is not to say that this alternative view is a perfect antidote for the age-old practices that were statist. The emergence merely shows the dissatisfaction with a model that relies entirely or mostly on force per se. The relation between the police and the polity is an important factor in deciding the nature of policing – a government's credential as a democratic political dispensation hinges crucially on the manner in which policing is carried out.

In a multi-ethnic, multi-lingual, and poly-religious society prone to conflict, the role of the police is of immense importance, and the institution is crucially dependent on skills that force alone would not provide. Further, in a world where civil society activism has attained critical heights, policing must seek to incorporate the emergent trends of a globalised world that has increasingly brought the activities of distant lands into the home and hearth of millions of Indians and with it the messages and stories of dissent, resistance, and rebuilding of polities and communities.

Paradoxically, the age of globalisation is also an age of conformity – market forces gradually penetrate the vast Indian hinterland, contributing to a uniformity of socio-economic practices that draw stiff resistance from diverse groups and classes. Market forces in search of resources and profits often cause displacement and misery for a vast number of people who find themselves left without access to livelihood. The 'Maoist problem' as it exists in the tribal-dominated areas of Chhattisgarh, Odisha, Andhra Pradesh, Maharashtra, and West Bengal is often a direct consequence of the failure of the democratic system to ensure justice and access to basic goods and services. However, the increasing marginalisation of the people and the feeling of alienation that has set in have spawned a violent armed movement that has triggered a state response equally violent and forceful. This undoubtedly has moved the discourse of policing away from community-oriented strategies to a more vigorous armed police-centric model that mirrors the colonial state response to internal dissent.

There is misunderstanding among academics and police personnel alike about the concept of the 'community-oriented' or 'community-policing' model (King and Brearley, 1996; Mawby, 1990). This chapter thus endeavours to analyse the various models of policing with special reference to India. Research into Indian policing is sparse and virtually non-existent, as opposed to research into other aspects of governance and law and order. This paucity is due to several factors – the secretive nature of police organisations with inherent reluctance to share information, the ignorance among police officers about the need to do research, and the fear of criticism from 'outside' the organisation. Although these factors are common to many police organisations across the globe, much of the problem in relation to research into Indian policing is firmly rooted in the colonial origins of the police which saw policing as an activity in isolation of the populace and, more critically, in opposition to the populace (Anderson and Killingray, 1991; Arnold, 1986; Mukhopadhyay, 1998). This historical baggage shapes the Indian police even sixty years after independence and is summarised by the failure of the state to find an alternative legislation to the colonial Police Act of 1861.

What does the Police Act of 1861 say? Or, more pertinently, what does it not say that should be said?

> [The] duty of every police officer (is) promptly to obey and execute all orders and warrants lawfully issued to him by any competent authority; to collect and communicate intelligence affecting the public peace; to prevent the commissioning of offences and public nuisances; to detect and bring offenders to justice; and to apprehend all persons whom he is legally authorized to apprehend and for whose apprehension sufficient ground exists [...].
> (cited in Mehra and Lévy, 2011: 39)

A close reading of the act would show that in the order of importance attached to policing duties, the police are not enjoined to be of service to the people, and neither is it their remit to garner trust and legitimacy for their acts. This, as shall be shown subsequently, is the gestalt of colonial policing strategy and it is ill suited to a democratic and independent country or a state where the civil society has made strong inroads to claim a stake not anticipated by the Police Act of 1861.

In political economic terms, the colonial British police was a strong arm of the government that was designed to be used primarily for rent extraction, which is reflected in the repressive provisions of the Act of 1861. For example, Section 15 of the Police Act provides for stationing additional punitive police where the area in question is disturbed by the inhabitants. More critically, the cost for such additional deployment was to be recovered through levies on the local populace and through sale of confiscated property of those who were proclaimed to be absconding. Anandswarup Gupta (1979) notes that the "Act made provision in detail only for two purposes, the establishment and administration, under strict magisterial control [. . .] and measures for using it to keep the people of the country effectively repressed" (Gupta, 1979: 7). It is significant that these legal measures were introduced at a time when the people were becoming increasingly strident in their resistance to British rule. The 'Indian mutiny' of 1857 must have been fresh in the memory of the colonial administration – not only did the civilian population rise against the British, but a substantial section of the colonial army had also become embroiled in the revolt. This must have sent panic signals in the then-colonial administration, and subsequently, the Indian police drilled along army lines became an auxiliary armed force of the state. In this context, scholars (Kudaisya, 1992; Yang, 1985; Arnold, 1985, 1986; Cartwright, 1995) working on colonial police administration and policing strategies have pointed out that policing was mainly concerned with upholding the authority of the state rather than protecting the life and property of the people.

The other imperative that must not be overlooked is the use of the police in effecting a more efficient system of revenue collection. The establishment of an effective police force, it was felt, would provide a better milieu for the collection of revenue. Warren Hastings, the first governor-general of India from 1773 to 1785, argued that the possible objections to the establishment of the police force on the grounds of expenses were not valid, as returns from security and order that a police force can obtain for colonial trade would be more profitable in the long run. Hastings stated:

> I am assured that many villages, especially in Jessore and Mahmudshahee, pay a regular malguzaree to the chiefs of the dacoits, from which if they can be freed, the reiats will certainly be better enabled to pay their rents to the Government, independently of the improvements which their lands may be expected to receive from a state of quiet and security.
>
> (cited in Griffiths, 1971: 55)

The control of crime and the compulsions of colonial politics therefore became intertwined – one played off the other – and indeed, as Arnold (1986) comments, they were inseparable from the colonial administration. Any dissent and revolt against the colonial rule was a challenge to the tenuous hold of colonialism and deserved the full wrath of the state's coercive arm. This made the police inseparable from the state and insulated from the people who were policed. Yet paradoxically, the colonial control did not require intensive policing. The police in rural India were to be brought into action only to prop up the state, which made policing an adaptive and selective enterprise. The colonial police appeared intimidating not only to those who were being policed, but also to those who were mere onlookers. Arnold puts the matter succinctly when he argues that

> ... the state relied upon the use of coercion to compensate for other deficiencies in rural policing, to magnify the impact of a limited police presence and to assist in the formation of a 'proper', that is a compliant and co-operative, 'public opinion'.
>
> (Arnold, 1986:147)

A study of British colonial police structures across the world reveals policing as a punitive force that would have salutary effect in terms of a show of arms and forcing into submission a sullen and restive populace. In Kenya, for example, the police were concentrated in the towns and centres of the settler communities. This pre-occupation with urban policing was a direct consequence of colonial trade and commerce (Anderson, 1994: 254). In India, with a rapid rise in trade, commerce, and industrial output that was integral and essential to the colonial economy, it was imperative for the colonial police to concentrate most of its resources on such centres of activity. As a corollary condition, and as a consequence of the use of the police by the colonial administration as a punitive force, all challenges to power, authority, and property were converted to a law-and-order paradigm, enabling a political economy conducive to colonial extraction to take shape. Basu (1994), in his work on labour in the mill towns of colonial Bengal, shows how the colonial police worked explicitly on the orders of the jute mill owners and managers. Further, police were used on a regular basis to break up strikes and meetings convened by workers protesting low wages and poor working conditions. Thus, a connection between profit, production, and policing practices was established in the process. The maintenance of state and class control was never so well articulated as in the political agenda of the Indian colonial state, where the police were given the task of maintaining this status quo.

This, however, gave rise to a "fund of subaltern bitterness" (Arnold, 1986: 235) against the police. The seething undercurrent of anger and bitterness created a relation of adversity between the police and the policed that, in the long run, undermined the efficacy of the institution and its legitimacy. Arnold argues that the colonial police were very expressive of the nature of colonial rule itself. There was a belief in a periodic show of arms, in the interplay of the police and military responsibilities, the equation of force with authority and that of opposition with crime, the absence of public accountability, the reliance on supervisory and classificatory systems of manipulation and control, and the innovatory nature of policing itself (Arnold, 1986: 235). Although this may have worked in favour of the colonial administration and government, it would, as will be shown in the subsequent section, also prove to be a recipe for disaster in an independent India.

Sigler and King (1992), researching into colonial policing, pointed out that the basic difference between policing in Britain and the colonies was that in Britain, policing was essentially dependent on consent and, therefore, could posit a model of unarmed policing, whereas in the colonies, police operations were based upon sanction of armed force. They suggest that colonial policing survived the end of colonialism insofar as colonial structures are seldom done away with. The colonial police structure allows the government to maximise control of the population by separating the police from the community and by having strangers policing strangers. This denies the police as an organisation a more integrated and legitimised role within the discourse of maintaining law and order and makes them illegitimate in the eyes of the populace.

It is in this context of decreasing legitimacy and increasing democratisation of the polity in independent India that the idea of community policing was mooted. A former officer, who had headed the Delhi police, writing on this issue felt that the Indian police would have to overcome the problem of a 'bad image' and argued in favour of reform in police culture. The space for this reform is to be found in the recognition within the force that it also has a "service-oriented, citizen-protection-oriented and crime-prevention-oriented" role (Roy, 1992: 53). According to him, if these roles were closely woven into the culture and ethos of the police, then "its credibility and acceptability in society would have been vastly better, despite its otherwise negative functions" (Roy, 1992: 53).

A service-oriented force would necessarily shed the adversarial image that colonialism has so effectively entrenched and bring to focus as a key area of concern the police–public interface. This would also change the culture of conflict management honed by the colonial administrative practices, for the post-colonial independent state had, by the inertia of its history, drawn upon such a discourse. Community policing strategies all over the world have tried to overcome this crisis of overt dependence on coercion and repression, as well as decreasing regime legitimacy by forwarding the agenda of meaningful engagement with the citizenry.

The Padmanabhaiah Committee on Police Reforms was set up by the Union Home Ministry in the year 2000. The committee was entirely made up of government bureaucrats and police officers and had a large remit. It, too, felt that the police–public relation needed to be improved and that the Indian police should adopt the philosophy of community policing. It also felt that the Union government should bring out a policy guideline on this issue and that training inputs should be incorporated for police personnel. In addition, it felt that the government of India should set up a permanent National Commission for Policing Standards as a body that would set up and maintain uniformity in police work. Like many police commissions before the setting up of the Padmanabhaiah Committee, it felt that the Police Act of 1861 should be replaced – that is, an act for the police in post-colonial India should be in consonance with the reality of the socio-economic and political conditions.

Several programmes and pilot projects tried to usher in community policing styles and philosophy. In West Bengal, for example, a pilot project was undertaken whereby two police stations of the State – East Bidhannagar in Salt Lake and Bolpur in the district of Birbhum – were to be transformed into model police stations. It was also the first attempt by a group of citizens backed by the government to engage with a core concern of the state: the policing strategy(s). The effort was to think in a manner that incorporated the concerns of the policed. Whereas the East Bidhannagar police station is located in Salt Lake, an extended suburb of Kolkata and highly urbanised, the Bolpur police station is largely rural and incorporates a great number of villages. Not much came out of this effort, which was funded by the Ford Foundation and had very accomplished retired senior police officers and serving academics on board. The failure of the programme to gather momentum and become a movement was largely due to the government failing to take cognisance of the project as much as it was a failure of those involved to inspire real change at the targeted police stations. Thus, the project, known as the 'Law Enforcement Reform and Good Governance in West Bengal', died an unsung death, as did many others in other parts of the country. Part of the failure to usher in community-oriented policing lies with the failure of the political system to see the changes in the police administration as leading to a system of 'Good Governance', although such gestures are also routinely made. A case in point is the efficient and reasonably successful manner in which the superintendent of police in the Murshidabad district of West Bengal turned the sullen and restive populace of Hariharpara Police Station into partners of the administration, thereby bridging the trust deficit that was once prevalent there. Part of the problem is also the inability to conceptualise a post-colonial police system in India, which entails reforms. A community-oriented police system may not emerge as a reality unless one understands what post-colonial policing is all about.

One of the more universal features of post-colonial policing is the heavy emphasis on the armed and paramilitary style of policing. This involves the application of quasi-military training, equipment, and organisation to questions of policing. The para-military style of policing often involves the imposition of a brutal public order and an admission that negotiation has broken down, or that there is a crisis of hegemony that is present. It is also related to regime representation through the control of public order. Although all post-colonial states do qualify as modern states, none of them has a private economy that can be reasonably called an 'advanced institution of capitalism'. As a corollary, it can be said that the bureaucracy, and by implication the police, brings a different dimension to authority and coercion, both physical and otherwise. Thus, even though the concepts of hierarchy, command structure, and public office separate from kin and other familial ties and the principles of positive and negative sanctions are all universally operative, the socio-economic milieu in which all these are embedded becomes transformed and even transmogrified in the context of post-colonial police and police administration. Drawing on Max Weber, it can be argued that in the absence of a fully fledged capitalist sector, post-colonial bureaucracy can only mimic the advanced capitalist societies morphologically without realising the gestalt of the structures in question. In other words, the nature of bureaucracy in post-colonial states, it can be argued following Max Weber, would be bureaucratic authority that would reinforce the statist nature of police and civil administration. The bureaucratic management that is predicated upon the growth of a capitalist economy, and which acts as a counterbalance to authority in capitalist societies, is obviously muted or absent in most post-colonial countries. Bureaucratic organisation usually comes to power, according to Weber, on the basis of a levelling of economic and social differences. The 'levelling' may be relative, but is an essential assumption for modern administrative functions. However, the postcolonial Indian state has not been able to out the differences and stark contrasts in the population with regard to inequalities in social status and economic wealth. With the liberalisation of the economy from 1991 onwards, the history of the postcolonial Indian state can be seen as entering a new phase with a distinct rupture from the trajectory that it had followed since 1947.

The formation of a polity that is underpinned by liberalisation and driven by globalisation did not 'level' out the differences that Weber understood to be the hallmark of an advanced capitalist society. The creation of enormous wealth has not been matched with an even distribution of resources, and access to public goods has remained out of bounds for many. Indeed, the government of India has of late been forced to acknowledge that about two decades after the 'opening up of the economy', inequality is a major concern, as is the uneven nature of the distribution of resources across the country (UNDP Report on HDI in India, 2011). The situation has become critical over time, and a new initiative has been launched to remedy the state of affairs – the programme of 'inclusive growth'. Thus, the post-colonial situation can be divided into two phases: one that can be traced from 1947 to 1991, and the other from 1991 to the present. It is during this second phase that globalisation manifests itself much more acutely and far-reaching connections between global developments and the situation in India can be observed.

The nomenclature notwithstanding, for the purpose of policing, India remains a divided society with intricate fractures and fissures that challenge the idea of Good Governance. The centralisation of power through economic gain and the waning of political resistance against the new dispensation of a liberalised economy have thrown up a variety of dangerous challenges to the Indian state, which have manifested themselves in various ways – ethnic strife, communal violence, and riots, as well as extreme Left militancy. Added to these largely internal or domestic concerns is international terrorism in the form of Islamic terror. The resultant reaction has been the increasing 'militarisation' of the police forces, thus relegating issues of community policing and service-oriented policing strategies to the background.

In the immediate aftermath of the 'opening of the Indian economy', Atul Kohli (1990) commented on the crisis of governability that the Indian state was going through and would continue to encounter in the future. Rajni Kothari had seen the Indian state in the grip of an 'unbalanced development' and the consequential unleashing of power of the state to contain the 'challenge of the unprecedented mobilisation of the masses' (Kothari, 1988). In today's India, the word development, which suggested moderation in the exploitation of natural resources, has been replaced by the more rapacious and faster notion of growth, and the challenge of the masses has perforce moved away from democratic methods of resistance to, as noted earlier, more militant ways and means. Issues of social management and political resolutions are branded law-and-order problems, and repression of the dissenting voices further erodes the credibility of the police force.

With liberalisation and the dynamism of the market, the Indian state, or more precisely, the Indian police, is now forced to face a dilemma – on the one hand, it senses that the reform of the police and its engagement with community-oriented policing is a solution that can retrieve its legitimacy in the eyes of the citizenry. On the other hand, the increase in militancy has created a discourse of police modernisation that increasingly centres on weapons and surveillance technology, thus increasing the distance between the police and the policed. France, which in many ways mirrors the armed style of policing known as the 'continental' style, has found great similarity with the Indian police insofar as over the years there have been efforts at reforms for a more community-oriented approach. However, neighbourhood policing, a concept that is close to the idea of community policing, was not considered a solution to the state-oriented armed style of policing (Lévy, 2011) – a situation similar to India's faltering on reforms in policing.

Interestingly enough, the police in England and Wales, known for their low-key, unarmed approach to policing, have been undergoing a quiet militarisation (Mukhopadhyay, 1998). Ever since the Brixton riots and the miners' strikes, ways to ensure public order have become increasingly removed from the community-based approach that the police in England were known for. Parallel to this development is the manner in which the polity in Britain has moved away from social welfare measures and plunged into the socio-economic policies of right-wing politics led by Margaret Thatcher, the then-Prime Minister of the United Kingdom and leader of the Conservative Party. This is ample proof that policing as a discourse is always in consonance with the greater political currents that flow through state and society. The discourse of policing and the discourse of politics are mutually influencing, creating the imperatives that drive forward the agenda. Therefore, when the Indian state decided on a particular economic programme after the collapse of the Soviet Union, it became imperative that policing also change with the political rhythm that was unleashed. But unlike in the United Kingdom, where there was an engaged debate about the role of the police and the expectations of the citizens from within the police, both serving and retired, in India, the debate over the role of the police and their approach has been muted post-1991. This stands in contrast with other watersheds in modern Indian history, for example, the Emergency rule (1975–77), in the aftermath of which the National Police Commission (NPC) was set up. Appointed on 15 November 1977, in the immediate wake of disruption of parliamentary democracy in India, the NPC was an expression of the desire to investigate the role of the police in the suspension of democracy. The NPC report was submitted to the government in five parts, but none of the recommendations were ever implemented.

Thus, the force/service dichotomy was never problematised and the question of 'over policing versus under policing', or militarisation of the police versus suggested reforms did not take place. A direct consequence of this was the acceptance of the view, *sotto voce* as it were, that modernisation of the force meant armament, and that combat tactics were needed in place of skills traditionally associated with the police. Thus, para-military tactics became the thrust area for police modernisation in lieu of reforms that would have brought to the fore the debate over service orientation and militarisation. It is instructive that the places where the armed militarised police have been sent to operate, the so-called 'liberated areas' under Maoist control, are precisely the areas where two of the most important developments in post-1991 India have taken place – the erosion of state legitimacy and the opening up of the forests and the interior to mining and mineral exploitation. With the insurrection in mind and the outside terrorist threat looming large, it would seem that the Indian police has once again lost the opportunity to reform itself and create a discourse of community-oriented policing strategy(s) that would have been in sync with the other development of contemporary India – the rise of a vocal civil society backed by a dynamic media that has been able to reach out to an unprecedented mass audience. With the rise of civil society activism, a strong audio-visual media, and an enhanced consciousness of human and civic rights, the confrontation between a police refusing to reform and a society fast transforming itself is bound to take place.

8 The problems of Statehood in Indian federalism
A case for territorial pluralism

Rekha Saxena

Introduction

The rapid pace of globalisation has arguably had a profound impact on Indian federalism and the socially and culturally heterogeneous States. Since the beginning of coalition governments at the Union level in the late 1980s and the economic decentralisation consequent upon the process of globalisation, the States have found a new space for themselves, and are now able to assert a greater influence than ever before (Bhattacharyya, 2011, 2009a; Sáez, 2002; Dua and Singh, 2003). The State governments have been able to see through the advantages of the new liberalisation scenario. In short, this process led to a greater degree of reorientation of the States' role as the national government shed its labyrinthine regulations (Mitra, 2007).

The reforms have involved opening up the economy, making it more competitive, reducing significantly the role of the Union government as the sole authority of regulation, and empowering the States to take more responsibility for their development. Further, in the realm of society, culture, and polity, economic liberalisation has infused a new layer of assertion and confidence amongst the States to create a distinct niche for themselves. This also made the study of State politics and identities within their domain an alternative parameter of analysis. This chapter seeks to discuss the ethno-national moorings and the struggle for Statehood in modern India in the age of India's reforms.

This theoretical idea of the States as independent sites of growth can be captured from the imagination of globalisation theorists like Kenichi Ohmae, who argues that the rise of States/sub-units in the global era needs to be seen as geographical clusters and as potential engines of huge regional economic growth (Ohmae, 1995). Baldev Raj Nayar contends that globalisation is nothing but a new incarnation of modernisation (Nayar, 2007: 26). He further argues that defying the predictions of both the supporters and critics of globalisation, the nation-state remains at the heart of the project to accomplish the developmental transition. Gupta and Sharma point out that the impact of globalisation on various States will be different, and transformation in each State is different. They note that we cannot overlook the political context and history of a particular State in order to understand the impact of globalisation in that State (Gupta and Sharma, 2006). Interestingly,

Linda Weiss argues that globalisation must be viewed as a politically, rather than a technologically, induced phenomenon. It is political in two senses. First, it is a result of governments, either willingly or unwillingly, conceding to the pressure from financial interests. Second, it is political in the sense that a number of states are seeking to directly facilitate, rather than constrain, the internationalisation of corporate activity (Weiss, 1997).

In the Indian context, policymakers hold that the process of liberalisation juxtaposed with the rise of coalition governments, a powerful judiciary, social movements, and a generally vibrant civil society have tilted the balance towards a more decentralised federalism in which the States have a renewed concern for development within its spheres (Watts, 2008; Bhattacharyya, 2009a).

One major impact of globalisation on Indian federalism has been a marked increase in class and regional disparities. Leela Fernandes (2000) argues that the invention of a hybridised form of globality is produced through the nationalist imagination in liberalising India and has been centrally linked to the production of public images of the urban middle classes. The urban middle classes are the central agents in the revisioning of the Indian nation, which is visible not least in the culture of consumption. Robert Jenkins (1995) contends that we should not overlook the autonomous political logic behind the economic adjustment reforms introduced by the Narasimha Rao government in 1991. The roots of this logic can be traced back to the populist policies introduced by Indira Gandhi. Liberalisation and decentralisation helped the Congress party gain its lost strength and vitality. Francine Frankel (2005) has done a comprehensive longitudinal study of India's political economy from 1947 to the mid-2000s wherein she highlights the tendency of India to move towards a dualistic economy as a consequence of its 'macro-economic reforms without redistributive change' since the early 1990s. The new economic strategy is widening class as well as regional economic disparities.[1] The inconsistency between rapid industrialisation and gradual agrarian reforms intrinsic in the Nehruvian strategy of development could not be brought back into balance either by the Green Revolution initiated in 1969, due to its narrow scope and run, or by the Janata Party that was in power for a brief period (1977–79), with its bias towards small farmers and traders (Frankel, 2005). However, from the mid-1980s onwards, a sustained growth rate of approximately 6 percent contributed to the emergence of a consumer class and the development of a sort of national market, including rural areas. Along with the industrial and agrarian sectors, there was a speedy growth of the information technology revolution relating to the expansion of the service sector. However, these developments were confined to certain classes, communities, and regions. This trait led directly to growth without redistribution and inclusion and hurried the slide towards two economies: "a smaller, yet sizeable affluent economy growing up in larger cities and spreading to self-contained islands of export-oriented, high technology parks", on the one hand, and " the larger predominantly agricultural economy, of landless, marginal and small farmers, many belonging to historically disadvantaged lower castes, minority religions, tribal groups and women", on the other (Frankel, 2005: 625). Frankel also comments on the distinct inclination to increase inter-State disparities, with Maharashtra and Gujarat demonstrating the probability of imitating the East Asian levels of annual growth in the 1990s, and Rajasthan, Madhya Pradesh, Tamil Nadu, and West Bengal growing above the national average, whereas Bihar, Uttar Pradesh, Odisha, and even the richer States of Haryana and Punjab experienced a decline in annual growth rates, with Rajasthan, Andhra Pradesh, and Karnataka remaining more or less as in the 1980s (Frankel, 2005: 604–605).

B. B. Bhattacharya and S. Sakthivel are of the view that

> . . . [w]hile advanced industrial states have tended to leapfrog in the reform years, other states have lagged behind [. . .]. We also note that the tertiary sector, rather than industry, has become the engine of growth in the last two decades [. . .]. Unfortunately, backward states with higher population growth are not able to attract investment – both public and private – due to a variety of reasons, like poor income and infrastructure and probably also poor governance
>
> (Bhattacharyya and Sakthivel, 2007: 475)

In Amaresh Bagchi and John Kurian's assessment, "a proximate cause of the widening regional disparities during the nineties was the grossly uneven flow of investment to various states after liberalization" (Baghci and Kurian, 2005: 336). Between August 1991 and March 2000, the percentage share of investment proposals netted by the Group I States comprising of Andhra Pradesh, Gujarat, Haryana, Karnataka, Kerala, Maharashtra, Punjab, and Tamil Nadu was 66.7 percent, whereas Group II States covering Assam, Bihar, Madhya Pradesh, Odisha, Rajasthan, Uttar Pradesh, and West Bengal were desired by investors for their project location only to a small extent (27.4 percent) of investment proposals. Group I States are also the hot spots for foreign direct investment (FDI). Five States – Andhra Pradesh, Gujarat, Karnataka, Maharashtra, and Tamil Nadu – together account for about 75 percent of the total FDI in India since liberalisation (Bagchi and Kurian, 2005: 336–339).

The impact of globalisation on human development indicators in India disaggregated along regional lines is also adverse and must be addressed by remedial public policies. The number of the working poor in India is quite large, and it is expected to rise in the event of the ongoing financial crisis. Although the adult literacy rate is increasing, it is distressing that public expenditure on education as percent of Gross Domestic Product (GDP) is more or less stationary (3.1 percent in 1995 and 3.2 percent in 2004–08). The same trend is evident in public expenditure on health as percent of GDP (0.7 percent in 1995 and 0.9 percent in 2006). The gender disparity profile is even more worrisome, with the female unemployment rate tending to increase rather than decrease. It was 3.9 percent in 1994–96 and increased to 5.3 percent in 2004–07 (Haq, 2010). Given India's very complex multi-ethnic mosaic and moorings, the reforms in India are not likely to augur well if adequate remedial measures, as indicated earlier, are in short supply.

The argument of this chapter is that whereas the newfound space of freedom of action, thanks to India's reforms, has benefited some States (though not all groups within them), many of the Indian States are not likely to reap the benefits, socially and culturally differentiated as they are. Also, in some cases, the smallness of the States in size, the still-differentiated social and cultural morphology, and the unfavourable geographic locations tend to affect negatively any move to attract capital and investment from the national market, let alone the international one.

Changing perceptions of Indian federalism

In retrospect, perceptions about Indian federalism can be said to have passed through two phases. Early on, there was an almost universal consensus regarding the Indian Constitution as federal in form and unitary in spirit. The most eminent statement along those lines was, of course, made by Sir Kenneth C. Wheare (1953). Another perception is most eminently represented by the American expert on the Indian Constitution and its working, Granville Austin, and the Canadian expert Ronald Watts, who were never in doubt that the Indian Constitution right from the Nehru era was federal (Austin, 1966, 1999; Watts, 1966, 1999). By now, of course, the consensus is that even if the Indian Constitution gives somewhat overriding powers to the Union government and the Parliament both in normal and emergency times, the Indian political system since at least the 1990s has become increasingly more federal in its working (Ray, 1970; Khan, 1992; Mukarji and Arora, 1992; Arora and Verney, 1995; Singh, 1992; Majeed, 2005; Narang, 1995; Bhattacharyya, 2001, 2009a; Saez, 2002; Dua and Singh, 2003; Saxena, 2003, 2006; Dhavan and Saxena, 2006). Even Douglas Verney, who maintains a distinction between federalism as an ideology and federation as a system and seems to consider the United States as the paragon of federalism (Verney 1995), rather surprisingly has gone to the extent of problematising India in the era of multi-party coalition governments as "quasi-confederal" (Verney, 2003).[2]

There is another subtle shift in Indian federal studies which is worth noting. This new shift is double pronged. Firstly, there is a growing realisation that even though the self-image of the Constitution of India is that it is a 'Union of States' (Article 1(1)), there are enough pointers in the text of the Constitution, as well as its working, that India can just as well be regarded an "ethnic federalism" or an "ethno-federalism" (Narang, 1995). Simultaneously, the recent decades have also brought to the forefront the fact that although federalism has been effective in guaranteeing minority rights and interests of provincial majorities, it has not been equally successful in protecting the rights and interests of micro-minorities or "minorities within minorities" and "discrepant majorities" (Singh, 2007).[3] The demolition of the Babri Mosque in Uttar Pradesh on 6 December 1992 and the communal rioting against Muslim minorities in Gujarat in 2002, both under Bharatiya Janata Party (BJP) State governments also stand out as major failings of the Indian federation to protect minority rights and interests. It is against this backdrop that the idea of territorial pluralism within the overall federal framework has caught the imagination of political scientists, legal experts, policymakers, and the media. For every State in the Indian Union is far from being internally and culturally homogeneous, even after several rounds of reorganisation of provinces and States in colonial and post-colonial India for more than a century. Hence, there is the necessity of protecting ethnic subcultures, not only through the device of symmetrical and asymmetrical federal solutions, but also through well-thought-out schemes of territorial pluralism in India and within the federating States. This task has been addressed by devices such as fundamental rights of linguistic and religious minorities, as well as of a variety of castes and tribal communities; the principle of secularism; legal provisions of various kinds; reservations in education, public employment, and legislatures; the institutions of national and States human rights commissions; and commissions for minorities, women, and children.

The struggle for Statehood

During the long period of British colonial rule in India, the territorial/administrative boundaries of the units did not, quite predictably, reflect ethno-cultural boundaries. The reorganisation that was nonetheless made was very marginal. Eleven units were created under the provisions of the Government of India Act, 1919: Madras, Bombay, Bengal, United Provinces, Punjab, Bihar, Orissa, Burma, Central Provinces, Assam, Delhi (Pylee, 1980: 66). This number increased to twelve under the Government of India Act, 1935: Assam, Bihar, Bengal, Bombay, Madras, United Provinces, Central Provinces, Berar, North-West Frontier Province, Orissa, Punjab, and Sind (Pylee, 1980: 95).

These boundaries remained unaltered until the partition and independence in 1947. The 561 princely states that survived until around the time of independence were, despite their 'notional' autonomy or suzerainty, for all practical purposes under the strong control of the British.

The Constituent Assembly (1946–49) was thus confronted with the formidable challenge of reorganising the vast and, socio-culturally speaking, very complex territory of India. The Dar Commission[4] appointed by the Constituent Assembly did not recommend in favour of unilingual units in view of the objective reality, but preferred a piecemeal process of reorganisation and identified three categories of States, or federating units: Part A/ I, Part B/ II, and Part C/ III. The first category included nine units, namely Assam, Bengal, Bihar, Bombay, Koshal-Vidarbha/Madhya Pradesh, Madras, Orissa (now called Odisha), Punjab, and United Provinces/ Uttar Pradesh. The second category comprised eight units largely coinciding with smaller but unitary princely States, namely, Bhopal, Bilaspur, Cooch Behar, Himachal Pradesh, Kutch, Manipur, Rampur, and Tripura. The third category consisted of larger but composite princely states, namely, Hyderabad, Jammu and Kashmir, Madhya Bharat, Mysore, Patiala and East Punjab States Union (PEPSU), Rajasthan, Saurashtra, Travancore-Cochin, and Vidhya Pradesh (Rao, 1968: 43–45).

The first States Reorganisation Commission (SRC) of 1953 launched the first-ever major reorganisation undertaken in post-independence India in the face of persisting demands from ethno-regional groups for linguistic States. The commission, however, broadly recommended in favour of maintaining multi-lingual

States only. Its list amounted to the following sixteen States: Madras, Kerala, Karnataka, Hyderabad, Andhra Pradesh, Bombay, Vidarbha, Madhya Pradesh, Rajasthan, Punjab, Uttar Pradesh, Bihar, West Bengal, Assam, Orissa, and Jammu and Kashmir (Report of the States Reorganisation Commission, 1955).

In partial acceptance of the SRC Report, the Union government conceded to the demand for unilingual States only in the case of Andhra Pradesh in deference to popular agitation ending in the death of Potti Sriramulu, a popular Telugu mass leader who, in 1952, died of starvation in his fast for a Telugu-speaking State of Andhra. Less pressing agitations for Gujarati-, Marathi-, Kananda-, and Punjabi-speaking States were ignored by the States Reorganisation Commission Act and the 7th Constitutional Amendment, both passed by Parliament in 1956. The list of reorganised States by the Government of India in 1956 (with territorial changes in parentheses) is provided in Table 8.1.

The dominant objective of the whole exercise seemed to further bring about as much linguistic homogenisation as the Centre thought desirable and necessary in the existing and newly created States. The State of Andhra Pradesh was carved out of the Madras presidency and it was merged with the Telangana region of the Hyderabad State, which was previously ruled by the Nizam.[5] The predominantly Marathi- and Guajarati-speaking State of Bombay (previously the headquarters of the Bombay presidency) was retained as bilingual, but the Marathi-speaking territories previously in the princely States of Saurashtra and Kutch, as well as the Marathi-speaking districts of the Nagpur division previously in Madhya Bharat,

Table 8.1 States reorganised in 1956

1. Andhra Pradesh (merging the Andhra and Telangana regions of the erstwhile Hyderabad State)
2. Assam
3. Bihar
4. Bombay (enlarged by the addition of Saurashtra and Kutch and Marathi-speaking districts of the Nagpur division. Southernmost districts of Bombay were transferred to Mysore State)
5. Jammu and Kashmir
6. Kerala (merging Travancore-Cochin State with the Malabar district of Madras State)
7. Madhya Pradesh (merging Madhya Bharat, Vindhya Pradesh, and Bhopal: Marathi-speaking districts of Nagpur division were transferred to Bombay State)
8. Madras
9. Mysore (enlarged by the addition of the Coorg State and the Kannanda-speaking districts from southern Bombay State and western Hyderabad State)
10. Orissa
11. Punjab (enlarged by the merger of PEPSU)
12. Rajasthan (Rajputana was renamed Rajasthan and enlarged by adding Ajmer-Marwar State)
13. Uttar Pradesh
14. West Bengal

Sources: The 7th Constitutional Amendment and SRC Acts, 1956.

were consolidated with Bombay. The Kannada-speaking State of Mysore was enlarged by adding on the Kannada-speaking Coorg State and areas with the same linguistic character as the parts of southern and western Bombay and Hyderabad States, respectively. The composite State of Indian Punjab was also enlarged by the merger of 'Patiala and East Punjab States Union' (PEPSU). A new State of Rajasthan was created out of Rajputana and the merger of Ajmer and Marwar States. The remaining States were left untouched.

The next major reorganisation of the States was made in the 1960s. In all, three new States were created during Nehru's premiership (Gujarat and Maharashtra in the 1960s, and Nagaland in 1963). The four other States were the creation of Prime Minister Indira Gandhi: Punjab, Harayana, and Himachal Pradesh in 1966, and Karnataka in 1968. The bifurcation of Bombay was forced upon the Nehru government in the face of persistent linguistic agitations by the Marathi- and Gujrati-speaking populations. Ironically, these linguistic agitations had made the Congress governments in New Delhi and Bombay unpopular, but once the Congress government at the centre conceded the demands, the Congress party emerged stronger as the newly mobilised linguistic agitations subsequently joined the Congress party in the newly created States of Maharashtra and Gujarat. The Nehru government also tried to accommodate the separatist Nagas by forming the State of Nagaland in 1963. This was the first such exercise in India's northeast.

The Union government, led by Indira Gandhi, conceded the long-standing demand for a Punjabi Suba agitated by the Shiromani Akali Dal in 1966. It was a demand couched in the name of Punjabi language, but in reality it asked for a Sikh majority State within the Indian Union. The fallout was the trifurcation of Punjab into Punjab, Haryana, and Himachal Pradesh. Another notable change was the renaming of the State of Mysore to Karnataka in 1968. The running thread in this reorganisation again was the linguistic principle so as to consolidate as much as possible the Punjabi-, Hindi-, and Kannada-speaking populations within the respective State boundaries.

The decade of the 1970s witnessed the further reorganisation of northeast India, with Assam decreasing in territory. Five new States were conceded: Manipur, Meghalaya, Mizoram, Arunachal Pradesh (all in 1972), and Sikkim (in 1975). Ironically, then-Prime Minister Indira Gandhi was at the helm of a highly centralised national state during the decade, yet she found it difficult to stem the tide of demands for the creation of tribe-based States in the northeast. After India's independence, the centre tried to experiment with granting sub-State autonomy to the hill districts of Assam under the provisions of the Sixth Schedule of the Constitution – an offer which was outright rejected by the Naga Hill district. Through politics mixed with insurgency and democratic political processes, these areas were gradually upgraded to separate Statehood. Mizoram gradually attained a comparable Statehood through a similar political path. Meghalaya also attained Statehood through a peaceful democratic process. After these formations, Assam was left with Brahmaputra and Surma valleys and two hill districts: Karbi Anglong and North Kachar. The North-East Frontier Agency (NEFA), which was a district administrative unit at the time of independence, gradually emerged as the State of Arunachal Pradesh. At the time of independence, Manipur and Tripura were princely States that were merged with the Indian Union as Group C States, with their institutional heritage of territorial councils. Subsequently, they first became Union territories and finally federal States. Sikkim, which was a princely State until 1975, became a federated democratic State through popular demand, and resolution to this effect was passed by its representative assembly.

The northeast thus became divided into rather small States (except for Assam) by the end of the 1970s. The ethnic diversities asserted themselves and turned into a complex ethnic and territorial mosaic. Centralised planning was considered difficult in such a situation, and thus a need for supplementary regional planning was required for the northeast. This prompted the creation of the North-Eastern Council by an Act of Parliament: the North-Eastern Council Act of 1971. In this sense, the northeast, despite its tenor of identity politics, is the only genuinely *political* region in the country, in that no other region of the country has such a common institutional forum. It is important to point out here that the northeast has gone in the direction of ethnic federalism to a much greater extent than have other parts of the country, despite the former's very small federating units often sending no more than one elected representative from the State to the Parliament. As will be shown later, the macro-regions of the country rely on territorial federalism rather than on ethnic federalism. Because of their large size and ethnically composite population, the need for territorial pluralism is very acutely felt there. In western India, Goa, which was a Union territory after its 'annexation' by the Indian Union in the early 1960s, was made a State in 1987. It is also a rather small State, formed on the basis of its distinct Indo-Portuguese cultural heritage and history, with a sizeable Catholic Christian population.

Another round of State creation took place in November 2000. It was the BJP-led National Democratic Alliance (NDA) government that granted three Statehoods on the basis of a long-drawn-out demand in Jharkhand, somewhat more recent agitation in Uttarakhand, and an almost non-existent pressing demand in Chhattisgarh.[6] Ironically, even in the cases of Jharkhand and Uttarakhand, the movements for Statehood had lately become dormant for all practical purposes. In all three cases, the ruling BJP at the head of the NDA government understood it as the actualisation of its long-standing demand for small States as mere administrative units, not based on any particular ethnic identity markers (Adeney, 2005). These three States were carved out of the parent States of Bihar, Uttar Pradesh, and Madhya Pradesh, respectively, but the instances do not fall along the patterns of either linguistic or tribal States per se. For although Jharkhand and Chhattisgarh have a substantial tribal population, the decisive factors appear to be regional economic backwardness in their respective parent State and party political considerations in favour of the BJP. As the party that conceded to these demands, the BJP won the popular acclaim of the backward regions that happened to be richly endowed in natural resources such as minerals and/or hydro-electricity, but are extremely disadvantaged in terms of socio-economic and human development indicators.

Despite the protracted bouts of the territorial reorganisation of States in India for over a century, the perplexing fact is that the dominant cultural policy of creating linguistically homogeneous States in the country has not achieved its objective in full. A glance at Table 8.2 makes this point amply clear.

Table 8.2 States and Union territories in India (2014)

Sl. No.	State	Area (sq km)	Population	Literacy (rate %)	Principal Language
1	Andhra Pradesh (1953, 1956, 1959)	276,754	76,210,007	60.5	Telegu/Urdu/Hindi
2	Arunachal Pradesh (1971)	83,473	1097	54.3	Nissi/Dafla/Nepali/Bengali
3	Assam (1951, 1962, 1971)	78,438	26,655,528	63.3	Assamese/Bengali/Bodo/Bora
4	Bihar (1950, 1956, 1968, 2000)	94,163	82,998,509	47.0	Hindi/Urdu/Santhali
5	Chhattisgarh (2000)	155,191	20,833,803	64.7	Hindi
6	Goa (1987)	3,702	1,347,688	82.3	Konkani/Marathi/Kannada
7	Gujarat (1960)	197,024	50,671,017	69.1	Gujrati/Hindi/Sindhi
8	Haryana (1966, 1979)	44,212	21,144,564	67.9	Hindi/Punjabi/Urdu
9	Himachal Pradesh (1966)	55,673	6,077,900	76.5	Hindi/Punjabi/Kinnauri
10	Jammu and Kashmir (1950)	222,236	10,069,343	54.5	Kashmiri/Urdu/Dogri
11	Jharkhand (2000)	79,714	26,945,829	53.6	Hindi/Santhali/Udu
12	Karnataka (1950, 1956, 1968)	191,791	52,850,562	66.6	Kannada/Urdu/Telegu
13	Kerala (1956)	38,863	31,841,374	90.9	Malayalam/Tamil/Kannada
14	Madhya Pradesh (1950, 1956, 2000)	308,000	60,348,023	63.7	Hindi/ Bhili/Bhilodi/Gondi
15	Maharashtra (1950, 1960)	307,713	96,878,627	76.9	Marathi/Hindi/Urdu
16	Manipur (1971)	22,327	2,166,788	70.5	Manipuri/Thangdo/Thangkhul
17	Meghalaya (1971)	22,429	2,318,822	62.6	Khasi/Garo/Bengali/Assamese
18	Mizoram (1971)	21,087	888,573	88.5	Lushia/Mizo/Bengali/Lakher
19	Nagaland (1962)	16,579	1,990,036	66.6	Ao/Sema/Konyak
20	Orissa (1952, 1960)	155,707	36,804,660	66.1	Orya/Hindi/Telegu
21	Punjab (1950, 1956, 1960, 1966)	50,362	24,358,999	69.7	Punjabi/Urdu/Hindi
22	Rajasthan (1950, 1956, 1959)	342,239	56,507	60.4	Hindi/Bhili/Bhilodi/Urdu

(Continued)

Table 8.2 (Continued)

Sl. No.	State	Area (sq km)	Population	Literacy (rate %)	Principal Language
23	Sikkim (1975)	7,096	540,851	68.8	Nepali/Bhutia/Lepcha
24	Tamil Nadu (1950, 1953, 1959)	130,058	62,405,679	73.5	Tamil/Telegu/Kannada
25	Tripura (1950)	1,049,169	3,199,203	73.2	Bengali/Tripuri/Hindi
26	Uttar Pradesh (1950, 1968, 1979, 2000)	236,286	166,179,921	56.3	Hindi/Urdu/Punjabi
27	Uttaranchal (2000)	53,483	8,489,349	71.6	Hindi/Garhwali/Kumoani
28	West Bengal (1950, 1954, 1956)	88,752	81,176,197	81.7	Bengali/Hindi/Urdu
Union Territories (UTS)					
1	Andaman and Nicobar (1950, 1956)	8,249	356,152	81.3	Bengali/Tamil/Hindi
2	Chandigarh (1966)	114	900,635	81.9	Hindi/Punjabi/Tamil
3	Dadra and Nagar Haveli (1961)	419	220,490	57.6	Gujrati/Hindi/Konkani
4	Daman and Dui (1987)	112	158,204	78.2	Gujrati/Hindi/Marathi
5	Lakshadweep (1956)	32	60,650	86.7	Malayalam/Tamil/Hindi
6	Pondicherry (1962)	492	974,345	81.2	Tamil/Malayalam/Telegu
7	National Capital Territory/Delhi State (1950, 1956)	1,483	13,850,707	81.7	Hindi/Punjabi/Urdu

Source: Adapted from O'Brian (2007) *The Penguin Reference Yearbook 2007*, New Delhi: Penguin.

Out of the twenty-eight States in Table 8.2 (until 2013; with Telangana in 2014, the number rose to twenty-nine), as many as five States are quadrilingual and twenty-one are trilingual; only Chhattisgarh is unilingual as per the latest census data (2001). Out of the seven Union territories – considerably smaller than States and some practically restricted to the municipal limits of a city or small islands – one is quadrilingual and the rest are trilingual. It is thus clear that territorial federalism, despite the belated acceptance of the principle of linguistic States, has not been successful in making the map of India linguistically homogeneous. There are still many more pending demands for the creation of new States that keep surfacing from time to time (Singh, 2003). Asha Sarangi and Sudha Pai also argue that with the creation of three new States in 2000 and the successful demand for Telangana Statehood, new dimensions and perspectives about State formation as a critical political practice have surfaced yet again in contemporary India (Sarangi and Pai, 2011). Louise Tillin opines in the context of the three States created in 2000 that

> ... the achievement of Statehood was not necessarily experienced on the ground as the direct or the tangible outcome of a collective popular struggle. Yet, the new States were the repositories of multiple and competing imaginings of what a new State could be.
>
> (Tillin, 2013: 200)

The foregoing discussion suggests that the real feasible solution to the problems of India's ethnic and cultural diversities remains territorial pluralism. The Indian experience therefore clearly suggests that whereas ethnic federalism may be considered the major premise on which States reorganisation in India is based, there is still considerable residue of territorial pluralism on the political map of India which demands solutions like sub-State regional development councils along devolutionary lines and protection of minority rights through the judiciary and National Human Rights Commission (first set up by an Act of Parliament in 1993), reservations for disadvantaged groups, and consociational democratic practices in power sharing and accommodation of elites in Cabinet formation and other pluralistic decision-making institutions at various levels (Lijphart, 1989, 1996).

Conclusion

In this chapter, an attempt has been made to draw attention to the fact that territorial pluralism was a much more important dimension of the Indian democratic experiment in the early post-independence decades. And what is more important is that it is still an aspect of the Indian political system which is not negligible. Given the complex ethnic and territorial mosaic that India still continues to be and will continue to be through much of the twenty-first century, its importance is likely to be not only maintained, but will possibly grow. This hypothesis is prompted by the fact that the recent phase of federalisation of the Indian political system against the backdrop of market economy and reforms has brought to the forefront difficult tasks of protecting the micro-minorities, discrepant majorities (national majorities that are regional minorities), and internal minorities within all castes, tribes, languages, and religions, which are interspersed throughout the territorial extent of the Indian federation. The complexity of this problem has been intensified due to the simultaneous impact of globalisation, regionalisation, and localisation of identities in India and the world.

Since the neo-liberal economic reforms and retreat of the role of the national/federal state in the economic domain and the dilution of redistributive criteria in public policies in general and fiscal federalism in particular, the incidence of class and regional disparities has been rising. If privatisation and globalisation have had a positive impact on the growth of GDP in aggregate terms, their negative impact on human development and class and regional disparities must be a cause of grave concern on account of social, political, and regional conflict potential, which India has only been slowly waking up to. With the onset of the global financial crisis in 2008, North America and Europe must also seriously rethink their farewell to Keynesian welfare-state capitalism and the embrace of neo-liberalism. Raymond Plant (2009) has persuasively argued that no politico-economic order can be sustainable without popular trust and loyalty, which, in turn, is not possible without democratic equality and participatory democracy:

> [Gross] material prosperity cannot in fact be the ultimate guarantor of popular legitimacy of the free market and loyalty outside of that and neo-liberal thinkers have, I believe, to accept that the source of trust and loyalty have to be found outside the market.
>
> (Plant, 2009: 267–270)

Notes

1 For a detailed discussion of regional disparities and globalisation, see the chapter by Jhumpa Mukherjee in this volume.
2 Verney (2003) uses the term 'quasi-confederal' in the sense of State governments in practice having acquired tremendous political leverage in the making and unmaking of the federal coalition governments.
3 The term 'discrepant majority' refers to a national majority which is a provincial minority in some States.
4 The Constituent Assembly of India constituted the Linguistic Provinces Commission, popularly known as the Dar Commission after its chairman, Mr. S.K. Dar, on 17 June 1948 to advise and recommend the former on the extent of linguistic considerations in forming federal units of India. The commission, however, did not straight away recommend in favour of the formation of provinces on the basis of language, but tended to take a cautious approach: "As soon as the Indian States have been integrated and the country has stabilized and other conditions are favourable, they may be re-formed and convenient administrative provinces set up" (quoted in Bhattacharyya, 2001: 99).
5 'Nizam' was the title of the princely rulers of Hyderabad, the most powerful princely State in south India under indirect British suzerainty.
6 For details on the creation of these three States, see Tillin, 2013.

9 Regional movements in India
Evaluating Telangana and Uttarakhand

Jhumpa Mukherjee

Introduction

The last two decades or so have witnessed the acceleration and intensification of the impact of globalisation on economic, political, cultural, ideological, and environmental aspects of life throughout the world. Few issues have given rise to more debates than the effects of globalisation on the prospects for development in India. Globalisation, or what is also called neo-liberal reforms in India, has challenged notions of development vis-à-vis identities, regions, citizenship, and governance; the protagonists of globalisation like to see in it new opportunities for development; the critics have looked at the subject as producing a kind of development that seems to negatively impact vulnerable countries and societies, and in particular, the socially and economically disadvantaged ones (Nayar, 2007).

The literature on the impact of globalisation on regional politics is burgeoning and has its own proponents and detractors. A survey of mainstream literature on globalisation focuses upon three strands of thought: *thesis* (hyper-globalists), *antithesis* (sceptics), and, converging the two, *synthesis* (transformationalists), each confident in its own sphere, leaving the reader to surmise his or her own idea in the process. Hyper-globalists visualise the emergence of a world in which all territorial claims and controls would evenly become outmoded and unfeasible, eventually leading to what they call 'unbundling territoriality'. With the increasing influence of international economic institutions, the sovereign state is gradually 'withering away' (Featherstone, 1990; Fukuyama, 1992; Ohmae, 1990, 1996; Wilson and Dissanayake, 1996). Sceptics reject the hyper-globalist perspective as a fanciful exaggeration and see ethno-cultural claims and demands for local justice stronger and more vocal in a globalised world. Identities would become more spontaneous, rather than fade away. Sceptics see territorial and cultural identities becoming stronger rather than weaker in large parts of the world (Hirst and Thompson, 1996; Huntington, 1996; Fleiner *et al.*, 2003). Violent conflicts are more likely to emerge where societies are marked by 'horizontal inequality' – the unequal distribution of income and political power between groups – defined by region, ethnicity, class, and religion (Stewart, 2004). Transformationalists appear to adopt a midway between the two opposite theses. Although they approve of the hyper-globalist argument that the sweep and influence of globalisation have been all-pervasive, they disagree with them that the traditional state has become obsolete. Rather, globalisation has created new opportunities for states to cater to newly emergent challenges. It operates on uneven tracts, creating both inclusions and exclusions (Giddens, 2002; Held, 1999; Rosenau, 2003; Stiglitz, 2007). No one, whether classes, communities, and cultures, could remain immune to the effects of globalisation.

Regionalism and regional movements grow from within society, and the embedded societal discontent provides the potent basis of ethno-regional self-assertions (Bhattacharyya, 2005b). The inquiry seeks to measure the extent of challenges of India's reforms to Indian society and culture so that regional movements and regional politics can assume newer dynamics now.

Regional autonomy movements are not a new phenomenon in India; the country has witnessed periodic spells of movements since the years following independence, if not before. The movements initially were directed towards the realisation of ethnic demands of the different cultural and linguistic communities. Since the 1990s, with the introduction of neo-liberal reforms in India, the identity movements acquired a new dimension, with the forces of globalisation permeating the country and making the regions more conscious of their identity and the need to compete with other areas of the state in order to develop and bring the regional identity issues to the fore. Rather than ethnic factors, the regional movements now revolve around the theme of 'backwardness'. The central argument of this chapter is thus that asymmetrical globalisation has given rise to a new politics of identity – in which the primordial cultural identity gets subsumed in the new economic or regional identity, leading to the unity of groups and classes. One prime concern is that the post-1991 economic reforms have negatively affected people in the so-called 'backward regions' who see the state as indifferent to their plight and thus have more easily extended support to movements led by the regional elites.

The chapter is divided into three parts. The first section focuses on the dynamics of neo-liberal reforms vis-à-vis India's regional growth. The second part attempts to explore the co-relationship between regions and identities and attempts by the state to accommodate cultural identities. The third section seeks to strike a balance between the theory and practice of globalisation by studying the Telangana and Uttarakhand movements in some detail in order to highlight the shifts and turns since the 1990s.

India's reforms and their impact on the regions

Since independence, the primary assumption of autonomy movements was that regions could be clearly delineated in terms of language, culture, tribe, and religion, to name but the most obvious markers. India's economic reforms that were set in motion in 1991 have led to the onset of new dynamics in the democratic processes and have resulted in the reconfiguration of its politics and economy and changed the notion of region and identities altogether. The emergence of a more genuinely decentralised democracy has led to the sharpening of the line of distinction between the well-off and marginalised regions within the same State. The marginal groups increasingly feel left out, with the central and the State governments within which they live withdrawing from the welfare activities and the market economy benefitting the already privileged regions at the expense of the backward ones. No doubt the liberalisation process has increased the States' bargaining power, but this does not mean that the States have been able to wrest concessions for all the regions: "[W]hile the relatively developed States complain of 'reverse discrimination', the peripheral regions of some of these states complain of being victim of 'internal colonialism'" (Kumar, 2011: 2).

Post-liberalisation India also saw rising inequalities between different regions (Deaton and Dréze, 2002; Singh *et al.*, 2003; Pal and Ghosh, 2007) within the same State. What is unique is that people of these regions have become quite assertive of their plight, and this has led to competition for resources between regions, with foreign direct investment (FDI) as the major instrument to take recourse to. As a consequence, the Indian federal debate (Chibber and Nooruddin, 1999; Pai, 2000; Yadav and Palshikar, 2008; Bhattacharyya, 2010; Kumar, 2011) has registered a marked shift from the centre to the regions, and regionalism has become a potent issue, with regions clamouring for more autonomy and increased participation. Movements for the creation of new States are now being garnered on issues of development rather than on core identity issues. Quite markedly, gears were shifted from the politics of language and culture to the politics of rights, resources, and recognition. This newly found assertion of regional movements gained momentum in the wake of the creation of the three new States of Jharkhand, Uttarakhand, and Chhattisgarh carved out of the original States of Bihar, Uttar Pradesh, and Madhya Pradesh, respectively, in 2000. C. P. Bhambri observed that the State governments are very important players in the economic development of the country, more pronounced, of course, since the 1990s (Bhambri, 2005: 84). Globalisation is encouraging more rights for the States, in the sense that they have more freedom of action with respect to adopting and implementing structural adjustment programmes (Bhattacharyya, 2009: 99–112).

The unfolding of the political processes reveals that liberalisation policies have led to a transformation in 'sub-national' roles (Sinha, 2010: 484). The agenda for regional development has ignited various forms of States' reassertion, such as Bhojpur (out of Uttar Pradesh and Bihar), Bodoland (out of Assam), Bundelkhand (out of Uttar Pradesh and Madhya Pradesh), Coorg (out of Karnataka), Gorkhaland (out of West Bengal), Harit Pradesh (out of Uttar Pradesh), Mahakaushal (out of Odisha), Mithilanchal (out of Bihar), Muru Pradesh (out of Rajasthan), Poorvanchal (out of Uttar Pradesh), Saurashtra (out of Gujarat), Telangana (out of Andhra Pradesh), and Vidarbha (out of Maharashtra). The new base of identity is 'backwardness' in relation to other regions within the State, and hence the renewed emphasis on 'development'. For instance, a look at Table 9.1 showing the human development indicators of Andhra Pradesh pre- and post-liberalisation demonstrates that the Telugu speakers dispersed in the three regions of Andhra Pradesh have not benefitted equally from the fruits of neo-liberal reforms.

Table 9.1 Human development indicators in the regions of Andhra Pradesh

Indicators	Year	Coastal Andhra	Telangana	Rayalseema
Population density per sq. km.	1961	170	102	94
	2007	367	288	213
Urban population (in percent)	1971	19	21	16
	2007	25	31	23
Rural literacy rate (in percent)	1961	24	14	21
	2001	58	49	58
Rural work participation rate (in percent)	1961	51	54	53
	2001	45	45	48

Source: Adapted from Amarender Reddy and MCS Bantilan, 'Regional Disparities in Andhra Pradesh', http://oar.icrisat.org/6224/7/reddy_Bantilan-26_11_11.pdf (accessed 5 September 2014).

Excluding Hyderabad, the Telangana region has not benefitted equally from State policies. The socio-economic profile clearly indicates that although the density of the population is high in Telangana, the human development index in terms of literacy and work participation is poor. In fact, the Telugu-speaking population may be united by language, but divided in terms of spatial distribution, literacy rate, and employment. Regional trends in population density, rural literacy, and work participation rates as presented in Table 9.1 over a period of forty years reflect a lower human development index in Telangana and Rayalaseema as compared to coastal Andhra. The percentage of the urban population is higher in Telangana than in the other two regions, primarily because Hyderabad shares a larger portion of the urban population. Although the gap in rural literacy has declined over the years, Telangana continues to lag behind in terms of education. Population density is higher in developed coastal Andhra as compared to Telangana and Rayalaseema due to better opportunities in terms of education and employment.

Thus, since the 1990s, the new identity concern seems to divide linguistic groups into divergent and conflicting regional groups joined by multi-linguistic/multi-cultural communities with a stake in the region. Interestingly, although in the 1950s and 1960s, language (and religion to some extent) united identities, the 1990s saw cultural identity not as an integrating force, but as circumscribed by concerns of development and deprivation. The pertinent point is that people speaking the same language are divided today in terms of region and development issues.

New dynamics of regional movements

The movements around Telangana and the Uttarakhandi *pahari* identity[1] existed well before contemporary globalisation made inroads into India and thus provide a good opportunity to study the changes these movements underwent as they were confronted with the new challenges of globalisation. Are the movements reactions against the negative effects of globalisation and neo-liberalism, or are they simply a continuation of the autonomy movements of the yesteryears? A study of the political processes and the issues of mobilisation at the regional level have therefore become imperative for understanding the relationship, if any, between globalisation and regional movements in India. There is a need to rethink regional politics at a theoretical level. It goes without saying that this is not the first time that questions of regional autonomy have been raised. The national government was confronted with demands for the reorganisation of the federal States immediately after independence. The following narrative seeks to examine the issues surrounding regional identity in the Telangana and Uttarakhand movements, the response of the centre, and the shifts since the 1990s.

The Telangana movement: then and now

The emergence of a distinct region is the outcome of specific national, regional, and local conditions conjoined with their specific socio-cultural, historical, institutional, and political legacies. Andhra Pradesh, one of the largest States in India, was formed in 1956 by merging three regions: Telangana, coastal Andhra, and Rayalaseema. The Telangana region occupies the largest geographical area of the State (42 percent), followed by coastal Andhra (34 percent) and Rayalaseema (25 percent).[2]

The genesis of the Telangana movement[3] can be traced back to the 1950s when the country was already rocked by various movements for the creation of linguistic States. It is specifically linked to the Andhra movement, where the political leaders were divided between the twin concerns of the formation of 'Vishalandhra' or the two States of Andhra Pradesh and Telangana. With the movement for the recognition of linguistic States gathering momentum, the demand for recognition of the legitimate rights of the people of the region also took a new course. In 1953, based on the recommendations of the States Reorganisation Commission (SRC), the Telugu-speaking areas of the former Madras State were separated to form Andhra Pradesh, India's first linguistic province. The SRC, which was set up by the government of India in 1953 to examine the question of reorganisation of the States, was, in fact, not in favour of merging the Telangana region with the then-Andhra State and creating Vishalandhra. After a careful study of the issues involved in Telangana, the SRC recommended that ". . .it will be in the interest of Andhra as well as Telangana, if for the present, the Telangana area is constituted into a separate State which may be known as the Hyderabad State" (SRC Report; Para 386).

The State of Andhra Pradesh was formed on 1 November 1956, ignoring the recommendations of the SRC and the aspirations and sentiments of the people of Telangana. However, to pacify the Telangana people, senior Congress leaders from the region and the Centre signed in 1956 a 'Gentlemen's Agreement'[4] which sought to provide some concessions for the region. It is a travesty of truth that the Gentlemen's Agreement, which sought to provide concessions for the people of Telangana, was scuttled by the men in power. The result was a massive revolt by the people of the region in 1968–69 demanding separation of Telangana from the

State of Andhra Pradesh, popularly designated as the 'Jai Telangana Movement'. Since the Gentlemen's Agreement was destroyed by the majorities, the then–Congress-led State government adopted a diplomatic stance, offering assurances that non-Telangana civil servants in the region would be replaced by *mulki*,[5] disadvantaged local people; furthermore, revenue generated from the region would be returned to the region itself. It is, however, ironic that the promises remained confined to paper. Dissatisfied by the developments, the people of the region took to violent techniques, with the agitation spreading. Simultaneously, the political elite of the Andhra region did not digest the corrective measures adopted by the central government. The subsequent years witnessed clashes between the supporters of the Jai Andhra and Jai Telangana movements. The leaders of the Jai Andhra movement demanded either doing away with the safeguards promised by the then–Congress-led State government to the people of Telangana, including the judgment of the Supreme Court of India on the legality of *mulki* rules,[6] or bifurcating Andhra Pradesh into Andhra and Telangana States. Yielding to this pressure, the government of India quashed almost all the protective measures promised to the people of Telangana, including the invalidation of the judgment of the Supreme Court on *mulki* rules,[7] thus depriving them of their legitimate share in the fruits of development and denying them any opportunity to voice their grievances before the government in the political process.

The so-called people's issues

The movement dynamics in recent years brings to the fore the concern of the common masses on matters affecting their daily lives. Whereas the movement of the 1960s divided people on linguistic grounds, the movement of the 1990s united them, as it were; now the cultural concerns seem to have been overruled by the developmental ones. However, the concerns of low income groups have been sidelined in the process.

The majority of the Telangana population, excluding Hyderabad, comprises the agricultural farmers whose livelihood revolves around the yearly produce from their lands, for which they are heavily dependent on the government for subsidies on fertiliser and irrigation facilities. Some of the reform policies led to a deterioration of the conditions of the poor farmers: withdrawal of subsidies, support prices, privatisation, and simultaneous increase in power tariffs, which create considerable difficulties to the farmers heretofore much dependent on government subsidy. Developmental policies have catered to the elite agri-business class, to the utter discontent of the millions of rural farmers. With the withdrawal of State subsidies on fertilisers, seeds, and other inputs, the cost of cultivation went up drastically. To supplement for the losses incurred, the farmers took to growing commercial crops and a multi-crop system which was highly water intensive. Thus, the poor farmers became heavily dependent on bore wells and other means of artificial water supply, which were extremely expensive and forced them to take loans, which increased their debts in the absence of the means to pay them off. The neo-liberal reforms led to open competition, with the well-off agri-business class and the multi-national corporations interested in land acquisition reaping high profits.

The number of farmer suicides speaks for itself: between May 2004 and November 2005, Telangana reported 663 suicides, Rayalaseema reported 231, and coastal Andhra stood at 174 out of a total of 1,068 reported suicides (Report of the Committee for Consultations on the Situation in Andhra Pradesh, Dec. 2010). The causes of farmer suicides are drought, higher investments in agriculture, decrease in government subsidies, and crop failures leading to indebtedness. Whereas the farmers in all regions have shown a stable income or income which has hardly changed, the real income of the agricultural wage labourers has declined considerably in Telangana and it has increased considerably in coastal Andhra. Similarly, whereas the Scheduled Castes (SCs), Scheduled Tribes (STs), and minorities in the Telangana region have suffered a decline in income during the past decade or more, these communities have gained substantially in coastal Andhra. In a study conducted by the Planning Commission in 2004, it was found that the high caste communities have gained considerably in Telangana, while there is a decline of relative income among the rich in coastal Andhra. Difficulties in wresting a livelihood from agriculture, especially in the dry areas of Telangana and Rayalaseema, have contributed to a general sense of dissatisfaction which, in Telangana, is a contributory, if not a direct, factor in the present movement.[8]

Another pertinent issue is that of sharing water resources. Andhra Pradesh is a riverine State with forty major, medium, and minor rivers – Godavari, Krishna, and Pennar are three major inter-State rivers which flow through the heart of the region. About 70 percent of the catchment area of the Krishna and close to 80 percent of the catchment area of the Godavari are located in the Telangana region (*The Hindu*, 16 January 2010). According to the Bachawat Tribunal[9] on the sharing of Krishna waters, Telangana should receive 555.54 TMC (Thousand Million Cubic Feet), but in reality Telangana gets 277.86 TMC – far less than the entitled amount (Kannabiran *et al.*, 2010). According to the Department of Irrigation and Command Area Development of the Government of Andhra Pradesh, the total amount spent on irrigation projects in Telangana from independence until 2004 is Rs. 2251 crore in nine districts of Telangana and Rs. 7126 in Rayalaseema and coastal Andhra. Thus, due to the apathy of the government, the region was deprived of its rightful share of water, so very essential for this semi-arid region.

The Srikrishna Committee reports:

> Economic inequality within the region is an important indicator of the unrest within communities. This analysis of income change in rural areas over a period of one decade suggests that, in Telangana, the relative income growth has occurred only amongst the richest; whereas the poorer and the most deprived have experienced considerably large declines in relative income over the reference period so far as the income change dynamics is concerned, the coastal Andhra region has moved over to a more equitable distribution of income where the deprived, the wage labourers, and the SCs/STs/minorities have gained income during the decades of 1990 and 2000; whereas these

communities were not able to improve their household income and living conditions in Telangana. This analysis provides credence to the fact that the most of the deprived communities in Telangana are facing hardship and therefore are vulnerable to mass mobilization on one pretext or the other, including political mobilization with promises which may or may not be met.[10]

Again, the new model of development has led to a massive migration of labourers who were displaced as a result of land acquisition by the Special Economic Zones (SEZ) Act, 2005.[11] Coupled with this is the State's withdrawal from education and health services and moving them into the hands of private service providers. This is one of the reasons why the main participants of the movement are the youth and the unemployed, who have been displaced from all economic opportunities. Despite several promises by political parties and representatives, progress in the region in terms of job creation has been slow, which is starkly visible in terms of FDI. The State of Andhra Pradesh attracted 124 billion Rs. of FDI between 1991 and 2010, of which 51 percent was invested in Telangana, but with a very high concentration in Hyderabad. The Telangana region, excluding Hyderabad, has received only 13 percent compared to 43.2 percent in coastal Andhra.

These instances of continuous deprivation definitely go against the constitutional obligation where the State is obliged to minimise inequalities of status, facilities, and opportunities, not only among individuals, but also among groups of people residing in different areas or engaged in different vocations (Article 38 of Directive Principles of State Policy). In post-liberalisation times, the state, which is expected to be a protector of the people and resources, has turned into a facilitator of global capital. This model of development has led to a widening of inequalities across the classes, rural, urban, and the forward and backward regions. It is these widening inequalities between the elite-urban and the marginalised segment, between metropolitan Hyderabad, coastal areas, and rest of the State, that unleashed new political forces. The revival of the Telangana movement is a direct fallout of this path of development (Haragopal, 2010: 56); thus, the movement, instead of being couched within ethno-cultural issues, has thrown open questions of equity, power, participation, and development quite distinct from the Jai Telangana movement of the 1960s. Thus, it seems that the Telangana movement has actually subdued the ethnic concerns and highlighted the economic and social concerns of the common people. Whereas the region witnessed a linguistic movement in the 1950s which united the speakers, the same Telugu community is today divided on issues of development. It is undeniable that globalisation has definitely reshaped identity concerns.

Along with new issues, the leadership of the movement registered a marked change since the 1990s which coincided with the era of coalition politics and regional parties playing a dominant role in national politics. Unlike the earlier Statehood movements, where the leadership was provided by the Indian National Congress, in the movements since the 1990s, the rise of regional parties and forums (the Telangana Development Forum was established by a group of Non-Resident Indians (NRIs) to sponsor the Telangana movement by providing financial assistance to its supporters) created new intersections between popular movements and politics throughout India, including Telangana. Statehood movements are popularised today by regional parties fighting for the cause of local issues and increasing their competitive space in the State. This, however, does not mean that the national parties are indifferent or oppose the cause of new Statehood demands. The leadership of the Telangana movement was taken up by the Telangana Rashtra Samiti (TRS), formed in 2001 under the leadership of K. Chandrasekhar Rao, whose primary agenda was the formation of a separate State of Telangana. The Congress party, however, showed an interest in Telangana and created a favourable climate; in the 2004 Lok Sabha elections, the Congress party formed an alliance with TRS to obtain a stronghold in Andhra Pradesh, competing with the Telugu Desam Party (TDP). The Congress agreed to fast-forward the creation of Telangana and even included it in the United Progressive Alliance (UPA) election manifesto. However, the UPA I could not further the cause of Telangana due to opposition from one of its allies, the Communist Party of India (Marxist) [CPI (M)]. Considering it to be a betrayal of the partnership, the TRS withdrew from the alliance with Congress. The TDP took this opportunity to forge an alliance with TRS against the Congress State government. In the 2009 elections, the party manifestos of the Congress, BJP, and TRS spoke of development as the main slogan and the need for the creation of Telangana. The Congress party's national leadership was undecided on this issue until the end of its tenure in May 2014, when because of electoral compulsions it was forced to cede Statehood for Telangana. Table 9.2, showing the results of the 2004, 2009, and 2014 Lok Sabha elections in Andhra Pradesh, definitely indicates the increasing predominance of regional parties, and the formation of Telangana just before the elections seemed to have worked in favour of the TRS. Whereas in 2004 and 2009, the election wave was in favour of the Congress party, primarily because of its alliance with a regional party and incorporation of the Telangana demand in the party manifesto, the 2014 elections seem to have eroded the base of the national parties in Andhra.

Table 9.2 Lok Sabha election results in Andhra Pradesh

Parties	2004 Seats	2009 Seats	2014 Seats
BJP	2		3
INC	29	33	2
TRS	5	2	11
TDP	5	6	16
All India Majlis-E-Ittehadul Muslimeen		1	
Yuvajana Sramika Rythu Congress Party		9	
CPI (M)	1		
Total	42	42	42

Source: Adapted from www.elections.in/parliamentary-constituencies/election-results.html (accessed 19 October 2014).

Whereas the TDP and TRS got a higher electoral mandate, the national parties – that is, the Congress and BJP – had to remain content with two and three seats, respectively, which was quite a downfall for the national parties. Thus, the Telangana struggle reflects the role of regional single-issue-based parties since the 1990s to capture votes by connecting themselves to the emotional quotient of the people and their region. Clearly, coalition politics has paved the way for regional parties to have a say in the agenda of national coalitions.

Uttarakhand: ecological reasons for Statehood

Uttarakhand, the twenty-seventh State of the Indian Union and comprising the hill districts of Uttarkashi, Chamoli, Rudraprayag, Tehri, Dehradun, Pauri, Pithorgarh, Bageshwar, Almora, Champawat, Nainital, Udham Singh Nagar, and Hardwar, was created in 2000 – after a long gap of twenty-five years since the last State was formed – in order to fulfil the aspirations of the people of the region and their needs for development in tune with the specific ecological considerations of the Himalayan region – the Uttaranchal. It raised newer questions regarding the bases of State creation because it seemed as if a deviation from the original linguistic premise occurred. As Louise Tillin observes, in the context of post-liberal reforms and the creation of three new States in 2000, the debate on smaller States has been favoured since territorial reorganisation acts as "a driver of further economic growth by spurring sub-national competition and policy innovation, or help[s] to address regional inequality" (Tillin, 2012).

On the face of it, the movement for a separate State for the people of the Garhwal region may apparently have nothing to do with globalisation; however, a perusal of the unfolding of events preceding the movement tells a story of the neoliberal impact on the region. The genesis of the demand for a separate hill State comprising Kumaon and Garhwal can be traced back to the proposal, surprisingly, made by the late P. C. Joshi, the General Secretary of the Communist Party of India in 1952, to Nehru who, although not in favour of dividing the State of Uttar Pradesh, nonetheless referred it to the SRC for consideration (Rangan, 2000:167). However, the movement did not take an organised shape in the absence of a single political organisation pursuing the goal of a separate State.

Indeed, the movement for Uttaranchal[12] had its genesis in the very failure of the state-led development process to bring about any substantive improvement to the lives of the rural poor. The so-called hill development projects have not only impoverished the hill districts, but have also added arduous ecological burdens on the people. For instance, when the Union government started the task of constructing new roads along the Himalayan frontier for easy transport of armed personnel and equipment to the border areas, construction work was given to the contractors from the plain land who, in turn, hire workers from the plains, thus denying the local people any employment; work, if at all given, was that of manual labour at paltry sums. For the people of Uttaranchal, the forests have always been the primary source of subsistence, but forest policies denied rights of common property resources[13] which was quite indicative of the hostile attitude of the State government. For years, 'scientific forestry'[14] stood for the maximum extraction of timber and forest products from the Himalayas by the government-sponsored private contractors, which brought misery to the hill people. In the name of progress, the hill areas saw significant deforestation; in the process the *paharis* were deprived of their right to the forest as a source of livelihood. By the 1990s, the rights of the people to their *jal jangal jameen* (water, forests, and land) were seriously eroded, popularising the era of privatisation of resources from local communities to rich business contractors in partnership with the State government.

Along with ecology, the policy of reservation in the post-Mandal era[15] served to ignite the sub-regional sentiments in the 1990s since it further skewed the already meagre economic opportunities available to the local hill youth. It was the extension of the 27 percent reservation quota for the so-called Other Backward Classes (OBCs) to the Uttarakhand region in Uttar Pradesh that sparked the agitation for a separate State in mid-1994 and strengthened the regional identity of the hill people. In July 1994, a mass movement began in the eight hill districts of Uttar Pradesh against the imposition of the 27 percent reservation for the OBCs, and for a separate hill State of Uttarakhand (Mawdsley, 1996). It was contended that since the hills of Uttarakhand comprise only 2 to 3 percent of the backward classes, providing 27 percent reservation for OBCs in addition to the existing reservation system would imply denial of government jobs and education to the hill people. In the absence of almost any significant secondary or tertiary sector employment locally (other than in the *terai* areas of Dehra Dun and Nainital), government posts provide the bulk of salaried employment in the region and are much sought after (Mawdsley, 1996: 205). As a consequence, agitation started for the removal of the 27 percent reservation in jobs. Even the Uttarakhand Kranti Dal (UKD), which was formed in 1979 with the aim of creating a separate hill State, started a campaign that entailed a 'fast unto death' by seven leaders of the UKD in the Pauri district to ensure the fulfilment of their demands.

Since the late 1990s, the anti-reservation movement has been overshadowed by the hill people's agitation for proper economic development of the area and a discriminatory attitude by both the Central and State government towards the population of the hill areas. The issue of statehood was now raised on the twin principles of 'development of underdevelopment' and 'peripheralisation of the periphery'. Furthermore, the Uttaranchal people also felt that they were subjected to socio-economic neglect and that even the administration of the State government adopted an antithetical standpoint towards them and kept them alienated from mainstream life. The main grievance which formed the basis of the protest movements in the mid- and late nineties was that

> ... economic and developmental marginalization of the hill area is due to the fact that plains based planners in the distant State capital of Lucknow are unable (as well as unwilling) to understand the development needs of the hill population, environment and economy.
>
> (Mawdsley, 1998: 42)

Therefore, only a separate hill State would help them solve their regional problem and at the same time consolidate the different "sub-regions within Uttarakhand which have distinct identities of their own" (Kumar, 2001). This would give the people of the Garhwal, Kumaon, Jaunsar-Bawar, Teraia, and the Doon valley a right to shape their own future in terms of development.

The distinctiveness of the Uttarakhand movement was that it was not confined to a particular segment of society, but rather cut across regions, castes, classes, and political parties.

> This new construction of a distinct regional identity was all encompassing and also included the *non-paharis*. For example, people belonging to Bania, Jain, and Punjabi communities who had migrated to the hill region long back and were engaged in small-scale business and trading now consider themselves also as Uttarakhandis.
>
> (Mukherjee, 2011: 119)

It is irrefutable that with the initiation of the era of liberal reforms, the indigenous people of the hills did not mind the support of the non-*paharis* and other cultural communities in their fight for security and development.

However, the movement gathered momentum with the help of the national parties. As far as the leadership is concerned, unlike the Telangana movement, the Uttarakhand movement was spearheaded by national parties like the Communist Party of India (CPI) in 1952, the Janata Party (JP) in 1970s, and the Bharatiya Janata Party (BJP) since the 1990s. Even the Rashtriya Swayamsevak Sangh (RSS) sided with the BJP, emphasising that "national security would be at risk in this border region without economic development" (Tillin, 2013: 103). In fact, the 1996 election manifesto of the BJP promised to carve out small states like Uttaranchal, Vananchal, Vidarbha, and Chhattisgarh, give them full Statehood and consider setting up a commission to examine the formation of smaller States (Election Manifesto, BJP, 1996: 10). Even some years before, L. K. Advani, the then-BJP president, in his presidential speech in 1987 emphatically maintained that administrative convenience should be the basis of Statehood.

> The need to redraw the political map of India with the needs of development and administration as the principal consideration; the ad hoc responses to agitations have resulted in having states varying in size from half a million to one hundred million. Some of the larger states are stagnating principally because of their unwieldy size. What would contribute more to the strengthening of our nation-state; a centralised federal polity as we have at present, or a decentralised unitary set-up, with power decentralised not merely to 20 odd states but to some 60 or so *janapadas* or provinces.
>
> (Tillin, 2013: 60–61)

The BJP was able to get the support of many umbrella organisations like the UKD and Uttarakhand Samyukt Sangharsh Samiti in the demand for Statehood.

The BJP calculated that regional issues should be at the forefront of the national agenda in the new era of coalition politics. Thus, the Uttarakhand movement received major support from the BJP and its Hindu nationalist allies to garner the support of regional elites with a local cause. Since the early nineties, the BJP had vociferously supported the cause of small States based on administrative and development needs, leading to the carving out of three new States of Jharkhand, Chhattisgarh, and Uttarakhand.

Conclusion

The experience of Telangana and Uttarakhand brings to the fore the definite changes in the dynamics of movements in terms of character, focus, leadership, and above all, the criteria of granting Statehood to regional movements since the days of India's neo-liberal reforms. The nature of identities has shifted from cultural concerns to economic, and especially to a development quotient. Above all, the leadership and the pace of movements brought to the limelight the question of control of local resources by local people and not necessarily by a centralised power structure remotely located in New Delhi.

As the analysis shows, globalisation has brought greater competition among and between States, as well as among the various regions within the same State. This has sharpened the regional identities who feel that unless their voice is raised and heard, they would be silenced by the dominant regions. Development, a share in resources, economic security, and educational and employment opportunities have subsumed affiliations on the grounds of religion, language, and ethnic divisions. During the 1950s and 1960s, socio-political movements raised cultural issues as reasons for separate Statehood, but shifted the focus in the new liberal environment, which pitted regions against regions and divided culturally homogeneous communities.

Demands for separate Statehood may appear to be upsetting the political equilibrium of the country, but they also serve as a platform for different groups to express their genuine concerns of neglect and marginalisation by the political authorities. The competitive attitude of the regions for autonomy is the 'new' identity base of regional movements. This competition has led to the erosion of primordial loyalties, which is most evident in the Uttarakhand movement that was shaped by the politics of rights, resources, and recognition. Telangana emerged as a State of the Indian Union in 2014, and the Garhwal-Kumaon region has already been quite successful in asserting its autonomy within a broad constitutional framework through the formation of a separate State in the year 2000. The political parties seem to have reaped the electoral dividends in the process, and as Amit Prakash notes, "Most political parties still seem to believe that narrower ascriptive identities will be subsumed into the national identity under the impetus of a faster and efficient development" (Prakash, 2001: 339). A politics of accommodation thus calls for balanced politico-economic power sharing and not just cultural recognition. It goes without saying that the erstwhile 'homeland' movements of the 1960s and 1970s have been replaced by movements for greater 'rights' economically and politically. The political journey of the Indian state since the 1990s, with a greater role for States in Structural Adjustment Programmes (SAPs), the popularity of regional parties, and their larger presence in coalition politics, definitely indicates that globalisation has created opportunities for more State rights, greater involvement of the States in decision-making, and above all, more competition between States and between regions and sub-regions over rights to resources.

The linkage of autonomy, region, and economy in the era of globalisation thus seems unavoidable. Seen from the perspective of the regional population, it can be said that globalisation has ushered in greater democratisation of the regions by giving eminence to local politics and cutting across language, religion, and ethnic concerns. The Constitution and the political system have continuously given recognition to these regional voices by providing them with the space to contest with other regions in terms of development, ultimately contributing to the progress of the State. Although the era of neo-liberal reforms has shifted the dynamics of regional movements and has increased inequalities within regions, it has also led to a greater role for the regions in the federal arrangement, something very different from the model of federalism in terms of a strong centre as intended by the makers of the Constitution. The Telangana and the Uttarakhand experiences truly show that globalisation has led to greater federalisation of regions through a new identity consciousness grounded in the need for socio-economic development.

Acknowledgement

The author is grateful to Professor Harihar Bhattacharyya and Dr. Lion König for their very insightful comments and suggestions and detailed editorial notes, which immensely helped improve the draft.

Notes

1. The *pahari* identity refers to the hill folk of the Tehri-Garhwal region, who developed a strong resentment against the plain people and the State government for their apathy to hill development which was depriving them of their right to livelihood.
2. The Telangana districts are Mahbubnagar, Hyderabad (Rangareddy and Hyderabad), Medak, Nizamabad, Adilabad, Karimnagar, Waranagal, Khammam, and Nalgonda; the four districts of Rayalaseema are Chittoor, Kadapa, Anantapur, and Kurnool; the nine districts of coastal Andhra are Srikakulam, Visakhapatnam (Visakhapatnam and Vizianagaram), East Godavari, West Godavari, Krishna, Guntur (Guntur and Prakasam), and Nellore.
3. The history of the Telangana struggle has been discussed in Sundarayya, 1972; Seshadri, 1970; Reddy, 2003; Simhadri and Rao 1997; and Pai, 2005.
4. The 'Gentlemen's Agreement of Andhra Pradesh' (1956) refers to an agreement signed by Telangana and Andhra leaders before the formation of the State of Andhra Pradesh in 1956. The agreement provided certain safeguards for preventing discrimination against Telangana by the Government of Andhra Pradesh. It provided for the establishment of a regional council for the general development of the Telangana region.
5. The Urdu term *mulki* refers to the 'residents of a nation'.
6. The *mulki* rules formed part of the Hyderabad Civil Services Regulations promulgated in obedience to the Nizam's Firman dated 25 Ramzan 1337 Hijri, corresponding to 1919 CE. The State of Hyderabad was then a native Indian State, which had not acceded

to the dominion of India after the Indian Independence Act, 1947. Article 39 of Hyderabad Civil Service Rules, as contained in Chapter III of the regulations, states that "no person will be appointed in any Superior or Inferior services without specific sanction of His exalted Highness, if he is not a Mulki".

7 *The Director of Industries and Commerce, Government of Andhra Pradesh vs. V. Venkat Reddy*, AIR 1973 Supreme Court 827.
8 Pattern of Development in India: A Study of Andhra Pradesh, SER Division Planning Commission, 2004.
9 The Krishna Water Disputes Tribunal was set up by the Government of India in 1969 under the Inter State Water Disputes Act of 1956 to resolve the disputes between the States of Karnataka, Maharashtra, and Andhra Pradesh over the sharing of Krishna river water. The tribunal was headed by R. S Bachawat, a former Supreme Court judge.
10 The Srikrishna Committee on Telangana or the Committee for Consultations on the Situation in Andhra Pradesh (CCSAP), headed by former Chief Justice B. N. Srikrishna, was set up on 3 February 2010 to look into the demand for separate Statehood for Telangana or to keep the State united in the present form, Andhra Pradesh. The committee recommended a number of possible solutions to resolve the problem.
11 The SEZ Act was enacted in 2005. The main objectives of the SEZ Act are (1) generation of additional economic activity; (2) promotion of exports of goods and services; (3) promotion of investment from domestic and foreign sources; (4) creation of employment opportunities; and (5) development of infrastructure facilities. Thus, this act aims to promote investment by domestic and foreign investors, thereby boosting economic activities, revenue generation, and employment opportunities. However, over the last few years, it has been observed that this has aggravated problems by increasing ecological pressures on existing cultivable land. In a bid to acquire land for developing SEZs, huge numbers of agricultural populations have been displaced, leading to loss of land and livelihood. This has not only had an adverse impact on food security, production, and livelihood for the agricultural farmers and labourers, but has also led to overexploitation and resultant exhaustion of land caused by additional population pressures on a smaller amount of land area, thereby adding to further ecological deterioration.
12 The names Uttarakhand and Uttaranchal have been used interchangeably because there was a politics of nomenclature associated with the new State. When the State was formed, the BJP-led NDA christened it Uttaranchal, but when the Congress-led UPA came to power, it rechristened it Uttarakhand in 2006.
13 Common Property Resources are natural resources owned and controlled jointly by a community rather than by individuals.
14 Scientific forestry was a method of forest management introduced in India by the colonial masters to control the forests and forest products and regulate the rights of forest dwellers by imposing restrictions on the use of forest products. The Indian government continued this policy even after independence so as to control the use of forest products, thus depriving the forest dwellers of their right to subsistence.
15 The Mandal Commission was established in India in 1979 by the Janata Party government under Prime Minister Morarji Desai and was headed by B. P. Mandal to 'identify the socially or educationally backward' and consider the question of seat reservations for people to redress caste discrimination. It used eleven social, economic, and educational indicators to determine backwardness. In 1980, the commission's report confirmed the affirmative action practice under Indian law whereby members of lower castes – known as Other Backward Classes (OBC), Scheduled Castes (SC), and Scheduled Tribes (ST) – were given exclusive access to a certain portion of government jobs and slots in public universities, and recommended changes to these quotas, by giving 15 percent reservation to SC, 7.5 percent to ST, and 27 percent to OBCs, thus increasing the quota to 49.5 percent.

10 Governing India's localities

Limits of structural and governance reforms

Harihar Bhattacharyya

Introduction

The global literature on 'comparative local governance' (Stoker, 2006: 495–513) suggests a few insights which are useful with respect to an analysis of the Indian case. Stoker (2006: 495) argues that although the study of local government, globally speaking, remains bogged down in a traditional institutional approach, the former has also received global attention and has been impacted by globalisation. The latter is evident in the shift from 'local government' to 'local governance', which means that the focus is now more on the "system of governance rather than formal institutions of government" (Stoker, 2006: 495): local governance, especially in respect to service delivery, is a shared responsibility of the government and the non-government agents – a relationship which is expressed in terms such as 'contracting out', public-private partnership', and 'new public management techniques' (Stoker, 2006: 502). It is also suggested that a slight impact of the neo-institutionalist perspective has been evident in understanding local government insofar as the recognition of the critical role of actors creating informal networks to affect the functioning of local governing is concerned (Stoker, 2006: 496).

What typically constitutes the congenial environment for the growth and flourishing of local government institutions? To be sure, if the governments at the regional and national levels show authoritarian tendencies, the local government's room to manoeuvre is greatly constricted. Judged in this light, one may argue that, unlike the previous century, this century has offered a more congenial atmosphere for the birth, growth, and working of the local governance system. If, at the beginning of the twenty-first century, nearly two thirds of all countries in the world are democratic (Diamond, 2003, quoted in Stoker, 2006: 500), this century seems to be favourable for local government. Added to this, the post-communist Polish case is interesting: the local government there has flourished since the decline of the communist regime in the late 1980s (Stoker, 2006: 500).[1]

India's reforms of local government

When placed in relation to the aforementioned global scenario, the Indian case is rather paradoxical. Despite the fact that India has been a democracy since 1952 (except for the brief interlude of the Emergency from 1975 to 1977), it is difficult to argue that local government below the State level has flourished here. Local government being a State competence, as per the Constitution, it was not until 1992 that a major reform of the local government was undertaken at the national level by way of the 73rd and 74th Constitutional Amendments for rural and urban local government, respectively. In common federal parlance, this is also called a kind of decentralisation. To be sure, local government reforms since 1992 have remained the major and most visible structural reforms in governance and have attracted considerable scholarly attention, which is, paradoxically, at variance with the success of the reforms. Since India embraced reforms in 1991, there have been reforms pertaining to the States' freedom of action in attracting foreign direct investment (FDI) and other kinds of investment in their domain, and to engage themselves in trade and commerce by leaving more space to the market. This has been done since the mid-1990s (after the relative failure of the first phase of reforms) (Bhattacharyya, 2009a) without formally changing the Constitution, but by the fiat of what is called 'executive federalism'. In common federal parlance, this is also called a kind of decentralisation. Not all States in India were willing to join the reform process, and of the States that have joined, often reluctantly, not all have benefitted equally (Bhattacharyya, 2009a: 99–112). However, the State-level reforms were not people empowering, participatory, and democratic. And this is where the special significance of local government reforms lies. It needs to be stressed here that India's major attempts at reforms of local government in 1992 were in a sense conjectural because the reform attempts of the local government structures and functions had been under way since the late 1980s, but eventually failed.[2] When it succeeded in 1992, India had joined the reforms process.

Therefore, the initial impulse for reforms in the realm of local governance was more indigenous. Nonetheless, the World Bank (1995) welcomed this structural reform, albeit with considerable scepticism.[3] The effectiveness, powers, autonomy, and capacity of the local governments in India remain, however, matters of considerable scholarly debate and differing opinions (Mukraji and Bandopadhay, 1993; Mukherjee, 1995; Jain and Hochgesang, 1995; Mitra, 2001; Bhattacharyya, 2002; Baviskar and Mathew, 2009; Jain, 2005; Govinda Rao and Singh, 2005; Jha and Mathur, 2000; Mathur, 2014). It cannot be claimed that this two-decade-old experiment has been a success story in all respects. However, its success in terms of some political empowerment – particularly of the socially disadvantaged, participation, and some 'development' in the rural areas – can hardly be underestimated.

This chapter examines the experience of India's rural local self-governments and points out the major limitations to the successful working of such democratically elected bodies (numbering about a quarter of a million), which elected over a million women representatives, mostly of the socially underprivileged – which itself is a remarkable record of sorts in terms of formal political empowerment. It also points out the major limitations to the effectiveness of self-governing bodies, which are systemic and environmental. The underlying hypothesis advanced here is that the success of the local self-government institutions holds an important key to the working of India's reforms because it is in rural India where the dominant majority of citizens (about 70 percent on a liberal estimate) reside. The theoretical underpinning here is that if a neo-Right turn through neo-liberal reforms demands a more restricted centralised state but at the same time demands more and fragmented decentralisation governments as the least state, then the Indian experience so far suggests that there is much to be desired.

The background to India's reforms

Any discerning observer of Indian politics since the 1990s will notice the challenges and constraints that India's federal democracy, ensconced as it is in a very complex multi-ethnic setting, placed before any smooth sailing of a neo-liberal globalisation.[4] India has embraced reforms officially since 1991, although the Indian economy had already been liberalised, domestically speaking, from the late 1960s in a variety of forms.[5] Paradoxically, India's adoption of globalisation and the rise of multi-party (most often of opposing views and policies, even on globalisation) coalition governments at the Centre have gone hand in hand, and the relations between the two have not, arguably, been harmonious and healthy. Aside from that, India's federal political system, itself quite complex, offers another challenge with respect to carrying out *or not* the project of globalisation, and the extent and effects of the same across India's regions have remained different (Kaviraj, 2010: 233–271;[6] Sáez, 2002; Bhattacharyya, 2009b; Dua and Singh, 2005). India's liberalisation remains problematic, however. Not all groups, segments of the population, and political parties hold the same or even a similar opinion on the phenomenon. There is also opposition to it from different ideological predispositions. The Indian ideological climate, which is itself very diverse, is marked by the exponents of redistribution rather than competition; the Gandhian would hold an anti-market opinion, and in politics, group equality rather than individual equality still hold greater sway. Sudipta Kaviraj has excellently brought out the previous point, but argues that in the midst of all these positions, the "logic of liberalization has developed a life of its own" (Kaviraj, 2010: 270).[7] This serves to point our direction to a major lacuna in the very perception of 'reforms' in India, one that is more oriented to a set of abstract positivistic instrumentalities of governance (or 'Good Governance') in governance reforms that grossly neglect to consider the social reality of India, on the one hand, and market reforms in the economy seeking to replace the well-entrenched, public-sector-oriented governance structures and practices (created and adapted to cater to the needs of India's complex social reality of groups, castes, Other Backward Classes [OBCs], quotas, etc.), on the other. Democracy's challenges to globalisation stem precisely from heightened mass mobilisation and bottom-up participation in the age of what Anthony Giddens calls "reflexive society" (Giddens, 1994). In Indian democracy, the electorates are a differentiated lot: they are divided along the lines of castes, regional identity, tribal affiliations, strong religious bonds, and so on, and are 'politically' so mobilised along those lines by the power-seeking politicians that they are reinforced rather than weakened.[8]

A crucial point in this context is that ultimately any reforms (of the market or of the governing structures) can hardly ignore the localities: regions, villages, and communities where most Indians live, and which provide for the backbone of any such major undertaking. Three issues here merit special attention: first, such localities are highly unequal and stratified, with strong attachments to primordial identities. So, asking for 'market equality' as the *sine qua non* of the World Bank–defined 'Good Governance' agenda in such contexts is really asking for too much. Second, Indians who are socio-economically disadvantaged have found of late a new weapon to fight for equality (caste rights, for example) in the very identity (Gupta, 2007) that hitherto condemned them in a hierarchical social order of castes. In other words, the *dalits* (former Untouchables and the Scheduled Castes), for instance, are resolutely fighting for their collective rights as enshrined in the Constitution and other legal pronouncements, as are India's *adivasis* (numbering some 100 million) who are asserting their collective rights and are striving for autonomy. Third, the globalisation-propelled reforms package in India does not contain any item or idea of reforms of the society of deeply rooted hierarchies and inequalities, of caste and communities, including their die-hard customs and practices, so that the former lack the required social support and legitimacy, and hence are limited in vision.

The Indian experiment with local government reforms

How are India's localities governed in the era of globalisation? Because the India of the twenty-first century is still an India of villages, the rural population holds the key to the success or failure of India's reforms. Again, if the countryside is aflame, no reforms will be durable and effective, as is evident in many parts of India that are infested with extremist violence. Therefore, a democratically governed rural India is a *sine qua non* of the country's move to reform and prosperity. David Williams (1997: 243) claims that governance is a "transformative ideology", where transformation constitutes the main objective. The Indian experience with reformed rural self-governing institutions would suggest otherwise. The detailed empirical studies undertaken so far in different States of the Indian federation (twenty-nine at present) would show how many traditional values, practices, and institutions, on the one hand, and political constraints, on the other, would seriously stand in the way of effective participation and empowerment of the socially underprivileged, despite constitutional mechanisms designed to ensure democratic participation and empowerment.

India's local self-governance structures are very complex and manifold. Although the Constitution of India (1950) has provided for varied forms of local self-governance, in particular for the aboriginal people, in order to accommodate diversity and ensure local participation in governance and development, a major constitutional reform of the local government bodies was undertaken in 1992 with the passage of the 73rd and the 74th Constitutional Amendments for rural and urban self-governing bodies, respectively (Bakshi, 2014; Mukherjee, 1994; Jha and Mathur, 2000; Bhattacharyya, 2002; Mitra, 2001). As per the provisions of Article 40 of the Indian Constitution (amended later in 1992), the institution and organisation of rural local self-government, known in India as *panchayats*, was left to the discretion of the State governments, and therefore, such institutional experiments have varied enormously across the States since independence.[9] The existing accounts also show that such experiments at the base of India's federal polity have passed through many generations (Bhattacharyya, 2002; Datta, 1992). Those not familiar with the intricacies of the Indian political system might not realise the difference between such experiments before and after 1992. Although in the pre-1992 phase, the State governments implemented the provisions of Article 40 (the Directive Principles of State Policy, which are not justiciable in the court of law) in their own ways, if at all, so that different States had different tiers of such bodies as it suited them; quite often, the Union government (federal/Central government) mandated the States to implement different developmental schemes of the latter.[10] There was, for instance, a time when *panchayats* were tied to 'community development' efforts of the central government as agencies of rural development (Webster, 1992; Lieten, 1992, 1996; Jha and Mathur, 2000). Also, not many State-level politicians appreciated the institutions as such, because many saw in them a potential challenge to their power and authority. Thus, successful experiments in the pre-1992 phase in many States in India were terminated, even by the same political parties ruling at the State level. During the same period, elections to form such bodies were not regular, and their functioning often remained confined to paper.

Institutional design

Designing representative political institutions, even with the best of intentions, is one thing, but making them work is a different matter. Also, institutional designs are not to be seen as merely drafting pieces of legislation; the process must be backed by the appropriate legacy and social and political support. India's *panchayats* have drawn considerable attention, not simply because these bodies perform a significant role, but more importantly because the institutions have enjoyed moral and political support for a long time. Mahatma Gandhi's ardent defence of the *panchayat* added further strength to the legacy. Greater participation of the people, particularly of the socially and economically underprivileged, has preserved the political dynamism of those bodies.

The pre-reform era

In the pre-reform era, the *panchayats* were somewhat neglected nationally and institutionalised at the State level without the seriousness that they deserved. Although the establishment of *panchayats* was a State competence, the Central government often also formed various committees to suggest ways of institutionalising them. But those reports of the committees seemed to have gathered a lot of dust in the corridors of power. The change of government at the central and the State level did not show the required political will to do otherwise. Nonetheless, the States that were more serious in institutionalising *panchayats*, such as Rajasthan, Andhra Pradesh, Maharashtra, Karnataka, Kerala (Raghavalu and Narayana, 1999: 117–131), and West Bengal (since 1978) (Kohli, 1987, 1991; Mitra, 2001; Bhattacharyya, 2002), developed distinct models of the institution.

In the post-Emergency phase, the establishment of *panchayati raj* for decentralisation and democracy became a rallying cry of political parties which were fighting the Lok Sabha elections in 1977. This was enmeshed with the political manifestoes of political parties for the restoration of democracy and devolution of power to the people. The first non-Congress, multi-party, Janata Party–led coalition government at the Centre (1977–80), although short lived, had made decentralisation its central pursuit in politics, administration, and economics in order to counter the ill effects of centralisation during the Emergency and to restore democracy and federalism. In this context, the long-term and sharp observers of Indian politics, Lloyd and Susanne Rudolph, noted:

> The Janata government formulated and attempted to implement and institutionalize a neo-Gandhian alternative to the centralized state and industrially oriented growth strategy associated with Congress rule. It took seriously Mohandas Gandhi's concern to decentralize the state and the economy [. . .]. The federal system and local and village administration were rejuvenated.
> (Rudolph and Rudolph, 1987: 163)

The Asok Mehta Committee (1978), formed by the Janata government, was the first to recommended politicised *panchayats*; that is, to allow multi-party competition in elections to form *panchayats*, and for a three-tier system at district, block, and village levels.

And yet, in the pre-reform era, the constitutional status of the *panchayats* did not change – they remained a subject of State competence. Therefore, how much power and responsibility would be devolved to the *panchayats*; whether elections to form them would be held or not; and the extent of reservation of seats for the Scheduled Castes (SCs), Scheduled Tribes (STs), and others were left to the discretion of the State governments. The available records suggest that there were wide variations with respect to these things (Raghavalu and Narayan, 1999: 117–131). Govinda Rao and Singh (2005: 299–300), looking at the phenomenon from the political economy perspective, argued that in the varied institutional changes at the State levels, the legislative assignment and the functional responsibilities in this regard hardly matched, so that despite the often long list of assignment of items to the *panchayats*, the *panchayats* in the pre-reform era were found to have played only a "very minor role relative to that of the State".

Post-reform institutional design

And yet, the tempo was not all lost. The groundswell of pressure from below for decentralisation remained active, particularly from the States ruled by anti-Congress parties. Indira Gandhi came back to power in 1980, the centre–State relations were reviewed, and accordingly, the Sarkaria Commission was formed in 1983. The Sarkaria Commission (1983–87), interestingly, went beyond its terms of reference and recommended decentralisation below the State level:

> Decentralization of real power to these local institutions would thus help defuse the threat of centrifugal forces, increase popular involvement all along the line, broaden the base of our democratic polity, promote administrative efficiency and improve the health and stability of inter-governmental relations.
>
> (quoted in Bhattacharyya, 2001: 152)

The 73rd Constitutional Amendment Act of 1992 (effective starting 24 April 1993), with the new Article 243A-K inserted for the *panchayats*, represented a major departure from the pre-reform era in that it is now obligatory for State governments to hold regular elections to form such bodies at different levels. The second reason why this piece of reform legislation attracted the popular political imagination is that it provided for the political empowerment of various weaker sections of society as obligatory too. The specific features of this reform legislation relating to political empowerment are:

- Direct election by the villagers to constitute *panchayats* for each tier;
- Provision of reservation of seats at each tier at the rate of 33 percent for women; SC and ST reservation shall be in proportion to their population;
- The electorate for each *panchayats* shall be known as *Gram Sabha*;
- Posts of Chair persons of each tier shall be governed by the State laws.

(The Constitution of India as quoted in Bhattacharyya, 2001: 153)

With regard to powers and responsibilities, the Eleventh Schedule, containing twenty-nine items relating to various basic services concerning the entire gamut of life of the rural populace, was inserted. But as in the pre-reform era, *panchayats* remain a State competence (under the State list), and any powers and responsibilities that are to be devolved to the *panchayats* ultimately depend on the State government. Consider the central part of the provision in this regard: "Subject to the provision of the Constitution, the State Legislature of a State, may, by law, endow the *panchayats* with such powers and authority as may be necessary to enable them to function as institutions of self-government" (Bhattacharyya, 2001:154).

It is true that in a vast country like India, and that, too, in a federal setup, the subject of local government could not conceivably operate as a Union subject. Also, the momentum of the *panchayati raj* experienced many ups and downs because some States at certain points in time kept up the experiment and devolved powers and responsibilities of various magnitude to the local bodies. The government of West Bengal, led by the Left Front (Communist Party of India [Marxist], or CPI-M), for example, maintained the experiment consistently from 1978 to 2011 by holding regular elections every five years and devolved many powers to such bodies, as well as development programmes (Meenakshisundaram, 1994: 65–69).

However, the institutional design of the *panchayats*, as outlined earlier, leaves the vital issue of financial capacity and autonomy (including administrative) to the State governments concerned, which is a structural limit to their operation as 'units of self-government', as provided for in the constitutional amendment for reforms.

Fiscal decentralisation at the sub-state level

The *panchayats* have very limited taxing and tax-raising powers. Govinda Rao and Singh pointed out that the local governments (including the urban ones) raised a very negligible 0.04 percent of the gross domestic product (GDP) in India around 1998 (Govinda Rao and Singh, 2005: 307). The expenditure share of the rural local bodies during 1997–98 was only 5 percent of the total public expenditure in India, of which the village (Gram) *panchayats*' share was only 1.40 percent (Govinda Rao and Singh, 2005: 307). Revenue collection by rural local bodies during the same period amounted to 0.20 percent of the total public expenditure (Govinda Rao and Singh, 2005: 3007).

The *panchayats*, therefore, are heavily financially dependent on the State government and the Union Finance Commission grants. The 1990s assessment of the *panchayats* pointed out the "very limited" financial decentralisation, as "resource flows are determined by the implementation guidelines of State- and central government anti-poverty schemes" (Robinson, 2005: 24). And it left a very limited role for the elected representatives to exercise any influence in matters of local development. In the first decade, the experience of local government reforms (both urban and rural) was succinctly summed up as follows: "Achievements from any political decentralization have not been matched either by financial or administrative decentralization. The powers and responsibilities of elected bodies remain highly circumscribed. Dominant interests at the village level continue to exercise considerable influence through proxy representatives" (Robinson, 2005: 27).

Hoshiar Singh (1994) expressed doubt about the kind of decentralisation that was to emerge from the reforms act, given the growing number and size of central government schemes to be implemented by the *panchayats*, a view substantiated by the recognition accorded to the *panchayats*' role by the Planning Commission (11th) Document and the successive Union Finance Commissions (UFCs).

Things did not improve much in the subsequent days, as the Punchi Commission (Second Centre – State Relations Commission) (2009) highlights under the sub-heading 'Separate Space for Local Bodies':

> Fiscal autonomy is essential for realizing the benefits of decentralization. Decision making at the local level will suffer in the absence of fiscal autonomy. The present system of almost total dependence of local bodies on higher levels of government does not promote accountability. Under Article 243-H and 243-X of the Constitution, the State legislatures are authorized to allow local bodies to levy and collect specific State taxes and to assign the proceeds

of specific taxes to local bodies. These provisions of the Constitution do not serve the purpose of empowering the local bodies financially [...]. The States have been by and large reluctant to part with financial powers.
(Government of India, Punchi Commission Report, 2010: 82)

It is no wonder that one of the recommendations of the said commission (under the headline 'Time Bound Devolution of Functions') was "State[s] have continued to drag their feet on the devolution of powers to *Panchayats* and Urban local bodies. There should be mandatory devolution of functions, and it must be done by the year 2015" (Government of India, Punchi Commission Report, 2010: 167).

Limits to political participation

India's villages, communities, castes, religions, tribes, and different language and dialect groups present themselves as heterogeneous and socially deeply discriminatory. Despite decades of democratic experience, the society has remained highly fragmented, with groups and sub-groups asserting themselves in terms of identity, recognition, and power (Gupta, 2007; Puri, 2012). Although this has served to exacerbate renewed caste consciousness among both the dominated and the dominant (both having their private armies), *panchayats*, and traditional rules of governance),[11] the modern, democratically elected, local self-government institutions such as the *panchayats* (with provisions of reservation of seats for the socially marginalised) are most vulnerable to such influences so that very often, democratic functioning of such bodies and their powers of social redistribution, as per the provisions of the Constitution, becomes the casualty.

The State of West Bengal, which would have paved the basis for the growth of self-governing institutions for the rural population, in reality was very often far removed from this goal. The first official report (1993) on the functioning of the *panchayats* in West Bengal lamented as much:

[...] *panchayats* have so far operated mainly in the field of development. There also, they have functioned more as implementing agencies of Union and State schemes than doing things on their own. Even as implementing agencies of such schemes, they have had to depend on departmental staff outside their control. On the face of it, the *panchayats* have resigned themselves to the situation, but there is a great deal of dissatisfaction.
(Mukarji and Bandopadhyay, 1993: 221)

Further, the authors of the report note that:

... [i]n our discussions with *panchayats* leaders at different levels, we found that the idea of self-government was new to them, so new that their eyes had a touch of disbelief as they avidly took in its implications. But after the initial hesitation they were invariably keen on discussions in which difficulties encountered in the present dispensation were elaborated and clarifications sought on what self-government would mean in practice.

(Mukarji and Bandopadhyay, 1993: 221)[12]

In the post-1992 reincarnation, the institution of *panchayats* (as well as of the municipalities for the urban areas) became mandatory for the States. The States were constitutionally mandated to hold regular elections to such bodies after an interval of five years, and the various schemes of both Central and State governments, both of a welfare and developmental nature, are implemented by the *panchayats*.

Unfortunately, during the more than three-decade-long experiments with the institutions of *panchayats* in West Bengal, when the Left Front Government led by the CPI-M was in power and in control over most of the institutions of *panchayats*, it was precisely the realm of democracy, or self-government, that became a casualty. My own research and writings on the subject since the late 1990s until 2011[13] (the CPI-M–led Left Front regime lost power to the Trinamool Congress coalition in May 2011) have confirmed that not casteism, as elsewhere in India, but the omnipotent and hierarchical control by the Communist parties, particularly the CPI-M, over such institutions stood, paradoxically, in the way of their development as institutions of self-government. It was a 'paradox' because the main credit for the revival and organisation of *panchayats* on a multi-party, democratic electoral basis immediately after the end of the Emergency went to the Left Front. Despite the fact that the 73rd Constitutional Amendment of 1992 (for *panchayats*) provided for a set of institutional mechanisms to ensure greater participation and empowerment of the weaker sections of society[14] (such as SCs, STs, and women), the actual operational dynamics of such bodies have been such that those sections, although popularly elected as per provisions of the Constitution, remained far removed from the realm of the exercise of power and authority, and hence have had little or no say in matters of decisions taken relating to various welfare schemes and development programmes. The insidious mechanisms of party control at all levels of the *panchayats* (Bhattacharyya, 1998, 1999, 2002, 2005a, 2007, 2013) saw to it that a small party committee, called the Panchayat Sub-Committee and known locally as the Guide Committee, operating secretly, took full control over the *panchayats* and all decisions prior to their being made formally on the floor of the *panchayats*, which served to overshadow the democratic functioning of these self-governing bodies. The party in command officially stated its position otherwise – that is, its aim was participation and empowerment of the common people – but its approach remained instrumental. Rather than develop them as institutions of self-government with the required autonomy, the committee deployed them for mass contact and mobilisation (read 'party building'). This, quite predictably, adversely affected the enjoyment of rights on the part of the elected representatives to represent their constituencies, the citizens' ability to take part in decisions in the designated institutional platforms such as *Gram Sabha* and *Gram Samsad* (the assembly of votes in a *panchayat* constituency), and the delivery of services to the target groups, which very often was vitiated by political discrimination (Bhattacharyya, 2007, 2005a).

The detailed empirical studies of such cases in fifteen States in the Indian Union contained in Baviskar and Mathew (2009) is the first-ever comprehensive study undertaken on the functioning of post-1992 *panchayats*, and the data contained therein show how deeply rooted the power of traditional bonds, social hierarchies, and loyalties, accompanied by a domination of sorts, can eat into the *élan vitae* of such democratic self-governing bodies. As far as the role of the SC members of *panchayats* is concerned, in such States as Haryana, Andhra Pradesh, Odisha, Uttar Pradesh, and Tamil Nadu, the dominant castes in the localities do not approve of the reservation for the SCs and humiliate the latter in various ways. For instance, in those States, it is a common practice for the *sarpanchs* (chairperson of *panchayats*, whether men or women) to not be allowed to sit on the chair during meetings; they have to sit on floor and while the dominant castes sit on chairs (Baviskar and Mathew, 2009: 8). For a variety of reasons, the SC *sarpanchs* are helpless to assert themselves; their poverty, ignorance, and economic dependence on the dominant castes stand in the way of equal treatment (Baviskar and Mathew, 2009: 8).

As far as women are concerned – about a million of whom have been elected to different tiers of the *panchayats* in the country as a whole – their proxy role of various kinds, all conditioned by gender divisions in society (often encouraged by different political parties too), has turned out to be the norm rather than the exception in almost all States in India. As Baviskar and Mathew (2009: 14) have noted, it is also a widespread practice for husbands to carry out the actual day-to-day official work of their wives as heads of the *panchayats*.

Conclusion

This discussion strongly suggests that the local government reforms in India's rural areas are victims of local party 'oligarchies'[15] (in the case where the ruling parties are in full control) and social oligarchies (where caste or gender domination has a greater sway in society). The small and secretly operating CPI-M subcommittees, composed mostly of members not elected by the local people, at each level of the *panchayats* are but party oligarchies over the little democratic bodies – so much so that the latter pale into insignificance for all practical purposes. Sadly, this is the scenario in a region in India known for its advanced social and cultural environment and for its many social reforms since the nineteenth century, and not known for casteism and major communal conflicts after the great Calcutta killing of 1946. In other regions of India, local government reforms have failed to produce the desired political effect, that is, participation and empowerment. James Manor (2010: 61–79), in his overall survey of 'local governance' in India, is at pains to conclude that despite many congenial preconditions here, democratic decentralisation has suffered from many 'limitations'; only a small minority of State governments have devolved powers to the local bodies to enable them to work well. He notes that the Indian example "may be chiefly remembered as a sad example of what might have been". In his global survey of 'comparative local governance', Stoker (2006: 511) raised doubts about the "quality of democracy that is established at the local level and the nature of the relationship between local politicians and citizens" even in advanced Western democracies. The study here of the Indian case does hold much to offer with respect to both. Contrarily, in many cases, overarching political and social control over such bodies have led to disempowerment and loss of human rights on the part of the socially under-privileged sections. To put it a little theoretically, this provides proof of why both Tocqueville and Marx were cynical of the consequences of democracy (Kaviraj, 2011). Paradoxical though it may seem, democracy's long journey since the times of the ancient Greeks has been enmeshed with forms of exclusion (Dunn, 1992; Held, 2006: 19–23) and discrimination. Despite all efforts of the policymakers and the institutional designs, smaller-sized, rural self-governing institutions have yet to emerge as what Robert Dahl calls "inclusive polyarchies" (Dahl, 1977: 81–103). If India's governance reforms are to work at all, there is a need for a serious rethinking of its reforms agenda.

Notes

1 This provides a lot of food for thought on why local government experiments in West Bengal did not flourish as democratic institutions despite their existence for more than three decades. This democratic deficit has been pointed out by Harihar Bhattacharyya in various writings (Bhattacharyya, 1998, 1999, 2002, 2005a, 2013).
2 The 64th Constitutional Amendment for rural self-government introduced by then-Prime Minister Rajiv Gandhi in 1989 fell through in the Rajya Sabha by one vote.
3 In its country study, the World Bank cautioned: "The 73rd Amendment [. . .] is an important and welcome change, aiming at increasing autonomy of local governments. However, it may accentuate fiscal indiscipline by establishing between the state and local governments a system of transfers similar to the one in place between the central and state governments" (quoted in Govinda Rao and Singh, 2005: 341).
4 Adam Przworski (2010) has brought out a series of challenges which limit the functioning and effectiveness of democracy as a form of self-government. He argues that democracy has failed on many accounts throughout the world, and has yet to recover from the congenital limits set in its very design, that is, the "fear of participation by the broad masses of the population" (p. 162).
5 The Approach Document of the Fourth Five Year Plan (which was itself problematic) had given an indication when it had stated that "within the broad framework of control in strategic areas, there is an advantage in allowing the market much fuller play" (Hardgrave and Kochanek, 2000: 373).
6 See Kaviraj (2010, chapter 8) for an excellent and original political theoretical analysis of the complexities of carrying out the project of what he calls 'liberalisation' in India.
7 Kaviraj notes that even the CPI-M in West Bengal nearly admitted that all public-sector industries operating at a loss were to be closed down, thus paving the way for the central government to make use of the space for implementing liberalisation programmes (Kaviraj, 2010: 268–270).
8 Decades of modernisation have failed, much to the disbelief of the theorists of modernisation writing on India since the 1950s, so much so that the same scholars have begun to revisit their categories (Rudolph and Rudolph, 2008: 100–119). See also Rajinder Puri 'Reversing Quota Policy', *The Statesman*, Kolkata, 3 May 2012 in which he argues that even today, the virulent manner of continuing with the reservation policy in India has been meant to "splinter society into thousands of small castes and sub-castes which are subtly encouraged to become antagonistic and mutually hostile" (p. 6).

Governing India's localities 137

9 See Bhattacharyya (1998, 2002); Mukherjee (1994); Mitra (2001); Jha and Mathur (1999); Lieten (1992, 1996); Webster (1992); Baviskar and Mathew (2009); Jain (2005).
10 However, there is a theoretical point made by Kaviraj (1991) which is to be stressed here. Kaviraj (1991: 72–100) argues that the lower echelons of the bureaucracy in India hardly share the rationality of the elites at the commanding levels, so the policies get modified as they are implemented locally (p. 84). This is particularly true in the case of India's brand of federalism in which the Union government is all staff, but no line. In other words, the State-level bureaucracy is responsible for implementing, apart from the laws and policies of the States concerned, many social welfare and developmental policies and programmes of the Union government. For further details, see his chapter in Manor (1991: 72–100).
11 See Kohli (1991: 205–238) for information on caste armies. *Khap panchayats*, which are traditional *panchayats* in North India – especially Haryana and Punjab- are examples of a caste-based system of governance, which often inflict inhumane punishment on their targets.
12 However, the report did highlight the achievements of the *panchayats* too, but not as an institution of self-government: In the decade and a half of their existence, the *panchayats* have achieved much that is tangible, especially in terms of land reform and rural development. But more than this, they have helped to generate social and political consciousness among the people and facilitated the development of new leadership. This intangible achievement has strengthened the roots of democracy (Mukerji and Bandopadhyay, 1994: 251). For more thoughts on the subject of self-government, see Bandopadhyay (2007: 131–189).
13 Bhattacharyya (1998, 2001, 2002, 2007, 2011).
14 See Bakshi (1991). The Eleventh Schedule added to the Constitutional Amendment Act of 1992 for the ambit of *panchayats'* powers and functions contains twenty-eight items relating to social justice, rural development, empowerment, and so on.
15 This reminds us what Robert Michels said on the basis of his study of socialist parties in Europe in the late nineteenth and early twentieth centuries: "Who says organization, says oligarchy" (Michels, 1915: 1–11, 400–408).

11 Conclusion

India's second 'tryst with destiny'

Harihar Bhattacharyya and Lion König

This volume has examined the impact of globalisation on Indian society, culture, and public institutions, and explored the interface between India's globalisation, on the one hand, and its society and public institutions, on the other. What kind of impact has globalisation produced on Indian society and its public institutions? How have Indian society and her public institutions responded to globalisation? Ten chapters have critically reflected on the problem from various perspectives with adequate hard data. Although India's experience with globalisation is a millennia-old history, the post-1991 changes have proven to be substantial. In the process, the state institutions have been reformed, various acts and amendments have been passed for facilitating India's reforms, and the 2014 abolition of the Planning Commission, a relic of the 'license permit raj', or the public-sector-dominated economy, is a major case in point. The 73rd and 74th Constitutional Amendments for rural and urban local self-governments (passed in 1992) and the Right to Information Act and the Special Economic Zones (SEZ) Act (both passed in 2005) constitute other significant markers of the policy changes connected with globalisation. Although the Constitution itself remained more or less the same, the Punchi Commission (2010), the second centre–State-related commission, which was appointed by the government of India in 2009, submitted its ten-volume report recommending changes to the Constitution in tune with India's globalisation as mandated. Without a doubt, the years since 1991 have been a period of profound changes.

India's struggle with globalisation has not been uncontested. It is a highly diverse country with extremes of regional unevenness of development, and India's reforms have to navigate through a federal democratic polity of many layers, in particular, the Union and the State governments, the latter with constitutionally guaranteed competence on some strategic subjects like policing and land reforms – the most important bone of contention in implementing India's macro-economic reforms. India's very active judiciary, a vibrant mass media, and an articulate civil society further contribute to the complexity of the picture. The States in India, which are ruled by different political parties with their respective political manifestos and mandates, are very often vehemently opposed to such reforms; some reluctantly go along with the reforms; others are not attractive at all to investors, both indigenous and foreign, because of their geographic position. Despite

India being a democracy, the major decision to embrace reforms in 1991 was not mandated by the people; it was rather superimposed on the people, the most disadvantaged sections of whom pay what Amartya Sen has called "the penalties of globalisation" (Sen, 2006: 131). In other words, the benefits of globalisation in India have been reaped very differentially by different classes of people, with those who are socially and economically privileged having benefitted most. The unequal outcome of the globalisation process has been observed acutely throughout the centuries by thinkers such as Joseph Stiglitz (2012) or earlier by Karl Marx, who in the first volume of *Das Kapital* pointed out that as a result of deregulation of the economy and the free market, increasing asymmetry of power between those who own and those who do not would produce "an accumulation of wealth at one pole" and "an accumulation of misery, agony of toil and degradation at the opposite pole" (quoted in Upadhyay, 2013: 16). Global-level writings have pointed out that the inequality of income has increased worldwide: in the United States in 2000, for example, the wealthiest 1 percent owned 35.6 percent of the national wealth (Upadhyay, 2013: 16). Also in India, economic inequality has increased manifold (Pal and Ghosh, 2007). Globalisation may not necessarily result in governance; in a country like India, the market is needed, but in view of the vast majority of poor people in the country, a proper social welfare state is required. Thus, leaving the delivery of goods and services to non-state actors (the market forces) leaves many questions unanswered.

In the light of this nexus between state and market, Mohit Bhattacharyya sought to engage with the conceptual issues of globalisation and decentralisation within the global context, with particular reference to India and the conceptual tool of 'glocalisation'. Bhattacharyya has argued that as a result of globalisation in India, as elsewhere, a 'noticeable move' towards decentralisation of fiscal, political, and administrative responsibilities to lower-level governments has taken place, and governments are seeking new ways of service delivery in response to rising public demand for public services. Glocalisation creates incentives for sub-national governments to play a more active role in attracting foreign investment, promoting trade, providing infrastructure, and enhancing human capital; yet on the other hand, various forms of centralisation are being endorsed by increasing the importance of macro-economic policy levers, especially monetary policies and other central bank–sponsored fiscal policies. In this respect, the parallel between globalisation and decentralisation is quite close and like globalisation, decentralisation carries a potential for large overall benefits as well as risks and losses for the more vulnerable areas and groups. However, in India, decentralised rural local government is a relatively late phenomenon, and its record of performance leaves much to be desired. Until now, the multi-partner coalitions at the Centre meant a hard struggle against many odds, domestic as well as international. More serious attention is called for in matters of framing well-designed decentralisation policies and bolstering local democratic governance to enable India's national efforts to face up to the challenges of globalisation. The chapter thus recommended that more pointed attention needs to be paid in terms of field-level empirical studies to clearly unravel the global-local interactions in real-life situations.

T. R. Sharma provided the political background for India's reforms of the early 1990s by taking into consideration the ongoing developments such the Right to Information and the Right to Education acts. He shows that over the past one and a half decades, the Indian voter has become more discriminating, and consequently, the vicious circle of incumbency does not operate with predictable patterns as it used to before. Although his account mostly deals with the period before 1991, he has also addressed the developments post-1991. He reveals that today, performance, whether real or perceived, features significantly, and factors like accountability and transparency and the issues of development have started weighing with the electorate; as a result, democracy in India has 'deepened', as it were. Marginalised sections of society, such as *dalits* and women, are now increasingly represented in political institutions at the regional, the State, and the national level, thus contributing to the diversification of democracy in the country. He has, however, noted further challenges such as social and communal violence, institutionalised caste hatred, and rural indebtedness leading to farmer suicides. The benefits of post-1991 economic growth, Sharma ruefully reminds us, are largely confined to the urban centres, with rural India lagging far behind.

Cultural globalisation is a concept which is explored in the contemporary Indian context by Lion König. The chapter argues that globalisation is not a one-way transfer, but a pluralistic process in which all people and countries participate to varying extents. Investigating the role of the media and everyday consumer items in the globalisation process, the chapter shows that economic globalisation, since it is led by revenue and business interests, must adapt to local conditions and requirements in order to be successful. Rather than pushing for a uniform consumption pattern of cultural achievements, a process of hybridisation takes place where cultural patterns are developed by adding to and altering existing practices. As the chapter shows, new forms of cultural expression developed outside India can further identity articulation on the part of the receiver. It is the receivers of the message who themselves become the senders. As various examples in the chapter show, the increasing flow of media products from India, which are equally modified and hybridised in the process, contribute to the emergence of a 'global culture', which, far from being monolithic, is the sum of many parts. In connection with this, the chapter also engages with the concept of glocalisation, which was also explored by Mohit Bhattacharyya and which König defines as "the hybrid results of the multi-directional flows through which ideas, images, and languages travel and often become parts of new, third entities". It is through this process of glocalisation, closely connected to hybridisation, that a cultural 'third space' comes into existence. In conclusion, the chapter shows that equating globalisation with homogenisation overlooks the potential of this phenomenon to facilitate an articulation of hitherto silent voices and act as a motor for the promotion of identities. Although closer economic cooperation between countries will also trigger cultural (ex)changes, cultures do not become indistinguishable in the process of globalisation. Culture is inherently dynamic and subject to constant change, but, as the chapter shows, at the same time also has a non-negotiable, identity-constituting core, which feeds into the global interplay of cultures rather than being absorbed by it.

Asok Kumar Mukhopadhyay's chapter, somewhat similar in tone to Sharma's, is centrally preoccupied with Indian democratic governance, which is referred to as an "unfinished symphony". In his analysis of challenges to democratic governance in India since the 1990s, the author takes a critical stance on globalisation processes, which he sees as directly related to the economic reforms of 1991. Mukhopadhyay outlines three major fault lines cutting across Indian society that call for urgent reconciliation: the aspiration for quick economic gain among the upper classes, the strong demand for inclusive growth, and a rising power of the people's voice. He notes that about 40 percent of the population still lives below the poverty line and despite the economy growing at 6 percent, poverty figures have hardly declined. Even though development projects such as the Mahatma Gandhi National Rural Employment Guarantee Scheme (MGNREGS), the Bharat Nirman development projects, the Integrated Child Development Scheme, the Sarba Siksha Abhiyana, and the National Rural Health Mission have been launched, implementation remains tardy and inefficient, not least due to substantial political corruption. It is this inefficiency of policy measures which, according to Mukhopadhyay, has further disadvantaged marginal sections of society and led to a "widespread suspicion about the sincerity of governance". Like T. R. Sharma, Mukhopadhyay also refers to the Right to Information (RTI) Act as a promising policy step towards transparency and Good Governance, but also draws attention to the need for more solid implementation. Reviewing the various economic reforms since 1991, the author concludes that economic development has led to very asymmetrical outcomes, where the vast majority of the population has found itself excluded from the process. Based on these findings, the chapter suggests that the Indian model of development is essentially a 'zero-sum game' where one actor's gain inevitably is another one's loss. In view of this scenario of socio-economic realities, Indian policymakers will have to rethink their conceptual understanding of 'development' and readjust the definition of 'poverty'. It is thus the achievement of fiscal discipline in the midst of avoidable economic profligacy and rampant political-administrative corruption, and the adoption of a consensual attitude to democratic conflict resolution, including the protection of civil liberties and the regard for the dignity of the individual, that constitute the major challenge to making globalisation work in India.

Mahendra Pal Singh brings a completely new perspective of the judicial discourse in contemporary India and links it with India's ongoing reforms. Following a comparative judicial approach that takes into account the experiences of the Western countries, he argues that even though the Constitution makers expected that judges would not act as a super-legislature or super-executive, by its very nature, the task of judicial review brings the judiciary into conflict with the executive and the legislature. With particular reference to some very important acts, such as the Patent Act (2005), the Trade Mark Act (1999), the Geographical Indications Act (2000), the Designs Act (2000), and the Special Economic Zones Act (2005), he points out that serious differences have occasionally cropped up between the courts and the political branches on several issues, particularly with respect to the rights of the weaker sections of the society, where the courts have either failed to give the expected effect to the affirmative programmes of the state or have invalidated political decisions in favour of industry or trade in disregard of the vulnerable sections of the society such as Scheduled Tribes, or the environmental effects of economic growth. For the author, a central concern in the exercise of power of judicial review is the fact that in recent years several questions have been decided in smaller benches of two or three judges, which, apart from creating conflict of interpretation, undermines the sanctity of the Constitution itself. The policy advice to emerge from this chapter is that if the Supreme Court fails to attend to this issue, it loses its claim to be the custodian of the Constitution and to question the decisions of the other two powers of the state. With socialism no longer on the agenda, Singh argues, the judiciary has found itself much closer to the other two wings of the government.

A theoretical exploration of the Indian political Left's attitude towards the phenomenon of globalisation is provided by Sobhanlal Datta Gupta in his chapter. Datta Gupta disentangles the term 'Left' and differentiates between the 'mainstream' and the 'extremist' camps. When critiquing globalisation, the mainstream distinguishes between modernist thrusts of globalisation and their appropriation by the proponents of neo-liberalism; however, the extremist Left is not inclined towards recognising this differentiation, since in their understanding, modernity, capitalism, and globalisation are the three components of a single whole. Second, there are different views on the best way forward in the inevitable encounter with the effects of a globalised world: in the mainstream Left's understanding, globalisation is to be encountered by radicalising and democratising the state, whereas in the Left extremist perception, development is people-centric rather than state-centric, since the Indian state as such is a structure of violence to be overcome. The chapter explores a range of questions regarding the triangle of the relationship between development, globalisation, and India's Left. It seeks to understand how globalisation has affected the rise of extremist violence in the so-called 'red corridor' and what the response of the Indian state has been. Second, it sets out to shed light on how the Communist Party of India (Marxist) [CPI (M)] views the phenomenon of Maoist violence and its bid for power, and third, attempts to understand the differences within the mainstream Left in regard to the Maoists.

While for the followers of Maoist ideology with their utopian vision of an agrarian revolution brought about by a violent seizure of state power, capitalist modernity is a taboo, for the mainstream Left, the challenge is far more complex. In today's globalised world, while accepting new technology and the compulsions of the market, the Left has to work out an appropriate strategy to channel the positive fruits of globalisation to the lowest levels of society, which have acted as the nurseries of Left extremism in India in recent times.

Surajit C. Mukhopadhyay examines a very crucial institution: he analyses the work of the police in India in the age of increased globalisation. The chapter investigates the shifts that have occurred in this institution since its inception in the colonial era. Although on a global scale, the change has been from the police serving the government to now serving the citizens, in India, this transformation is still incomplete. Such a change towards a self-understanding of the police as a service provider to the individual citizen would, however, be necessary, since, as the chapter argues, "in a multi-ethnic, multi-lingual, and poly-religious society prone to conflict, the role of the police is of immense importance, and the institution is crucially dependent on skills that force alone would not provide'. Mukhopadhyay establishes a direct connection between processes of economic globalisation and the police: as the market spreads to even the remotest parts of India, streamlining socio-economic practices, it faces resistance from diverse groups and classes. SEZs, also discussed by Jhumpa Mukherjee as one of the expressions of market forces, can lead to displacement of a vast number of people. One of the reactions to this is Maoist violence, which the author sees as a direct consequence of the failure of the democratic system to ensure justice and access to basic goods and services. This particular kind of resistance, however, has spawned a violent armed movement that has triggered an equally violent and forceful state response. It is this response, the chapter argues, that has moved the discourse of policing away from community-oriented strategies to a more vigorous, armed, police-centric model that mirrors the colonial state response to internal dissent. Surveying the current outlook and performance of the police and the relevant policymakers, where the increase in militancy in some parts of India has created a discourse of police modernisation that increasingly centres on weapons and surveillance technology, thus increasing the distance between the police and the policed, Mukhopadhyay concludes that the Indian police has lost the opportunity to reform itself and create a discourse of community-oriented policing strategies that would have been in sync with the other development of contemporary India – the rise of a vocal civil society backed by a dynamic media that has been able to reach out to an unprecedented mass audience.

Exploring the 'complex ethnic territorial mosaic' that is India, Rekha Saxena suggests that the importance of federal pluralism 'is likely to be not only maintained, but will possibly grow'. Like Jhumpa Mukherjee in the following chapter, Rekha Saxena does not perceive the States as socio-cultural monoliths, but argues that the recent phase of federalisation of the Indian political system against the backdrop of the market economy and reforms has "brought to the forefront difficult tasks of protecting the micro-minorities; discrepant majorities (national majorities that are regional minorities); and internal minorities within all castes, tribes, languages, and religions that are interspersed throughout the country". Due to the simultaneous impact of globalisation, regionalisation, and localisation of identities in India and the world, these challenges have intensified, and India will have to address them in a way that balances neo-liberal economic reforms, redistributive public policies, and fiscal federalism.

Jhumpa Mukherjee has looked at the impact of globalisation from the regional perspective. She has ably analysed two recent success stories of sub-regional movements in India which resulted in the creation of the States of Uttarakhand and Telangana. These are discussed in close connection with the various ways in which globalisation has affected India. The asymmetrical process of globalisation gives birth to a politics of identity in which the primordial gets subsumed in the new economic or regional identity, leading to a unity of certain groups and classes. India's liberalisation, it is argued, has produced both inter-regional and intra-regional inequalities which have prepared the new bases for demanding territory for development. Drawing on the two cases, the chapter concludes that there have been changes in the dynamics of sub-national movements in terms of character, focus, leadership, and, above all, in the criteria of granting Statehood to regional movements since the days of India's neo-liberal reforms. Development, share in resources, economic security, and educational and employment opportunities have subsumed affiliations on the grounds of religion, language, and ethnic divisions. It is thus globalisation and its economic expressions which have led to greater federalisation of regions through a new identity consciousness grounded in the need for socio-economic development.

In the final chapter, Harihar Bhattacharyya takes yet another look at the local level within the global-level comparative local governance discourse, as well as the post-1992 discourses on local government experiments and experience. The chapter, written from a modified neo-institutionalist approach, examines the experience of India's rural local self-governments and points out central limitations to the successful working of such democratically elected bodies. The chapter contends that the success of the local self-government institutions holds an important key to the working of India's reforms. If a neo-Right turn through neo-liberal reforms demands a more restricted centralised state but requires more and fragmented decentralisation governments as the *least state*, then the Indian experience so far suggests that there is much to be desired. Investigating the complexity of India's local self-governance structures, the chapter emphasises the shift that has occurred with the passage of the 73rd Constitutional Amendment as a major departure from the pre-reform era in the sense that it is now obligatory on the part of State governments to constitute such bodies after an interval of five years. Also, this piece of reform legislation provided for political empowerment of various weaker sections of society as obligatory. However, with a new caste consciousness, political empowerment, and reservations for the socially marginalised, the democratic functioning of the *panchayats* and their powers of social redistribution, as per the provisions of the Constitution, like governance at the local level, has become the casualty. A set of substantive problems remains: local government reforms in India's rural areas falling victim to local party 'oligarchies' is a widespread phenomenon. In addition, women, about a million of whom were elected to different tiers of the *panchayats* in the country, are often represented in the *panchayats* by their husbands or male family members (often condescendingly called '*pati-panchayats*'), thus reflecting the gender divisions along patriarchal lines and furthering the sense of disempowerment on the part of female officeholders. In the light of such disillusioning empirical facts, it is found that actors, the context, and the inappropriate institutional designs have combined to serve as a severe challenge to such budding bodies, with transparency, accountability, and participation suffering.

In 1947, Jawaharlal Nehru announced India's independence in his historic speech 'Tryst with Destiny', which was a masterpiece in rhetoric, but strongly suggestive of the inauguration of an era:

> [A]t the stroke of the midnight hour when the world sleeps, India will awake to life and freedom. A moment comes, which comes but rarely in history,

when we step out from the old to new, when an age ends, and when the soul of a nation, long suppressed, finds utterance.

(quoted in Mitra and Singh, 1999: 17)

The 'destiny' that Nehru and his political colleagues had in mind was the inauguration of a command economy with public sectors dominating, an omnipotent social welfare state, and an open democratic polity towards the goal of a 'socialist pattern of society' via democratic means. This unique model continued for decades, with a 'Hindu rate of growth', as the 3 to 4 percent rate was often condescendingly referred to. From 1991 onwards, India 'stepped out' of the Nehruvian era to one that is its reverse under the leadership of the same Congress party of which Nehru once headed. The journey through a (liberal-)democratic polity with an economically dominant state was the first 'tryst with destiny'; India's post-1991 embrace of globalisation, opening up the protected economy, was the second tryst. This journey since 1991 has not been smooth because the party system changed from a one-party dominant system to multi-party coalition governments. The units of federation are today more conscious and assertive and are run by political parties whose policies and political manifestoes are often at variance with globalisation and macro-reforms. Even now many States remain virtually outside the net of reforms and receive very little, if any, private investment from abroad. India's globalisation, or neo-liberal reforms, has already created the basis for extreme inequality among the States in terms of the Human Development Index (HDI). The so-called 'forward States' have received more private investment, mostly Foreign Direct Investment (FDI), whereas the so-called 'backward ones' get very little. The very definition of Indian federalism thus known as 'cooperative' is being changed into a market-oriented 'competitive federalism'. Lawrence Sáez (2002) sees it as a transformation from inter-State cooperation into "inter-jurisdictional competition" among the federal units to attract more private investment, particularly FDI. Competition between the States is an issue: during the entire period of India's neo-liberal reforms since 1991, the States in the east and the northeast received very little FDI, except for Odisha; the same is true for Kerala, whose record in terms of poverty reduction and social development is otherwise outstanding. But then today aggressive reformers seek to radically change the criterion of development: in the cacophony of 'developmentalism', the overemphasis is on economic growth via investment, especially foreign, rather than poverty reduction and good performance in terms of social development indicators. And yet, the Indian experience with reforms until 2011 was less than attractive for investors in terms of institutional bottlenecks. The World Bank's 'Doing Business Survey' (2011) shows India second to last in enforcing the contract which includes forty-six procedures that take about four years to complete, and costs around 40 percent of the claim (Tendulkar and Bhavani, 2007: 198). Another survey, 'Asia Business and Politics' (2010), by the Hong Kong–based Political and Economic Risk Consultancy Private Limited (PERC) lists India as one of the most 'over-regulated' countries in the world (score: 9.16 out of 10) (Tendulkar and Bhavani, 2007: 198). The results of these surveys are confirmed by the fact that during the first decade of reforms (1991–2001) the total public-sector employment in fact recorded a growth of about 1 percent (Tendulkar and Bhavani, 2007: 51). This debunks the myth of 'deregulation' as one of the '3 Ds' of India's reforms (the others being disinvestment and denationalisation), and suggests once again that major institutional reforms are called for in making globalisation work in India.

In looking at things from the other side, Atul Kohli (2009) made two pertinent points which are worth mentioning. First, he argued that the real beginning of India's neo-liberal reforms and state-capital alliance ('shift away from socialism') for growth can be traced to Indira Gandhi's last inning in the 1980s as prime minister, which accelerated growth one decade before the liberalisation of the economy.[1]

This is corroborated by the annual growth figures since 1980: 1980–81 (7.17 percent); 1983–84 (7.68 percent); 1988–89 (10.43 percent); and 1989–90 (6.70 percent) (Tendulkar and Bhavani, 2007: 210), and leaves little room for underemphasising Nehru's considerable achievement in the growth of heavy industries (Kohli, 2009: 12), as is done nowadays by the mandarins of neo-liberal reforms. Second, Kohli shows that on a comparative estimate of the Indian States, it was West Bengal and Kerala – two States that have been dominated by the Left for a long time – which received very little FDI and do not figure among the 'forward States', but have effectively reduced poverty (Kohli, 2009: 15). Following Drèze and Sen's notion of a 'virtuous circle' (rather than a 'vicious circle'), Kohli remarked:

> A more pro-poor regime interacted with a more efficacious citizenry [. . .]. This created both a supply of and a demand for a variety of successful pro-poor public policies including land reforms, higher investments into and better implementation of education and health policies, and greater gender equality.
>
> (Kohli, 2009: 16)

But then the Left governments were dislodged from power in both States in 2011.[2] Ensuring economic growth and politically selling it are two completely different matters. Even though confirmed political stability at the Centre since 2014 (with a majority multi-party coalition government led by the Bharatiya Janata Party [BJP]) is a congenial factor to maintain the growth momentum, given India's complex diversity and the federal political structure that renders the States relative autonomy on some vital and strategic areas, much also depends on the realities, which are not very promising. If only the so-called 'forward States' could reap all or most of the benefits of globalisation, then this would also accentuate regional imbalances in development. A recent report shows that regional disparities and inter-State inequality have acquired the 'greatest salience' in India (Bakshi, Chawla, and Shah, 2015: 44–51). This is most apparent in areas inhabited by India's more than 100 million aboriginal peoples living in about 100 of the 257 districts across the country (Bakshi, Chawla, and Shah, 2015: 50). The Oxfam report (2014), 'Even It Up: Time to End Extreme Poverty', recorded that since the time of India's reforms, whereas India's billionaires have increased from only two in the 1990s to sixty-five in 2014, as much as 37 percent of India's population lives below the official poverty line, which is defined as Rs. 816 per month in rural areas and Rs. 1000 per month in cities (*Times of India* Calcutta, p. 8, 11 January 2014).

Finally, we seek to raise the issue of democracy in India in the 'era of reforms'. For one thing, democracy did not have much of an agency role during the days of Nehru when the omnipotent 'social welfare' state occupied most space and rendered democracy secondary for governmental change through elections. Today, democracy's space, institutionally speaking, has been reduced even further to the functional 'political society', as opposed to the 'civil society', which is less interested in the dynamic role of democracy (Chatterjee, 2004; 2011). Democracy thus seems to play only a surrogate role for supplying legitimacy to the rulers. No wonder that India's late political philosopher Rajni Kothari (2010: 152) hoped as much: "[D]emocracy could well become a legitimate instrument for transformative politics, based on an incipient movement for democracy, informed by an ethical imperative, leading individuals and societies towards world transformation". To what extent Kothari's agenda for 'emancipatory democracy' is adhered to by the reformers in the country remains an open question. Without a doubt, India's second 'tryst with destiny' is moving towards an unknown and rather uncertain path.

Notes

1 Biplab Das Gupta (2005) confirmed that the late Indira Gandhi had applied for a US$5 billion structural adjustment loan from the International Monetary Fund (IMF) with conditionalities and signed the contract. This was, according to Dasgupta, not that necessary, judging by the satisfactory records of industrial and agricultural growth in the decade (Das Gupta, 2005: 5–6).
2 Ironically, the United Progressive Alliance (UPA)-II was also dislodged from power at the Centre in 2014 when India's GDP growth in the preceding years was rather good: 2005–06 (9.5 percent); 2007–08 (9.6 percent); and 2010–11 (8.6 percent) (Tendulkar and Bhavani, 2007: 232).

Contributors

Harihar Bhattacharyya, MA (First Class First and Gold Medalist), PhD (LSE, London), is a Professor of Political Science, and former Dean of the Faculty of Arts, Commerce, Law, and Management at the University of Burdwan. Professor Bhattacharyya has also taught at the South Asia Institute, University of Heidelberg, Germany; Hull University, UK; the Institute of Federalism, Fribourg, Switzerland; and Delhi University. As an international expert, he has taken a leading role in peace-making for Sri Lanka, Burundi, and Nepal, helping the latter in its constitution-making process. A recipient of many national- and international-level assignments and author of over eighty research papers and ten books, his recent publications include *Federalism in Asia: Indian, Pakistan and Malaysia* (Routledge: London and New York, 2010) and (jointly edited) *The Politics of Social Exclusion in India: Democracy at the Crossroads* (Routledge: London and New York, 2010). His latest (co-edited) book is *The Politics of Citizenship, Identity and the State in South Asia* (New Delhi: Samskriti, 2012). He completed a research project funded by the Indian Council of Social Science Research (ICSSR, New Delhi) (2011–13) titled 'Asymmetric Federalism, Tribal Identity and the Left in Tripura' (2011–13). Currently, he is associated with the international research project 'Dealing with Territorial Cleavages in Transitional Constitutions' (2013–15) (based at New York University's Law faculty, as India Expert). He is a Lead Researcher of 'Continuity and Change in India Federalism in India in the Age of Coalitions Governments' (2014–17) based at the University of Edinburgh.

Mohit Bhattacharya, MA, PhD (Calcutta), is the former vice-chancellor of Burdwan University and Centenary Professor of public administration at Calcutta University. Professor Bhattacharya is widely known for his work in the field of public administration, with a special focus on urban and local government studies. He has been a research fellow in urban studies at the Institute of Public Administration, New York, and an honorary fellow of the Institute of Local Government Studies at the University of Birmingham. He was one of the founding members of the Urban Studies Centre at the Indian Institute of Public Administration (IIPA), New Delhi, where he was later appointed Professor of organisational studies. Later, he was selected as a national fellow of the ICSSR, New Delhi. Among his latest publications is *Contemporary Decentralization Discourse* (Progressive Publishers, Calcutta, 2011).

Sobhanlal Datta Gupta, MA, PhD (Calcutta), former Surendra Nath Banerjee Professor of political science, University of Calcutta (India), is working on the intellectual history of Marxism and issues concerning Left movements and Politics in the developing world in general and in India in particular. Some of his recent publications include *Comintern and the Destiny of Communism in India: 1919–1943. Dialectics of Real and a Possible History* (Kolkata: Seribaan, 2006). He is the editor of *The Ryutin Platform: Stalin and the Crisis of Proletarian Dictatorship* (Kolkata: Seribaan, 2010), and the author of *Marxism in Dark Times: Select Essays for the New Century* (London: Anthem Press, 2012).

Lion König, MA, PhD (Heidelberg), studied political science of South Asia and English philology at Heidelberg University (Germany) and at the University of Edinburgh (UK). He was awarded a PhD in political science by Heidelberg University for his thesis entitled 'Cultural Citizenship and the Politics of Censorship in Post-Colonial India'. Lion König has been a scholarship holder in the Graduate Programme for Transcultural Studies (GPTS) at the Cluster of Excellence: 'Asia and Europe in a Global Context' at Heidelberg University. He has held research fellowships at the Institute for Defence Studies and Analyses (IDSA) in 2011, as well as at the Institute of Social Sciences (ISS), and at the Centre for Social Sciences and Humanities (CSH), New Delhi, in 2014. Lion König has been affiliated with the Centre for the Study of Law and Governance, Jawaharlal Nehru University; and the Centre for Culture, Media, and Governance, Jamia Millia Islamia, as a visiting lecturer and an adjunct faculty, respectively. He is the co-editor of *Politics of the Other in India and China: Western Concepts in Non-Western Contexts* (London: Routledge, 2016) and of *The Politics of Citizenship, Identity, and the State in South Asia* (New Delhi: Samskriti, 2012).

Jhumpa Mukherjee, MA (Gold Medalist), PhD (Burdwan), is Assistant Professor of political science at St. Xavier's College (Autonomous), Calcutta. She was awarded the Principal Sudarshan Singha Memorial Prize, as well as the National Scholarship for securing the highest marks in political science at the graduation level at Burdwan University. She was also awarded the Dhirendra Jitendra Medal and the University Gold Medal for her achievement at the master's level. In addition, she has obtained a post-graduate diploma in human rights from the Indian Institute of Human Rights, New Delhi. She was awarded a PhD from the University of Burdwan for her thesis entitled 'Multicultural Decentralization in India', which was examined by Ronald Watts (Queen's University) and Gurpreet Mahajan (JNU). Her publications include *Conflict Resolution in Multicultural Societies: The Case of India* (New Delhi: Sage, 2014).

Asok Kumar Mukhopadhyay, MA, PhD (Calcutta), PhD (London), is an ex-emeritus fellow in political science for the University Grants Commission and a retired Netaji Subhas chair in political science, Calcutta University. An internationally known scholar on public administration and Indian politics, he taught at the Indian Institute of Public Administration, New Delhi, and at Calcutta University. He has published widely on Indian politics and public administration, and has formerly edited the *Calcutta Journal of Political Studies* and the *West Bengal Political Science Review*.

Surajit C. Mukhopadhyay, MA, MPhil (JNU), PhD (Leicester), is a sociologist. He taught sociology at the University of Burdwan for about two decades before taking up the position of Registrar of the West Bengal National University of Juridicial Sciences, Kolkata. He was a commonwealth staff scholar at Leicester University, UK, for his PhD on Indian policing. In 1991 he was a NORD scholar at the University of Oslo, and South Asian regional fellow for post-doctoral work awarded by the Social Science Research Council, New York, in 2003. His publications include 'Contemporary Concerns in Indian Policing: Can the Force Shift to Community Policing?', in: Harihar Bhattacharyya and Abhijit Ghosh (eds.) *Indian Political Thought and Movements: New Interpretations and Emerging Issues* (Kolkata: K.P. Bagchi, 2007), 303–14.

Sudha Pai, MA, MPhil, PhD (JNU) is Professor at the Centre for Political Studies, Jawaharlal Nehru University, New Delhi. Currently she is also the Rector (pro-vice-chancellor) of the university. She joined the Centre for Political Studies in 1980 as an Assistant Professor. Her graduation and post-graduation was from the University of Delhi, and her MPhil and PhD were from the Centre for Political Studies. She was a Lecturer from 1972 to 1975 at Gargi College for Women, Delhi University. Since joining the Centre for Political Studies, she has taught courses and guided research in the field of Indian politics and comparative politics. Her research interests include *dalit* politics, State politics in India, agrarian politics, globalisation, and legislative governance. She was a senior fellow at the Nehru Memorial Museum and Library, Teen Murti, New Delhi (2006–09).

Rekha Saxena, MA, PhD (Delhi University), is Professor at the Department of Political Science, University of Delhi. She is a recipient of the Shastri Indo-Canadian Institute's Doctoral (1999–2000), Faculty Research (2003), and Faculty Enrichment (2011) awards to visit Canada, where she was affiliated with the Department of Political Studies and Institute of Intergovernmental Relations at Queens University, University of Toronto, and McGill University. She was twice appointed a country co-coordinator for India on the Global Dialogue Programs of the Forum of Federations, Canada, on the themes of 'Legislative and Executive Governance in Federal Countries' and 'Intergovernmental Relations in Federal Countries'. She was also appointed a member of a task force of the Second Commission on Centre-State Relations set up by the Union Ministry of Home Affairs, Government of India. She is the author of *Situating Federalism: Mechanisms of Intergovernmental Relations in Canada and India* (New Delhi: Manohar, 2006) and has edited the volume *Varieties of Federal*

Governance: Major Contemporary Models (New Delhi: Cambridge University Press, 2011).

T. R. Sharma, MA, PhD, is Professor Emeritus of Political Science, Panjab University, Chandigarh. He has specialised in State politics in India, particularly with regard to Punjab and Himachal Pradesh. From 1997 to 1999 he was regional coordinator on Punjab for the DFG Project on Governance in India directed by Professor Subrata Kumar Mitra, Department of Political Science, South Asia Institute, University of Heidelberg, Germany. He has published research articles in international-level journals, such as *Modern Asian Studies, Pacific Affairs*, and the *Australian Journal of Politics and History*. He served as a member of the Committee on Political Philosophical/Political Theory of the International Political Science Association (IPSA). Currently he is editing three books on different aspects of northeast India, including *The Nature of Inter- and Intra- Tribal Conflicts, Reforming Education*, and *The Issues of Inclusive Development of the Region*.

Mahendra Pal Singh, BA, LLB (Agra), LLM (Columbia), LLM, LLD (Lucknow), is currently the chairperson of Delhi Judicial Academy. Until recently, he was the Vice-Chancellor at the National University of Juridical Sciences, Kolkata. Earlier he taught at the University of Delhi from 1970 to 2005, where he was also Head and Dean of the Faculty of Law from 1994 to 1997. From 1980 to 1982 and again in 1985 he was Alexander-von-Humboldt Fellow at Heidelberg University. He was visiting professor and Head of the Law Division at the South Asia Institute, University of Heidelberg, from 1987 to 1988 and Visiting Professor at the Faculty of Law, Heidelberg University, and a Fellow at the Max Planck Institute for Comparative Public Law and International Law, Heidelberg. He has held visiting professorships at the University of Hong Kong and the City University of Hong Kong; Kansai University, Osaka; National University of Singapore; Renmin University, China; and Jawaharlal Nehru University, New Delhi. He was a Fellow at the Institute for Advanced Studies, Berlin, and at the Indian Institute of Science, Bangalore. He was also Director of the Indian Law Institute, New Delhi, in 1997. His publications include *Town, Market, Mint and Port in the Mughal Empire* (New Delhi: Adam, 2007) and *Outlines of Indian Legal and Constitutional History* (Meerut: Western Law House, 1984).

Bibliography

Adeney, Katherine. 2005. 'Hindu Nationalism and Federal Structure in the Era of Regionalism', in: Katherine Adeney and Lawrence Sáez (eds.) *Coalition Politics and Hindu Nationalism* (London: Routledge).
Ahire, Philip Terdoo. 1991. *Imperial Policing: The Emergence and Role of the Police in Colonial Nigeria, 1860–1960* (Milton Keynes: Open University Press).
Aiyer, Swaminathan S. Anklesaria. n.d. 'KFC Is Just a Chicken Pakora', accessible at: http://swaminomics.org/?p=455 (last access: 24 March, 2012).
Alam, Javeed. 2013. *Who Wants Democracy?* (New Delhi: Orient Blackswan).
Ambedkar, B. R. 1994. *Writings and Speeches*, volume 13 (Bombay: Education Department, Government of Maharashtra).
Amin, Samir. 2004. *The Obsolescent Capitalism: Contemporary Capitalism and Global Disorder* (London: Verso).
Anderson, David M. 1994. 'Policing the Settler State: Colonial Hegemony in Kenya, 1900–1952', in: Dagmar Engels and Shula Marks (eds.) *Contesting Colonial Hegemony: State and Society in Africa and India* (London: British Academic Press).
—— and David Killingray. 1991. *Policing the Empire: Government, Authority and Control, 1830–1940* (Manchester: Manchester University Press).
Arnold, David. 1985. 'Bureaucratic Recruitment and Subordination in Colonial India: The Madras Constabulary, 1859–1947', in Ranajit Guha (ed.) *Subaltern Studies: Writing on South Asian History and Society IV* (New Delhi: Oxford University Press).
——. 1986. *Police Power and Colonial Rule, Madras 1859–1947* (New Delhi: Oxford University Press).
Arora, Balveer and Douglas Verney (eds.). 2003. *Multiple Identities in a Single State* (New Delhi: Konark).
Austin, Granville. 1966. *The Indian Constitution: Cornerstone of a Nation* (New Delhi: Oxford University Press).
——. 1999. *Working a Democratic Constitution: The Indian Experience* (New Delhi: Oxford University Press).
Aydin, Ahmet Hamdi. 1995. *A Comparative Study of Police Organisation in England & Wales and Turkey: The Case for Centralisation and Decentralisation* (University of Leicester, Centre for the Study of Public Order: Unpublished Ph.D. thesis).
Bagchi, Amaresh and John Kurian. 2005. 'Regional Inequalities in India: Pre-and Post-Reform Trends and Challenges for Policy', in: Jos Mooij (ed.) *The Politics of Economic Reforms in India* (New Delhi: Sage).
Bakshi, P. M. 2014. [1991]. *The Constitution of India* (New Delhi: Delhi Law House).

154   Bibliography

Bakshi, S. Chawla and M. Shah. 2015. 'Disparities in India: A Moving Frontier', *Economic and Political Weekly*, 50(1), 44–53.

Balibar, Étienne and Immanuel Wallerstein. 1991. *Race, Nation, Class: Ambiguous Identities* (London: Verso).

Bandopadhyaha, Debabrata. 2007. *Land, Labour and Governance: An Anthology* (Kolkata: Worldview).

Banerjee, Sumanta. 1980. *India's Simmering Revolution* (London: Zed).

———. 2010. "Stationer nam Maobad" [in Bengali], *Anik*, July.

Banerjee, T. K. 2010. *The Naxalite Movement: Currents and Crosscurrents* (Kolkata: Progressive Publishers).

Bardhan, Pranab. 1984. *The Political Economy of Development in India* (New Delhi: Oxford University Press).

———. 2002. 'Decentralization of Governance and Development', *Journal of Economic Perspectives*, 16(4).

———. 2007. 'Poverty and Inequality in China and India: Elusive Link with Globalization', *Economic and Political Weekly*, September 22.

——— and Dilip Mookherjee. 2006. 'The Rise of Local Government: An Overview', in: Pranab Bardhan and Dilip Mookherjee (eds.) *Decentralization and Local Governance in Developing Countries: A Comparative Perspective* (New Delhi: Oxford University Press).

Baruah, Sanjib. 2005. *Durable Disorder: Understanding the Politics of Northeast India* (New Delhi: Oxford University Press).

——— (ed.). 2009. *Beyond Counter-Insurgency: Breaking the Impasse in North-East India* (New Delhi: Oxford University Press).

——— (ed.). 2010. *Ethnonationalism in India: A Reader* (New Delhi: Oxford University Press).

Basu, Subho. 1994. *Workers Politics in Bengal, 1890–1929: Mill Towns, Strikes and Nationalist Agitations* (University of Cambridge, Darwin College: Unpublished Ph.D. thesis).

Baviskar, B. S. and George Mathew (eds.). 2009. *Inclusion and Exclusion in Local Governance: Field Studies from Rural India* (New Delhi: Sage).

Baxi, U. 1991. 'Constitutional Perspectives on Privatization', *Mainstream*, 6 July.

Baxi, Upendra. 1998. 'The State and the Human Rights Movements in India', in: Manoranjan Mohanty, Partha Nath Mukherji, with Olle Törnquist (eds.) *People's Rights: Social Movements and the State in the Third World* (New Delhi: Sage), 335–353.

Berthet, Samuel and Girish Kumar (eds.). 2011. *New States for a New India: Federalism and Decentralization in the States of Jharkhand and Chhattisgarh* (New Delhi: Manohar).

Béteille, André. 2011. "Stateless Societies", *The Telegraph*, Kolkata, 30 August.

Bhabha, Homi K. 2007. *The Location of Culture* (London: Routledge).

Bhagwati, Jagdish. 2004. *In Defence of Globalization* (New Delhi: Oxford University Press).

———. 2007 'In Defence of Globalization: It *Has* a Human Face', in: Baldev Raj Nayar (ed.) *Globalization and Politics in India* (New Delhi: Oxford University Press), 149–157.

Bhambri, C. P. 1989. 'Indian State: Conflicts and Contradiction', in: Zoya Hasan, Shree Nagesh Jha, and Rasheeduddin Khan (eds.) *The State, Political Processes and Identity: Reflections on Modern India* (New Delhi: Sage), 73–88.

———. 1996. 'Working of Indian Parliamentary System: A Diagnosis', Paper presented at a National Seminar on Indian Politics held at Punjab University, Chandigarh (unpublished).

Bibliography 155

———. 2005.*Globalization India: Nation, State and Democracy* (New Delhi: Shipra).
Bhattacharyya, B. B. and S. Sakthivel. 2007. 'Regional Growth and Disparity in India: Comparison of Pre- and Post-Reform Decades', in: Baldev Raj Nayar (ed.) *Globalization and Politics in India* (New Delhi: Oxford University Press), 458–476.
Bhattacharyya, Harihar. 1992. 'Deinstitutionalization of Indian Politics: A Micro Critique', *Journal of Socio-Political Studies* 1(1), 64–85.
———. 1998 *Micro-Foundations of Bengal Communism* (New Delhi: Ajanta).
———. 1999. 'Contradictions of Grassroots Democracy in West Bengal: The Case of Panchayats', in: Asish Ghosh (ed.) *Dalits and Peasants: The Emerging Caste- Class Dynamics* (New Delhi: Gyan Sagar).
———. 2001. *India as a Multicultural Federation: Asian Values, Democracy and Decentralization (in comparison with Swiss Federalism)* (Basel: Helbing & Lichtenhahn).
———. 2002. *Making Local Democracy Work in India Social Capital, Politics and Governance in West Bengal* (New Delhi: Vedam Books).
———. 2005a 'Grassroots Democracy and Civic Participation in Rural West Bengal: The Case of Gram Sansad', in: D. Sen Gupta and S. Ganguly (eds.) *Theme India: Essays in Honour of Prasant Kumar Ghosh* (Kolkata: Arambag Book House), 63–76.
———. 2005b. 'Federalism and Regionalism in India: Institutional Strategies and Political Accommodation of Identity', in: *Heidelberg Papers in South Asian and Comparative Politics*, 27.
———. 2007. 'Approaches to Local Government: Arguing a Case for Human Rights', *West Bengal Political Science Review*, 2(2), 1–14.
———. 2009a. 'Globalization and Indian Federalism: Re-Assertions of States' Rights', in: Hans Lofgren and Prakash Sarangi (eds.) *The Politics and Culture of Globalization Indian and Australia* (New Delhi: Social Science Press), 99–119.
———. 2009b. 'Globalization and National Identity: Towards an Indian Perspective', in: *Society and Change*, 14, (1–4), 15–29.
———. 2011. 'UPA (2004–) and Federalism: A Paradigm Shift?', in: Lawrence Sáez and Gurharpal Singh (eds.) *New Dimensions of Politics in India: The United Progressive Alliance in Power* (London: Routledge), 26–39.
———. 2012. 'A Nation of Citizens in a Fragmented Society: Citizenship as Individual and Ethnic Entitlements in India', in: Harihar Bhattacharyya, Anja Kluge and Lion König (eds.) *The Politics of Citizenship, Identity and the State in South Asia* (New Delhi: Samskriti), 23–41.
———. 2013. 'Marxist Democratic Problematic and the Decline of the Left in West Bengal', in: Priya Singh (ed.) *Asia Annual* 2011. Democracy in Asia: Discourses and Counter-Discourses (New Delhi: KW Publishers), 101–117.
———, Partha Sarkar, and Angshuman Kar (eds.). 2010. *The Politics of Social Exclusion in India: Democracy at the Crossroads* (London: Routledge).
Bhaumik, 1998. 'North-East India: The Evolution of a Post-Colonial Region', in: Partha Chatterjee (ed.) *Wages of Freedom* (New Delhi: Oxford University Press), 310–327.
Brar, Bhupinder, Ashutosh Kumar and Ronki Ram (eds.). 2008. *Globalization and the Politics of Identity in India* (New Delhi: Pearson Longman).
Butcher, Melissa. 2003. *Transnational Television, Cultural Identity and Change: When STAR Came to India* (New Delhi: Sage).
Cartwright, J. P. 1995. *The Evolution of the Hong Kong Police as a British Colonial Police Force 1898–1941* (University of Leicester, Centre for Study in Public Order: Unpublished MA dissertation).
Chakrabarti, Dipankar. 2010. "Samaj bodoler larai, shashastra sangram o ajker Bharat" [in Bengali], *Anik*, July.

Chandhoke, Neera. 2003. 'Governance and the Pluralisation of the State: Implications for Democratic Citizenship', *Economic and Political Weekly*, 38(28), 2957–2968.

Chatterjee, Partha. 1999. 'Introduction—The Wages of Freedom: Fifty Years of the Indian Nation-State', in: id. (ed.) *Wages of Freedom: Fifty Years of the Indian Nation-State* (New Delhi: Oxford University Press), 1–22.

——. 2004. *The Politics of the Governed: Reflections on Popular Politics in Most of the World* (New Delhi: Permanent Black).

——. 2011. *Lineages of Political Society: Studies in Postcolonial Democracy* (New Delhi: Permanent Black).

Chatterjee, Saikat. 2010. 'Hollywood Goes Bollywood as U.S. Studios Target India Filmgoers', *The Seattle Times*, 5 June; accessible at: www.seattletimes.nwsource.com (last access: 24 March 2012).

Chenoy, Anuradha. 2007. "Alarm Bells Ringing Everywhere", *The Telegraph*, 1 July.

Chibber, Pradeep K. and Irfan Nooruddin. 1999. 'Party Competition and Fragmentation in India', in: Ramasray Roy and Paul Wallace (eds.) *Indian Politics and the 1998 Elections: Regionalism, Hindutva and State Politics* (New Delhi: Sage).

Chowdury, Supriya Roy. n.d. 'Decentralization and Globalization' [unpublished paper].

Communist Party of India. 2012. *Draft Political Resolution (adopted by National Council in Its Session at Hyderabad from January 4 to 6, 2012)*. New Delhi.

Communist Party of India (Marxist). 2012. *Political Resolution adopted at the 20th Congress of CPI (M), Kozhikode, Kerala, April 4–9, 2012*; accessible at: www.cpim.org/content/political-resolution-adopted-20th-congress (last access: 18 May 2012).

——. 2012a. *Resolution on Some Ideological Issues (adopted at the 20th Congress of CPI (M), Kozhikode, Kerala, April 4–9, 2012)*; accessible at: www.cpim.org/content/resolution-ideological-issues-20th-congress (last access: 18 May 2012).

Corbridge, Stuart and John Harriss. 2000. *Reinventing India: Liberalization, Hindu Nationalism, and Popular Democracy* (Malden: Polity).

——, Glyn Williams, Manoj Srivastava, and René Véron. 2005. *Seeing the State: Governance and Governmentality in India* (Cambridge: Cambridge University Press).

Dahl, Robert Alan. 1977. *Modern Political Analysis* (New Delhi: Prentice Hall).

Dasgupta, Biplab. 2005. *Globalization: India's Adjustment Experience* (New Delhi: Sage).

Datta, Prabhat Kumar. 1992. *The Second Generation Panchayats in India: With Special Reference to West Bengal* (Calcutta: Calcutta Book House).

Datta Gupta, Sobhanlal. 2012. 'The Politics and Ideology of Maoism in Today's India: Some Reflections', in: Abhijit Guha (ed.) *Maoism in India: Ideology and Ground Reality* (Jhargram: Indian National Confederation and Academy of Anthropologists).

de Souza, Peter R., Suhas Palshikar, and Yogendra Yadav. *State of Democracy in South Asia: A Report* (New Delhi: Oxford University Press).

Deaton, Angus, and Jean Drèze. 2002. 'Poverty and Inequality in India: A Re-examination', *Economic and Political Weekly*, 37(36), 3729–3748.

Dhavan, Rajeev and Rekha Saxena. 2006. 'Republic of India', in: Katy Le Roy and Cheryl Saunders (eds.) *A Global Dialogue on Federalism, Legislative, Executive, and Judicial Governance in Federal Countries*, volume 3, (Quebec: McGill – Queen's University Press).

Diamond, Larry. 2003. 'Universal Democracy?', *Policy Review*, 119, June–July.

D'Mello, Bernard. 2014. 'Where Is the Magazine? Indian Semi-Fascism and the Left', *Economic and Political Weekly*, 49(41), 36–50.

Drèze, Jean and Amartya Sen. 1995. *India: Development and Social Opportunity* (New Delhi: Oxford University Press).

———. 2002. *India: Development and Participation* (New Delhi: Oxford University Press).
Drèze, Jean, M. Samson, and S. Singh (eds.). 1997. *The Dam and the Nation: Displacement and Resettlement in the Narmada Valley* (New Delhi: Oxford University Press).
Dua, B. D. and Mahendra Prasad Singh (eds.). 2005. *Indian Federalism in the New Millennium* (New Delhi: Manohar).
Dunn, John (ed.). 1992. *Democracy: The Unfinished Journey: 508 BC to AD 1993* (Cambridge: Cambridge University Press).
Dutta, Prabhat Kumar. 1992. *The Second Generation Panchayats in India: With Special Reference to West Bengal* (Kolkata: Calcutta Book House).
Featherstone, Mike (ed.). 1990. *Global Culture: Nationalism, Globalization and Modernity*, (London: Sage Publications).
Federation of Indian Chambers of Commerce and Industry (FICCI). n.d. *Task Force Report on National Security and Terrorism*, volume I. New Delhi.
Fernandes, Leela. 2000. 'Nationalizing "the global": Media Images, Cultural Politics and the Middle Class in India', *Media, Culture & Society* 22(5), 611–628.
Fleiner, Thomas, Walter Kälin, Wolf Linder, and Cheryl Saunders. 2003. 'Federalism, Decentralization and Conflict Management in Multicultural Societies', *Politorbis* 32(1), 13–26.
Frankel, Francine. 2005. *India's Political Economy 1947–2004* (New Delhi: Oxford University Press).
Friedman, Thomas. 2000. *The Lexus and the Olive Tree* (New York: Anchor Books).
———. 2005. *The World Is Flat: The Globalized World in the Twenty-First Century* (London: Allen Lane).
Fukuyama, Francis. 1992. *The End of History and the Last Man* (New York: Free Press).
Galeota, Julia. 2004. 'Cultural Imperialism: An American Tradition', *Humanist* (May/June), 22–24, 46.
Ganguly, Sumit and Kanti Bajpai. 1998. 'Kashmir: A Strategic Crisis or Ethnic Nationalism', in: Subrata K. Mitra and Alison R. Lewis (eds.). *Subnational Movements in South Asia* (New Delhi: Segment Books).
Garrett, Geoffrey and Jonathan Rodden. 2000. 'Globalization and Decentralization'. Paper presented at the Annual Meeting of the Midwest Political Science Association, April 27–30.
Ghosh, Buddhadeb. 2000. 'Panchayati Raj – Evolution of the Concept', *ISS Occasional Paper Series*, 25.
Giddens, Anthony. 1990. *The Consequences of Modernity* (Stanford: Stanford University Press).
———. 1994. *Beyond Left and Right: The Future of Radical Politics* (Cambridge: Polity).
———. 2002. *Runaway World: How Globalisation Is Reshaping Our World* (London: Routledge).
Gilpin, Robert. 2000. *The Challenge of Global Capitalism: The World Economy in the Twenty-First Century* (Princeton: Princeton University Press).
Government of India. 1971. *North-Eastern Council Act* (New Delhi: Lok Sabha Secretariat).
Government of India. n.d. 'Pattern of Development in India: A Study of Andhra Pradesh' (New Delhi: SER Division; Planning Commission), accessible at: planningcommission.gov.in/reports/sereport/ser/std_patternAP.pdf (last access: 22 December 2011).
———. 1955. *Report of the States Reorganization Commission* (Chair Fazal Ali), (New Delhi: Ministry of Home Affairs).

———. 2008. *Development Challenges in Extremist Affected Areas. Report of an Expert Group to Planning Commission.* New Delhi.

———. 2010. *Report of the Committee for Consultations on the Situation in Andhra Pradesh*; accessible at: http://mha.nic.in/pdfs/CCSAP-REPORT-660111.pdf (last access: 22 December 2011).

Govinda Rao, Marapalli and Nirvikar Singh. 2005. *The Political Economy of Federalism in India* (New Delhi: Oxford University Press).

Graham, John, Bruce Amos, and Tim Plumptre. 2003. *Principles for Good Governance in the 21st Century* (Ottawa: Institute on Governance) (accessible at: http://unpan1.un.org/intradoc/groups/public/documents/UNPAN/UNPAN011842.pdf) (last access: 16 May 2015).

Griffiths, Percival. 1971. *To Guard My People: The History of the Indian Police* (London: Benn).

Guha, Abhijit (ed.). 2012. *Maoism in India: Ideology and Ground Reality* (Jhargram: Indian National Confederation and Academy of Anthropologists).

Guha, Ramachandra. 2000. *Environmentalism: A Global History* (New Delhi: Oxford University Press).

———. 2007a. *India after Gandhi: The History of the World's Largest Democracy* (New York: Harper Collins).

———. 2007b. 'Adivasis, Naxalites and Indian Democracy', *Economic and Political Weekly*, 42(32), 3305–3312.

Guhan, S. 1995. 'Federalism and the New Political Economy in India', in: Balveer Arora and Douglas V. Verney (eds.) *Multiple Identities in a Single State: Indian Federalism in Comparative Perspective* (New Delhi: Konark), 237–271.

Guibernau, Montserrat. 2001. 'Globalization and the Nation-State', in: Montserrat Guibernau and John Hutchinson (eds.) *Understanding Nationalism* (Cambridge: Polity), 242–268.

——— and John Hutchinson (eds.) 2001. *Understanding Nationalism* (Cambridge: Polity Press).

Gupta, Akhil and Aradhana Sharma. 2006. 'Globalization and Postcolonial States', *Current Anthropology*, 47(2), 277–307.

Gupta, Anandswarup. 1979. *The Police in British India: 1861–1947* (New Delhi: Concept Publishing).

Gupta, Dipankar (ed.). 2007. *Caste in Question: Hierarchy or Identity?* (New Delhi: Sage).

Gupta, S.P. 2006. *Globalization, Economic Reforms and Employment Strategy in India* (New Delhi: Academic Press).

Guven, Halil. 2006. 'Globalization and the Clash of Civilizations', in: B. N. Gosh and Halil Guven (eds.) *Globalization and the Third World: A Study of Its Negative Consequences* (New York: Palgrave), 53–67.

Hale, William and Eberhard Kienle. 1997. *After the Cold War: Security and Democracy in Africa and Asia* (London: Tauris Academic Studies).

Haq, Mahbub-ul. 2010. *Human Development Centre, Human Development in South Asia 2009* (New Delhi: Oxford University Press).

Haragopal, G. 2010. 'The Telangana People's Movement: The Unfolding Political Culture', *Economic and Political Weekly*, 45(42), 51–60.

Hardgrave, Robert L. and Stanley A. Kochanek. 2000. *India: Government and Politics in a Developing Nation* (Orlando: Harcourt College Publishers).

Harrison, Selig. 1960. *India: The Most Dangerous Decades* (Madras: Oxford University Press).

Hasan, Zoya. 2011. 'Political Parties', in: Niraja Gopal Jayal and Pratap Bhanu Mehta (eds.) *The Oxford Companion to Politics in India* (New Delhi: Oxford University Press).
Held, David. 1999. *Global Transformations: Politics, Economics and Culture* (Cambridge: Polity Press).
———. 2006. *Models of Democracy* (Cambridge: Polity).
——— and Anthony McGrew (eds.). 2003. *The Global Transformations Reader* (Oxford: Polity Press).
Hirst, Paul Q. and Grahame Thompson. 1996. *Globalization in Question: The International Economy and the Possibilities of Governance* (Cambridge: Polity Press).
Huntington, Samuel P. 1996. *The Clash of Civilizations and the Remaking of the World Order* (New York: Simon and Schuster).
International Council on Human Rights Policy. 2006. *India Country Report on Decentralization Effectiveness and Human Rights*; prepared by Harihar Bhattacharyya, Geneva.
Jain, L. C. (ed.). 2005. *Decentralization and Local Governance: Essays for George Mathew* (Hyderabad: Orient Longman).
Jain, S. P. and Thomas W. Hochgesang (eds.). 1995. *Emerging Trends in Panchayati Raj* (Hyderabad: National Institute of Rural Development).
Jayal, Niraja Gopal and Pratab Bhanu Mehta (eds.). 2010. *The Oxford Companion to Politics in India* (New Delhi: Oxford University Press).
Jayaram, N. (ed.) 2005. *On Civil Society: Issues and Perspectives* (New Delhi: Sage).
Jenkins, Robert. 1995. 'Theorising the Politics of Economic Adjustment: Lessons from the Indian Case', *Commonwealth and Comparative Politics*, 33(1), 1–24.
Jha, S. N. and P. C. Mathur (eds.). 1999. *Decentralization and Local Politics in India* (New Delhi: Sage).
Johnson, Craig, Priya Deshingkar and Daniel Start. 2005. 'Grounding the State: Devolution and Development in India's Panchayats', *The Journal of Development Studies*, 41(6), 937–970.
Joshi, P. C. 1989. *Culture, Communication and Social Change* (New Delhi: Vikas).
Kakar, Sudhir (ed.). 1979. *Identity and Adulthood* (New Delhi: Oxford University Press).
Kannabiran, K., S. R. Ramdas, N. Madhusudan, S. Ashalatha, and M. Pavan Kumar. 2010. 'On the Telangana Trail', *Economic and Political Weekly*, 45(13), 69–82.
Karan, V. 1992. 'A Case for a Cultural Revolution of India's Police', in J. Guha Roy (ed.) *Policing a District* (Delhi: IIPA).
Karat, Prakash. 1998. "The Communist Manifesto: Globalisation, Nation-State and Class Struggle", *The Marxist*, 14(4), accessible at: www.cpim.org/marxist/1998-manifesto-class-struggle.pdf (last access: 18 May 2012).
Kaviraj, Sudipta. 2010. *The Trajectories of the Indian State* (Ranikhet: Permanent Black).
———. 2011. *The Enchantment of Democracy and India* (Ranikhet: Permanent Black).
Kazim, Hasnain. 2007. 'Deutsch-Indische Klatschblätter: "Bunte" aus Bollywood', available at: www.spiegel.de/kultur/kino (last access: 28 March 2012).
Kee, Sung-Bok. n.d. 'Administrative Reform in Decentralization and Globalization for the Twenty-first Century'; (Kon-Kuk University, Thailand; unpublished paper).
Kellner, Douglas. 2002. 'Theorizing Globalization', *Sociological Theory* 20(3) (November), 285–305.
———. 2012. *Theorizing Globalization* (New Delhi: Critical Quest).
Khan, Rasheeduddin. 1992. *Federal India: A Design for Change* (New Delhi: Vikas).
Khondker, Habibul Haque. 2004. 'Glocalization as Globalization: Evolution of a Sociological Concept', *Bangladesh e-journal of Sociology*, 1(2), 12–20.
King, Mike and Nigel Brearley. 1996. *Public Order Policing: Contemporary Perspectives on Strategy and Tactics* (Leicester: Perpetuity Press).

Bibliography

Kohli, Atul. 1987. *The State and Poverty in India* (Cambridge: Cambridge University Press).

——. 1990. *Democracy and Discontent: India's Growing Crisis of Governability* (Cambridge: Cambridge University Press).

——. 1997. 'Can Democracies Accommodate Ethnic Nationalism? Rise and Decline of Self- Determination Movements in India', *Journal of Asian Studies* 56(2), 325–344.

—— (ed.). 2001. *The Success of India's Democracy* (Cambridge: Cambridge University Press).

——. 2009. *Democracy and Development: From Socialism to Pro-Business* (New Delhi: Oxford University Press).

Kothari, Rajni. 1974. 'The Congress System Revisited: A Decennial Review', *Asian Survey*, 14(12), 1035–1054.

——. 1989. *State against Democracy: In Search of Humane Governance* (New Delhi: Ajanta).

——. 2012. *Rethinking Democracy* (New Delhi: Orient Blackswan).

—— (ed.). 1967. *Party System and Election Studies* (Bombay: Allied).

Krishnaswamy, Sudhir. 2009. *Democracy and Constitutionalism in India: A Study of the Basic Structure Doctrine* (New Delhi: Oxford University Press).

Kudaisya, Gyanesh. 1992. *State Power and Erosion of Colonial Authority in Uttar Pradesh, India: 1930–42* (University of Cambridge, Churchill College: Unpublished Ph.D. thesis).

Kumar, Ashutosh (ed.). 2011. *Rethinking State Politics in India: Regions within Regions*, (Routledge: New Delhi).

Kumar, Himanshu. 2009. 'Who Is the Problem, the CPI (Maoist) or the Indian State?', *Economic and Political Weekly*, 44(47), 8–12.

Kumar, Pradeep. 'Uttarakhand's Challenge', in *Seminar*, accessible at: www.india-seminar.com/2001/497 (last access: 10 October 2007).

Lechner, Frank J. and John Boli. 2008. *The Globalization Reader* (Malden: Blackwell).

Lenin, Vladimir I. 1966 (1920). 'Our Foreign and Domestic Position and the Tasks of the Party; Speech delivered to the Moscow Gubernia Conference of the R. C. P. (B), November 21, 1920', in: id. *Collected Works*, volume 31 (Moscow: Progress Publishers).

Lévy, René. 2011. *A Comparison of the Indian and the French Police: Some Thoughts in State and Society* (New Delhi: Pearson Longman).

Lieber, Robert J. and Ruth E. Weisberg. 2002. 'Globalization, Culture, and Identities in Crisis', *International Journal of Politics, Culture and Society* 16(2), Winter, 273–296.

Lieten, Georges Kristoffel. 1992. *Continuity and Change in Rural West Bengal* (New Delhi: Sage).

——. 1996. *Devolution, Democracy and Development Village Discourse in West Bengal* (New Delhi: Sage).

Lijphart, Arend. 1989. 'Democratic Political Systems: Types, Cases, Causes, and Consequences', *Journal of Theoretical Politics* 1(1), 33–48.

——. 1996. 'The Puzzle of Indian Democracy: A Consociational Interpretation', *American Political Science Review* 90(2), 258–268.

Lobo, Lancy, Mrutuyanjaya Sahu, and Jayesh Shah (eds.). 2014. *Federalism in India: Towards a Fresh Balance of Power* (Jaipur: Rawat).

Maddison, Angus. 2007. *Contours of the World Economy, 1–2030 AD: Essays in Macro-Economic History* (Oxford: Oxford University Press).

Majeed, Akhtar. 2005. *Federal India: A Design for Good Governance* (New Delhi: Manak).

Manor, James. 2010. 'Local Governance', in: Niraja Gopal Jayal and Pratab Bhanu Mehta (eds.) *The Oxford Companion to Politics in India* (New Delhi: Oxford University Press), 61–79.

——. 2012. 'Did the Central Government's Poverty Initiatives Help to Re-elect?', in: Lawrence Sáez and Gurharpal Singh (eds.). *New Dimensions of Politics in India* (London: Routledge).

—— (ed.). 1991. *Rethinking Third World Politics* (London: Longman).

Marx, Karl and Friedrich Engels.1975. [1948]. *The Manifesto of the Communist Party* (Moscow: Progress Publishers).

Mathur, K. 2014. *Panchayati Raj in India* (New Delhi: Oxford University Press).

Mawby, R. 1990. *Comparative Policing Issues: The British and American Experience in International Perspective* (London: Unwin Hyman).

Mawdsley Emma. 1996. 'Uttarakhand Agitation and Other Backward Classes', *Economic and Political Weekly*, 31(4), 205–210.

——. 1998. 'After Chipko: From Environment to Region in Uttaranchal', *Journal of Peasant Studies*, 25(4), 36–54, accessible at: http://eprints.bbk.ac.uk/218/ (last access: 10 October 2014).

Mazumdar, Jaideep. 2007. 'The Hills Are Alive: A Local Lad on National TV Unites a State', *Outlook*, October 1.

McLuhan, Marshall and Quentin Fiore. 2001. [1968]. *War and Peace in the Global Village* (Corte Madera: Gingko Press).

Meenakshisundaram, S. S. 1994. *Decentralization in Developing Countries* (New Delhi: Concept).

——. 2005. 'Rural Development for Panchayati Raj', in: L. C. Jain (ed.) *Decentralization and Local Governance: Essays for George Mathew* (Hyderabad: Orient Longman), 417–433.

Mehra, Ajay K. and René Lévy. 2011. *The Police, State and Society: Perspectives from India and France* (New Delhi: Pearson).

Mehta, Nalin. 2008a. 'Introduction: Satellite Television, Identity and Globalisation in Contemporary India', in: Nalin Mehta (ed.). *Television in India: Satellites, Politics and Cultural Change* (London: Routledge).

——. 2008b. *India on Television: How Satellite News Channels Have Changed the Way We Think and Act* (New Delhi: HarperCollins).

Menon, Vapal Pangunni. 1957. *The Transfer of Power in India* (Princeton: Princeton University Press).

Michels, Robert. 1915. *Political Parties: A Sociological Study of the Oligarchical Tendencies of Modern Democracy* (New York: Dover).

Mitra, Subrata K. 2001. 'Making Local Government Work: Local Elites, Panchayati Raj and Governance', in Atul Kohli (ed.) *The Success of India's Democracy* (Cambridge: Cambridge University Press), 103–127.

——. 2007. 'Federalism's Success', in: Sumit Ganguly, Larry Jay Diamond, and Marc F. Plattner (eds.) *State of India's Democracy* (Baltimore: Johns Hopkins University Press), 89–106.

——. 2011. 'From Comparative Politics to Cultural Flow: The Hybrid State, and Resilience of the Political System in India', in: Phillip Stockhammer (ed.). *Conceptualising Cultural Hybridization: A Trans-Disciplinary Approach* (Heidelberg: Springer).

—— and V. B. Singh. 1999. *Democracy and Social Change in India* (New Delhi: Sage).

—— and V. B. Singh. 2009. *When Rebels Become Stakeholders: Democracy, Agency and Social Change in India* (New Delhi: Sage).

―― and R. Alison Lewis (eds.). 1998. *Subnational Movements in South Asia* (New Delhi: Segment Books).

Modelski, George. 2003. 'Globalization', in: David Held and Anthony McGrew (eds.) *The Global Transformations Reader: An Introduction to the Globalization Debate* (Cambridge: Polity Press), 55–59.

Mohanty, Manoranjan, Partha Nath Mukherji, with Olle Törnquist (eds.). 1998. *People's Rights: Social Movements and the State in the Third World* (New Delhi: Sage).

Morris-Jones, W. H. 1967. *The Government and Politics of India* (London: The Hutchinson Press).

Mukarji, N. and D. Bandopadhyay. 1994. 'New Horizons of West Bengal Panchayats (A Report to the Government of West Bengal)'; reprinted in: Amitava. Mukherjee (ed.) *Decentralization Panchayats in the Nineties* (New Delhi: Vikas).

―― and Balveer Arora (eds.). 1992. *Federalism in India: Origins and Development* (New Delhi: Vikas).

Mukherjee, A. (ed.). 1994. *Decentralization Panchayats in the 1990s* (New Delhi: Bikash).

Mukherjee, Pampa. 2011. 'The Creation of a Region: Politics of Identity and Development in Uttarakhand', in: Ashutosh Kumar (ed.) *Rethinking State Politics in India: Regions within Regions* (New Delhi: Routledge), 107–127.

Mukherji, Dhurjati Prasad. 1947. *Modern Indian Culture: A Sociological Study* (Bombay: Kitabs).

Mukherji, Nirmalangshu. 2012. 'Resistance and Democracy', in: Abhijit Guha (ed.) *Maoism in India: Ideology and Ground Reality* (Indian National Confederation and Academy of Anthropologists).

Mukhopadhyay, Asok Kumar. 2011 'Public-Private Partnership for Good Governance', *Calcutta Review*, 13(1&2), 9–25.

―― (ed.). 2007. *Right to Information* (Kolkata: Administrative Training Institute, Government of West Bengal).

Mukhopadhyay, Surajit C. 1998. 'Importing Back Colonial Policing Systems? The Relationship between the Royal Irish Constabulary, Indian Policing and Militarization of Policing in England and Wales', *Innovation*, 11(3), 253–266.

Narang, A. S. 1995. *Ethnic Identities and Federalism* (Shimla: Indian Institute of Advanced Study).

――. 1996. *Indian Government and Politics* (New Delhi: Gitanjali).

Nayar, Baldev Raj (ed.). 2007. *Globalization and Politics in India* (New Delhi: Oxford University Press).

Nayar, Pramod K. 2006. *Reading Culture: Theory, Praxis, Politics* (New Delhi: Sage).

O'Brian, Derek (ed.). 2007. *The Penguin India Reference Yearbook* (New Delhi: Penguin).

Ohmae, Kenichi. 1990. *The Borderless World: Power and Strategy in the Interlinked Economy* (New York: Harper Business).

――. 1995. *The End of the Nation State: The Rise of Regional Economies* (New York: Free Press).

Pai, Sudha. 2000. *State Politics: New Dimensions* (New Delhi: Shipra).

――. 2002. *Dalit Assertion and the Unfinished Revolution: The Bahujan Party in Uttar Pradesh* (New Delhi: Sage).

――. 2005. *State Politics: New Dimensions (Party System, Liberalization and Politics of India)* (New Delhi: Shipra).

Pal, Parthapratim and Jayati Ghosh. 2007. *Inequality in India: A Survey of Recent Trends*, DESA Working Paper No. 45, accessible at: www.un.org/esa/desa/papers/2007/wp45_2007.pdf (last access: 14 January 2015).

Parsons, Talcott and Edward A. Shils (eds.). 1951. *Toward a General Theory of Action: Theoretical Foundations of the Social Sciences* (New Jersey: Transaction Press).

Patnaik, U. 2004. 'A Crisis Rooted in Economic Reform', *Frontline*, 21(5), 5–16.

Pieterse, Jan Nederveen. 2010. 'Globalization and Culture: Three Paradigms', in: George Ritzer (ed.) *McDonaldization: The Reader* (Los Angeles: Pine Forge Press), 341–345.

Plant, Raymond. 2009. *The Neo-Liberal State* (New York: Oxford University Press).

Pollock, Sheldon. 2014. 'What Is South Asian Knowledge Good For?', *South Asia Institute Papers*, 1, 1–23.

Prakash, Amit. 2002. *Jharkhand: Politics of Development and Identity* (Hyderabad: Orient Longman).

Priolkar, Anant Kakba. 1958. *The Printing Press in India: Its Beginnings and Early Development* (Bombay: Marathi Samshodhana Mandala).

Przeworski, Adam. 2010. *Democracy and the Limits of Self-Government* (Cambridge: Cambridge University Press).

Puri, Rajinder. 2012. 'Reversing Quota Policy', *The Statesman*, Kolkata, May 8.

Putnam, Robert D. with Robert Leonardi and Raffaella Y. Nanetti. 1994. *Making Democracy Work: Civic Traditions in Modern Italy* (Princeton: Princeton University Press).

Pylee, Moolamattom Varkey. 1980. *Constitutional History of India: 1600–1950* (New Delhi: S. Chand & Co).

Raghavalu, C. V. and E. A. Narayan. 1999. 'Reforms in Panchayati Raj: A Comparative Analysis of Andhra Pradesh, Karnataka and West Bengal', in: S. N. Jha and P. C. Mathur (eds.) *Decentralization and Local Politics in India* (New Delhi: Sage), 117–131.

Raghavan, P. 2011. 'Gear Up for the $2 Trillion Dollar Economy', *The Indian Express*, 2 March 2011, accessible at: http://archive.indianexpress.com/news/gear-up-for-the2trillion-economy/756615/) (last access: 27 April 2015).

Ramakrishnan, V. 2014. 'Now the Real Agenda', *Frontline* 31(25), December 26, 4–8.

Ramanujan, A. K. 1990. 'Is There an Indian Way of Thinking? An Informal Essay', in: McKim Marriott (ed.) *India through Hindu Categories* (New Delhi: Sage), 41–58.

Ramesh, M. and Scott Fritzen (eds.) 2009. *Transforming Asian Governance: Rethinking Assumptions, Challenging Practices* (London: Routledge).

Rangan, Haripriya. 2000. *Of Myths and Movements: Rewriting Chipko into Himalayan History* (London: Verso).

Rangarajan, C. 2006. 'Responding to Globalization: India's Answer'; 4th Ramanbhai Patel Memorial Lecture by Chairman, Economic Advisory Council to the Prime Minister, Ahmedabad, February 25.

Rao, B. Shiva (ed.). 1968. *The Framing of India's Constitution: A Study [with] Select Documents*, volume 5 (New Delhi: IIPA).

Rao, Nagendra. 2005. 'The Role of Early Indian Traders in Global Trade Network', in: id. (ed.). *Globalization: Pre Modern India* (New Delhi: Regency Publications), 56–68.

Ray, Amal. 1970. *Tension Areas in India's Federal System* (Calcutta: World Press).

Ray, Prasanta. 1991. *Conflict and State: Exploration in the Behaviour of the Post-colonial State in India* (Calcutta: Sarat Book House).

Reddy, A. Amarender and M. C. S. Bantilan. 2013. 'Regional Disparities in Andhra Pradesh, India', *Local Economy: The Journal of the Local Economy Policy Unit* 28(1), 123–135.

Reddy, G. K. 2010. 'Telangana: Inevitable and Desirable', January 16, accessible at: www.thehindu.com/todays-paper/tp-opinion/telangana-inevitable-and-desirable/article 684342.ece (last access: 14 October 2014).

Reddy, V. Ratna. 2003. 'Irrigation: Development and Reforms', *Economic and Political Weekly*, 38(12 &13), 1179–1189.

Bibliography

Ritzer, George. 2010. *McDonaldization: The Reader* (Los Angeles: Pine Forge Press).
Robertson, Roland. 1992. *Globalization, Social Theory and Global Culture* (London: Sage).
Robinson, M. 2005. 'A Decade of Panchayti Raj Reforms: The Challenges of Democratic Decentralization in India', in: L. C. Jain (ed.) *Decentralization and Local Governance: Essays for George Mathew* (Hyderabad: Orient Longman), 10–31.
Rogaly, Ben, Barbara Harriss-White, and Sugata Bose (eds.). 1997. *Sonar Bangla? Agricultural Growth and Agrarian Change in West Bengal and Bangladesh* (New Delhi: Sage).
Rosenau, J. N. 2003. *Distant Proximities: Dynamics beyond Globalization* (Princeton: Princeton University Press).
Roy, Jaytilak Guha. 1992. *Policing a District* (New Delhi: Indian Institute of Public Administration).
Rudolph, Lloyd I. and Susanne Hoeber Rudolph. 1967. *The Modernity of Tradition: Political Development in India* (Chicago: The University of Chicago Press).
———. 1987. *In Pursuit of Lakshmi: The Political Economy of the Indian State* (Chicago: The University of Chicago Press).
———. 2001. 'Redoing the Constitutional Design: From an Interventionist to a Regulatory State', in: Atul Kohli (ed.) *The Success of India's Democracy* (Cambridge: Cambridge University Press), 127–162.
———. 2008. *Explaining Indian Democracy: A Fifty-Year Perspective, 1956–2006*, volume 1 (New Delhi: Oxford University Press).
Saberwal, Satish. 1986. *India: The Roots of Crises* (New Delhi: Oxford University Press).
Sáez, Lawrence. 2002. *Federalism without a Centre: The Impact of Political and Economic Reform on India's Federal System* (New Delhi: Sage).
——— and Gurharpal Singh (eds.). 2012. *New Dimensions of Politics in India* (London: Routledge).
Sarangi, Asha. 2009/2010. 'Reorganization, Then and Now', *Frontline*, 26(26), 19 Dec 2009–1 Jan 2010.
——— and Sudha Pai (eds.). *Interrogating Reorganization of States: Culture, Identity and Politics in India* (New Delhi: Routledge).
Sarkar, Sumit. 1983. *Modern India (1885–1947)* (New Delhi: Macmillan).
Saxena, Rekha. 2006. *Situating Federalism: Mechanisms of Intergovernmental Relations in Canada and India* (New Delhi: Manohar).
——— (ed.). 2003. *Mapping Canadian Federalism for India* (New Delhi: Konark).
Sen, Amartya. 2005. *The Argumentative Indian: Writings on Indian Culture, History and Identity* (London: Penguin).
———. 2006. *Identity and Violence: The Destiny of an Illusion* (London: Allen Lane).
———. 2007 'Global Inequality and Human Security', in Baldev Raj Nayar (ed.) *Globalization and Politics in India* (New Delhi: Oxford University Press), 117–132.
Seshadri, K. 1970. 'The Telangana Agitation and the Politics of Andhra Pradesh', *Indian Journal of Political Science*, 31(1), 60–81.
Shah, Ghanshyam. 2004. *Social Movements in India: A Review of Literature* (New Delhi: Sage).
Shahani, Parmesh. 2008. *Gay Bombay: Globalization, Love and (Be)longing in Contemporary India* (New Delhi: Sage).
Sharma, Chanchal Kumar. 2009. 'Emerging Dimensions of Decentralization Debate in the Age of Globalization', *Indian Journal of Federal Studies*, 1, 47–65.
Sharma, T. R. 1984. 'Collapse of Political Institutions in India: Search for a Perspective', *The Punjab Journal of Politics*, July–December.

Shils, Edward. 1957. 'Primordial, Personal, Sacred, and Civic Ties', *British Journal of Sociology* 8, 130–145.

Shiva, Vandana. 2005. *Globalization's New Wars: Seed, Water and Life Forms* (New Delhi: Women Unlimited).

Sigler, Robert T. and David J. King. 1992. 'Colonial Policing and Control of Movements for Independence', *Policing and Society* 3(1), 13–22.

Simhadri, S. and P. L. Vishweshwer Rao (eds.). 1997. *Telangana: Dimensions of Underdevelopment* (Hyderabad: Centre for Telangana Studies).

Singer, Milton B. 1972. *When a Great Tradition Modernizes: An Anthropological Approach to Indian Civilization* (New York: Praeger).

Singh, Ajay Kumar. 2003. 'Federalism and State Formation: An Appraisal of Indian Practice', in: B. D. Dua and M. P. Singh (eds.) *Indian Federalism in the New Millennium* (New Delhi: Manohar).

Singh, Hoshiar. 1994. 'Constitutional Base for Panchayati Raj in India: The 73rd Amendment Act', *Asian Survey*, 34(9), 818–827.

Singh, Mahendra P. 1992. 'India: Searching for a Consensus by Amending the Constitution?', *Governance: An International Journal of Policy, Administration, and Institutions*, 5(3), 358–373.

——. 2000. 'Securing the Independence of the Judiciary: The Indian Experience', *Indiana International and Comparative Law Review*, 10, 245–292.

——. 2007. 'A Borderless Internal Federal Space and Reorganization of States in India', *India Review*, 6(4), 233–250.

—— and Rekha Saxena. 2013. *Federalizing India in the Age of Globalization* (New Delhi: Primus).

Singh, Nirvikar, Laveesh Bhandari, Aoyu Chen, and Aarti Khare. 2003. 'Regional Inequality in India: A Fresh Look', *Economic and Political Weekly*, 15 March, 1069–1073.

Singh, S. S. and Suresh Mishra. 1994. 'Public Law Issues in Privatisation Process', *Indian Journal of Public Administration*, 3.

Sinha, Aseema. 2010. 'The Changing Political Economy of Federalism in India: A Historical-Institutional Approach', in: Baldev Raj Nayar (ed.) *Globalization and Politics in India* (New Delhi: Oxford University Press), 477–515.

Spivak, Gayatri Chakravorty. 2000. 'Can the Subaltern Speak?', in: Diana Brydon (ed.) *Postcolonialism: Critical Concepts in Literary and Cultural Studies*, volume IV (London: Routledge).

Sridharan, Eswaran. 2011. 'The Party System', in: Niraja Gopal Jayal and Pratap Bhanu Mehta (eds.) *The Oxford Companion to Politics in India* (New Delhi: Oxford University Press), 117–138.

—— (ed.). 2014. *Coalition Politics in India: Selected Issues at the Centre and the States* (New Delhi: Academic Foundation).

Srinivas, M. N. 1952. *Social Change in Modern India* (Chicago: The University of Chicago Press).

State Institute for Panchayats and Rural Development. 2007. *Annual Administrative Reports* (Kalyani, West Bengal).

Stewart, Francis, 2004. 'The Root Causes of Conflict: Some Conclusions', Working Paper 16, in: James Putzel (ed.) *The Political Impact of Globalization and Liberalization: Evidence Emerging from Crisis States Research*, Discussion Paper No. 7, November. Accessible at: www.crisisstatespaper.com (last access: 27 January 2012).

Stiglitz, Joseph E. 2003 *Globalization and Its Discontents* (New York: W. W. Norton).

———. 2007. 'The Overselling of Globalization', in: Baldev Raj Nayar (ed.) *Globalization and Politics in India* (New Delhi: Oxford University Press), 133–148.

Stoker, Gerry. 2006 'Comparative Local Governance', in: R. A. W. Rhodes, S. A. Binder, and B. A. Rockman (eds.) *The Oxford Handbook of Political Institutions* (Oxford: Oxford University Press), 495–514.

Stubbs, Richard and Geoffrey R. D. Underhill (eds.) 2005. *Political Economy and the Changing Global Order* (Toronto: Oxford University Press).

Sundarayya, P. 1972. *Telangana People's Struggle and Its Lessons* (Calcutta: Desraj Chadha).

Tendulkar, Suresh D. and T. A. Bhavani. 2007. *Understanding Reforms: Post-1991 India* (New Delhi: Oxford University Press).

Thomas, Amos Owen. 2006. *Transnational Media and Contoured Markets: Redefining Asian Television and Advertising* (New Delhi: Sage).

Thompson, John B. 2003. 'The Globalization of Communication', in: David Held and Anthony McGrew (eds.) *The Global Transformations Reader: An Introduction to the Globalization Debate* (Cambridge: Polity Press), 246–259.

Thorat, S. 2007. *Human Poverty and Socially Disadvantaged Groups in India* (New Delhi: Sage).

Tillin, Louise. 2012. 'Principles and Prospects of Resizing India's States', in: *Politics, Society and Culture*, accessible at: https://casi.sas.upenn.edu/iit/tillin accessed on 18/10/2014.

———. 2013. *Remapping India: New States and Their Political Origins* (New Delhi: Oxford University Press).

Tilly, Charles. 1995. 'Globalisation Threatens Labour Rights', in: M. R. Ishay (ed.) *The Human Rights Reader* (New York: Routledge).

Times of India. 2011. 'Will Burn Down First Wal-Mart Store: Uma Bharti', (26 November 2011), available at: http://articles.timesofindia.indiatimes.com/2011-11/-26/lucknow (last access: 29 March 2012).

Tomlinson, John. 2010. 'Globalization and Cultural Identity', in: David Held and Anthony McGrew (eds.). *The Global Transformations Reader: An Introduction to the Globalization Debate* (Cambridge: Polity Press), 269–277.

Tremblay, R. C. 2003. 'Globalization and Indian Federalism' in: B. Dua and M. P. Singh (eds.) *Indian Federalism in the New Millennium* (New Delhi: Manohar), 335–350.

Turner, Bryan S. 2010. 'McDonalidzation: The Major Criticisms', in: *McDonaldization: The Reader* (Los Angeles: Pine Forge Press), 77–78.

Tyrrell, Heather. 2008. 'Bollywood versus Hollywood: Battle of the Dream Factories', in: Frank J. Lechner and John Boli (eds.) *The Globalization Reader* (Malden: Blackwell), 327–334.

United Nations. 2001. *World Public Sector Report: Globalization and the State* (New York: United Nations).

Upadhyay, V. 2013. 'The Class Question in the Growth and Equity Debates', *Economic and Political Weekly*, 48(21), 14–16.

Vaidyanathan, A. 2006. 'Farmers' Suicides and the Agrarian Crises', *Economic and Political Weekly*, 41(38), 4009–4013.

Verney, Douglas. 1995. 'Are all Federations Federal? The United States, Canada, and India', in: Balveer Arora and Douglas Verney (eds.) *Multiple Identities in a Single State: Indian Federalism in a Comparative Perspective* (New Delhi: Konark), 19–59.

———. 2003. 'From Quasi-Federation to Quasi-Confederacy? The Transformation of India's Party System', *Publius: The Journal of Federation*, 33(4), 153–171.

Wallerstein, Immanuel. 1974. *The Modern World System* (New York: Academic Press).
Waters, Malcolm. 1996. *Globalization* (London: Routledge).
——. 2002. *Globalization* (Routledge: London).
——. 2010. 'McDonaldization and the Global Culture of Consumption', in: *McDonaldization: The Reader* (Los Angeles: Pine Forge Press), 347–353.
Watson, James L. 2008. 'McDonald's in Hong Kong', in: Frank J. Lechner and John Boli (eds.) *The Globalization Reader* (Malden: Blackwell), 126–134.
Watts, Ronald L. 1966. *New Federations: Experiments in the New Commonwealth* (Oxford: The Clarendon Press).
——. 2008. *Comparing Federal Systems* (Montreal: McGill-Queen's University Press).
Webster, Neil. 1992. *Panchayati Raj and the Decentralization of Development Planning in West Bengal* (Kolkata: K. P. Bagchi).
Weiss, Linda. 1997. 'Globalization and the Myth of the Powerless State', *New Left Review*, 225, 3–27.
Wheare, K. C. 1953. *Federal Government* (Oxford: Oxford University Press).
Williams, B. 1997. 'Good Governance and the Ideology of Transformation', in: W. Hale and E. Kienle (eds.) *After the Cold War Security and Democracy in Asia and Africa* (London: I. B. Tauris), 227–250.
Wilson, R. and W. Dissanayake (eds.). 1996. *Global/Local: Cultural Production and the Transnational Imaginary* (Durham: Duke University Press).
Xaxa, Virginius. 2005. 'Politics of Language, Religion and Identity: Tribes in India', *Economic and Political Weekly*, 49(13).
Yadav, Yogendra. 2011. 'Representation', in: Niraja Gopal Jayal and Pratap Bhanu Mehta (eds.) *The Oxford Companion to Politics in India* (New Delhi: Oxford University Press), 347–360.
—— and Suhas Palshikar. 2008. 'Ten Theses on State Politics in India', *Seminar*, 591, accessible at: www.india-seminar.com/semsearch.htm (last access: 24 September 2014).
Yang, Anand A. (ed.). 1985. *Crime and Criminality in British India* (Tucson: The University of Arizona Press).
Yechury, Sitaram. 2001. 'Globalisation and Impact on Indian Society', accessible at: http://cpim.org/node/1369 (last access: 18 May 2012).
Zins, Max J. 1989. 'The Emergency: 1975–77', in: Zoya Hasan, Shree Nagesh Jha, and Rasheeduddin. Khan (eds.) *The State, Political Process and Identity: Reflections on Modern India* (New Delhi: Sage), 150–180.

Index

Figures are indicated with an f. following the page locator.

Administration xiii, 17, 19, 23, 27, 61 f., 70, 82, 91, 94, 120 f., 130
   civil administration 94
   colonial administration 91 f.
   maladministration 81
Advani, L. K. 121
Alienation 48, 63, 79 f., 90
All India Radio (AIR) 11
Americanisation 42
Andhra Pradesh 79, 90, 100, 103, 106, 112 f., 114–118, 123 f., 130, 135
   coastal Andhra Pradesh 113 f., 116 f., 123
Armed police-centric model 12, 90, 96, 143
   un-armed policing 92
Asok Mehta Committee 130
Austin, Granville 52, 69, 76 f., 101
Authority 17, 19, 22, 23, 29, 34, 41, 67, 74, 77, 87, 90, 91 f., 92, 94, 98, 121, 131, 134
   relocation of authority 16
Authoritarianism 31–33, 125
   creeping authoritarianism 32
Autonomy xvii, 18, 23, 25, 36, 102, 114, 128, 134
   autonomy and participation 17
   fiscal autonomy xviii, 28, 132
   local autonomy 16, 126, 136
   loss of autonomy 21
   national autonomy 21
   regional autonomy 13, 111 f., 114, 122 f.
   State autonomy 146
   sub-State autonomy 104

Babri Masjid 36, 101
Backwardness 79, 88, 105, 111 f., 117, 124
   backward classes 70, 120, 124
backward regions 13, 105, 111 f., 117
backward States 8, 100, 145
Bahujan Samaj Party (BSP) 37, 41
BALCO Employees Union 74
Bengal Gazette 44
Bhabha, Homi K. 51 f.
Bharatiya Janata Party (BJP) xvi, 14, 35 f., 40, 46, 66, 101, 105, 118 f., 121 f., 124, 146
Bihar 56, 79, 100, 102 f., 105 f., 112
BIMARU States xvi
Bollywood 48–50
BRICS 58

Capitalism xv, 2, 5, 9, 11 f., 36, 56, 59, 63 f., 72 f., 78, 85, 87, 94 f., 109, 142
Caste xiii, xvi, xiii, 8–10, 13, 28, 33–35, 37, 79, 83, 99, 102, 108, 116, 121, 124, 127 f., 133, 135–137, 143 f.
   caste consciousness 133, 144
   caste discrimination 7, 37, 124, 140
   caste domination 7, 135
   casteism 134 f.
centre-State relations 130
Chhattisgarh 56, 63, 84, 90, 105–107, 112, 121 f.
China 12, 19–21, 24, 44, 53, 58,
Citizenship 6 f., 87, 110
   consumerist citizenship 7
Civil society xvii, 4, 7, 14, 22, 43, 64, 87, 90, 97, 99, 138, 143, 147
   civil society activism xvi, 38, 89
Clientelist politics 26
Coalition politics xvi f., 10, 15, 29 f., 36, 58, 98 f., 101, 109, 119, 122 f., 127, 134, 139, 145 f.
Coalitions and regional parties 117, 119, 130

Index

Cold War 6, 31
Colonialism xviii, 11 f., 27, 31, 39, 69, 89–93, 102, 112, 124, 142 f.
  post-colonialism 34, 83, 85, 93–95, 102
Command polity 31 f.
Common man (*aam admi*) 61, 87 f.
Common Minimum Programme 24
Communism 83 f., 88, 125
Communist Party of India 119
  Communist Party of India (Marxist) (CPI-M) 78 f., 81, 118, 131, 134, 142
Competition Act 75
Conflict xvi, xviii, 3, 8, 11, 13, 28, 46, 65, 72 f., 74 f., 77, 80, 83, 89, 93, 109 f., 113, 135, 141–143
  Conflict between courts and government 70 f., 76, 141
  Conflict resolution 65, 141
Constituent Assembly 52, 56, 69, 102, 109
Constitution xvii, 6, 8, 11–13, 25, 28, 32, 40 f., 52, 56, 65, 67, 68–77, 86, 101, 104, 117, 122 f., 126, 128, 130–134, 138, 141 f., 144
  'basic structure' of the Constitution 40, 70 f.
  sanctity of the Constitution undermined 77, 142
Constitutional Amendments 40, 70–73, 76, 137 f.
  7th Constitutional Amendment 103
  42nd Constitutional Amendment 70, 74
  64th Constitutional Amendment 136
  73rd Constitutional Amendment 25 f., 28, 40, 126, 128, 131, 134, 136, 138, 144
  74th Constitutional Amendment 25 f., 28, 40, 126, 128, 138
Cultural difference 32, 43
Cultural hybridity 11, 43, 48 f., 51 f., 54, 140

Dalits xvi, 37, 78 f., 81, 83 f., 128, 140
Decentralisation i, xv, 9 f., 16–19, 22–23, 25–27, 29, 98 f., 126 f., 130–132, 135, 139, 144
  democratic decentralisation 28, 135
  fiscal decentralisation 132
  political decentralisation 132
Demand polity 31 f.
Democracy i, xvi, xix, 1, 5, 7–9, 11, 12, 28, 30–40, 55 f., 65, 72 f., 81, 84–88, 96, 111, 125, 127, 130, 134–137, 139 f., 147
  democracy and the 73rd and 74th Amendments 28

democracy from below 34, 88
democracy in the era of reforms 127, 147
democracy wave 17
democracy's challenge to globalisation 127
federal democracy xiii, 5
participatory democracy 18, 109
Democratic legitimacy 8
Designs Act 75, 141
Development xvi–xix, 1, 5, 7–14, 16 f., 22–26, 28, 30, 37 f., 43 f., 58–64, 74 f., 77–81, 84 f., 87, 95, 98 f., 100, 105, 108–110, 112 f., 115, 117–124, 126, 128, 131–134, 137 f., 140–146
  corporate model of development 80
  regional development 108, 112
  socio-economic development 3, 5, 7, 33, 56–58, 112, 123, 141, 144
Diaspora 48
Directive Principles 65, 71, 117, 129
Discrepant majorities 101, 108, 143
Disneyfication 42
Disparities 36, 100
  class disparities 99, 108f.
  economic disparities 99
  regional disparities xviii, 14, 99 f., 108 f., 113, 146
Doing Business Survey 145
Doordarshan 11, 45, 53

Easternisation of the West 51
Economy i, xvii f., 6–9, 16, 18, 21 f., 24, 27, 30–33, 36, 56–60, 63 f., 66, 72–76, 88, 92, 94 f., 98 f., 108, 111 f., 120, 123, 127, 130, 138 f., 141, 143, 145
  agricultural economy 99
  command economy i, 145
Education xvii, 40 f., 45, 57, 60, 70, 100, 102, 113, 117, 120, 122, 124, 144, 146
  Education Act 41, 140
Eleventh Schedule 25, 131, 137
Elites xvi, xviii f., 7, 27, 31, 37, 39, 58, 63, 108, 111, 115, 117, 137
  elite revolt xix, 58
  local elites 29
  political elites xix, 31, 115
  regional elites xvii f., 111, 122
Emergency rule (1975–1977) 32 f., 70, 96, 126, 130, 134
Employment 24, 32, 60, 63, 75, 100, 102, 113, 119 f., 122, 124, 144, 146

Engels, Friedrich 2
Equity 1 f., 14, 17, 23, 37, 56, 117
Ethnic conflict 8, 46
Ethnicity 61, 83, 85, 110
Exclusion 83, 111, 136
    social exclusion 37

Farmer suicide 37, 61, 116, 140
Federalism i, xvi, 6, 8 f., 13, 32, 75, 98 f., 101, 105, 107 f., 123, 126, 130, 137, 143, 145
    ethnic federalism 101, 105, 108
    executive federalism 8, 126
Federalisation 108, 123, 143 f.
Federation of Indian Chambers of Commerce and Industry (FICCI) 79 f.
feeble capacity 40
Five-Year Plans 32, 56 f.
Force/service dichotomy 96
Foreign Direct Investment (FDI) 46, 75, 100, 112, 126, 145
    FDI inflow 72
Foreign Exchange Management Act 75
Forest 62–64, 79 f., 85, 97, 119 f., 124
    Forest Rights Act (2006) 62
Forward States 145 f.
Friedman, Thomas 1–3

G-20 58
Gandhi, Indira 32 f., 71, 99, 104, 130, 146 f.
Gandhi, Rajiv 55, 58, 71, 136
Gender 28, 35, 83, 100, 135, 144
    gender equality 3, 15, 146
General Agreement on Tariffs and Trade (GATT) i, 6
Giddens, Anthony 2, 7, 111, 127
Global vs. local xv, 1 f., 5, 9, 16, 18 f., 22, 29, 43, 48 f., 52, 139 f., 144
    global communication 2, 44
    global interactions 1
    global movement of ideas 1
    global village 14, 43
Globality 99
Globalisation i, xiii, xv–xix, 1–6, 8–14, 16–23, 25, 27, 29, 30, 36, 42–55, 63, 66, 71, 75, 78–83, 85, 87–89, 95, 99 f., 108–114, 117, 119, 122 f., 125, 127 f., 138–146
    asymmetrical globalisation 111
    contested globalisation 88, 138
    cultural globalisation 10, 43, 47, 49, 52, 140
    digital divide and globalisation 21
    economic globalisation 3, 42, 140, 143
    globalisation and inequality 8, 20, 57, 95, 139, 145 f.
    globalisation-induced development and Maoism 79 f.
    hyper-globalisation 110
    impact of globalisation on development indicators 100, 109, 145
    impact of globalisation on India and China 19–21, 24, 53, 58
    impact of globalisation on Indian polity xv, xix, 2 f., 5 f., 9, 13, 19, 24, 28, 98–100, 111, 125
    penalties of globalisation 3, 55, 63, 139
    positive effects of globalisation xviii, 48, 88, 108, 142
    prerequisite for globalisation 47
    sociological accounts of globalisation xvii, 2
    unequal benefits of globalisation 3, 8, 21, 27, 37, 80, 101, 112, 139, 146
    Yechury on globalisation 82 f.
Glocalization 3, 10, 18 f., 49, 139 f.
Global management 17
Governance i, xiii, xv–xix, 2–7, 9–11, 13 f., 16–18, 22–25, 27, 29–31, 33, 37–40, 55 f., 61–65, 87, 89 f., 94 f., 100, 110, 125–128, 133, 135–137, 139, 141, 144
    Comparative local governance 125, 135, 144
    Good Governance xvi, 14, 18, 30, 94 f., 127 f., 141
    local governance 22, 25, 125 f., 135
    poor governance 40, 100
    sites of governance 16
Government xvi–xviii, 3–7, 9, 11–19, 21–26, 28 f., 31 f., 36–38, 40, 56, 63 f., 66, 68–72, 74 f., 79–81, 84 f., 87, 89–96, 98 f., 101–105, 109, 112, 114–116, 118–120, 123–139, 142, 145–147
    self-government 5, 40, 126, 129, 131–134, 136–138, 144
    self-governing bodies 126, 128, 134 f.
Government of India Act (1919) 102
Government of India Act (1935) 68, 102
Great Britain 39, 44 f., 92, 96
Green Revolution 33, 99
Gross-Domestic Product (GDP) 32, 55–57, 58 f., 64, 66, 100, 108, 132, 147
Growth xviii, 1, 3, 8 f., 13, 21 f., 24, 28, 32, 36 f., 55–60, 64–66, 80, 94, 95, 98–100, 108, 111, 116, 119, 125, 130, 133, 140–142, 145–147

172 Index

growth of GDP 32, 59, 64, 66, 147
growth with stability 21
growth-with-equity 17
inclusive growth 11, 36, 55 f., 95, 141
Gujarat 62, 100 f., 104, 106, 112

Hastings, Warren 44, 91
Hazare, Anna xvi, 38
Hindu Marriage Act (1955) 33
Hindu rate of growth 145
Hindu Succession Act (1956) 33
Hollywood 48, 53
Homogenisation 43, 52, 83, 103, 140
Human Development Index (HDI) 95, 145
Human Development Report (HDR) 57
Huntington, Samuel P. 17, 110
Hybridity 51 f.

Identity xiii, xv f., 6–10, 12 f., 43, 46 f., 51, 54, 56, 81, 83, 87, 105, 111–114, 117, 120–123, 127 f., 133, 140, 143 f.
  ascriptive identity 122
  cultural identity 10, 80, 110 f., 113
  identity articulation 46, 140
  identity politics 12, 83, 85, 105
  new identity consciousness xvi, 113, 122 f., 144
Illiteracy 7, 14 f., 31, 55, 59–61
Indian National Congress (INC) 36, 56, 117
  hegemony of Indian National Congress 35
Inequality 8, 20, 57, 95, 116, 119, 139, 145 f.
  horizontal inequality 110
Informal networks 125
Institutional design 38 f., 129 f., 132, 136, 144

Jal Jangal Jameen 120
Janata Party 35, 99, 121, 124, 130
Jawaharlal Nehru National Urban Renewal Mission (JNNURM) 24
Joshi, P.C. 43, 119
Judicial activism 30
Judiciary i, 9–11, 30, 38, 40, 69–71, 77, 99, 108, 138, 141 f.

Kerala 15, 27, 77, 100, 103, 106, 130, 145 f.

Language xv, xviii, 27, 45, 49 f., 54, 64, 72, 104, 106–109, 111–113, 122 f., 133, 140, 143 f.

Law Day (Speech of the Chief Justice (India) 65
Left Front Government, West Bengal 79, 81, 131, 134
Left, political i, 9, 11 f., 35 f., 63 f., 78 f., 81–85, 87 f., 95, 131, 134, 142, 146
  the Left and alternative paths of development 78
  extremist Left 12, 142
  Fragmentation of the Left 35, 78
  Left extremist concept of democracy 87 f.
  mainstream Left 9, 12, 78 f., 81, 84 f., 87 f., 142
Lenin, V.I. 88
Liberalism 7, 72
Liberalisation xiii, xvii f., 6, 8, 10, 24, 27, 51, 55, 58, 63, 65, 87, 95 f., 98–100, 112, 117, 127, 136, 143
License permit raj 138
local nationalism 2
Lok Sabha 118, 130

Madhya Pradesh 56, 79, 100, 102 f., 105 f., 112
Maharashtra 46, 60, 77, 79, 90, 100, 104, 106, 112, 124, 130
Mahatma Gandhi National Rural Employment Guarantee Scheme (MGNREGS) xviii, 61, 141
Mandal Commission 120, 124
Maoism xviii, 12, 37, 61, 63, 78, 82–88, 90, 97, 142 f.
  FICCI report on Maoism 79 f.
  Maoism as anti-modernist 85
  Maoist Communist Centre of India (MCC) 78
  Maoist violence 61, 79, 81, 85 f., 142 f.
  one-dimensionality in Maoism 85
  post-colonialism and Maoism 83
Marginalisation 29, 37, 45, 61, 63, 90, 112, 117, 120, 122, 133, 140, 144
Market economy xvii f., 9, 22, 63 f., 75, 108, 112, 143
Marx, Karl 2, 83, 136, 139
McDonaldization 42, 52 f.
Media xvi, xix, 7, 11, 38, 42, 44–47, 49, 97, 102, 138, 140, 143
Modernity 12, 43, 47 f., 51, 58, 78, 83, 87 f., 142
  bad modernity 88
  homogenous modernity 51
  modernisation 7, 21, 35, 42, 96, 98, 136, 143

Index

modernity and democracy 12, 85
post-modernism 83
Modi, Narendra 4, 66
Monetary policy 19
Movements xv f., xviii, 8 f., 12 f., 23, 35, 44–46, 61 f., 64, 84–86, 90, 94, 99, 105, 111–123, 143 f., 147
   Chipko movement 23
   ecological factors in movements 119, 124
   grassroots movements 23
   regional autonomy movements 13, 111, 114
   regional movements xv, 8, 13, 111–114, 122 f., 144
   social movements 35, 45, 99
   sub-regional movements 143
   swadeshi movement 52
   Telangana movement 114 f., 117 f., 121
   Uttarakhand movement 111, 114, 121 f.
Multinational Corporations (MNCs) 27, 42, 60, 62 f., 81, 87, 116
Multi-party competition xvi, 130

Nagaland 63, 104, 106
Narmada Bachhao Andolan 23
Narodniks 88
National Democratic Alliance (NDA) 14, 36, 66, 105
National Human Rights Commission 108
National Police Commission (NPC) 96
National sovereignty (and globalisation) 20
Nation-state xv, 2, 5, 16, 18, 44, 72, 83, 98, 121
Naxalism 78–85, 87
Nehru, Jawaharlal 33, 45, 51, 71, 101, 104, 119, 144–147
   Nehruvian xvi, 10, 31, 99, 145
Neo-institutionalism 144
Neo-liberalism xvi, 78, 81 f., 109, 114, 142
New Economic Policy (NEP) 11, 71 f., 75
   NEP and constitutionality 11, 72, 74–76
Non-governmental Organization (NGO) xv, 14, 16, 22, 38, 87
North-East India 46, 63 f., 67, 104 f., 145
North-Eastern Council 105

Odisha 56, 63, 79, 82, 90, 100, 102 f., 106, 112, 135, 145
Oligarchy 137
Ordered autocracies 2
Other Backward Classes (OBCs) xvi, 57, 120, 124, 127

Padmanabhaiha Committee 93
Panchayat 13, 19, 25 f., 31, 129–135, 137, 144
   gram panchayat 132
   khap panchayat 137
   panchayat sub-committee 134
   Panchayati raj 25, 130 f.
   pati panchayat 144
   sarpanch 135
Participation xviii, 6 f., 14, 17 f., 28, 34 f., 86, 112 f., 117, 126 f., 128 f., 134–136, 144
   political participation xviii, 35, 133 f.
Patent Act (2005) 75, 141
People's War Group 78
Percolation theory 37
Peripheralisation 120
periphery 38, 112, 120
Planning Commission 57, 64, 116, 132, 138
Police 9, 12, 61, 81, 84 f., 89–97, 142 f.
   community-oriented policing 12, 89 f., 94, 96 f., 143
   Police Act (1861) 90 f., 93
   police and revenue collection 91
   police as a punitive force 92
   police as a service provider 142 f.
   police as statist 89, 94
   police during British colonialism 91, 93
   post-colonial police system 94
Political economy i, 8 f., 30 f., 64, 72 f., 92, 99, 130
   political economy and judicial review 11, 76 f.
Polity xiii, xv–xii, 7, 9–12, 27, 31–37, 64, 89, 93, 95 f., 98, 121, 129, 131, 138, 145
Popular Front 63
Post-traditional societies 2, 5
Poverty xv, 1, 7, 14 f., 20, 24, 40, 56–58, 60, 62, 64, 78 f., 81, 86, 132, 135, 141, 145 f.
   poverty line 56, 58, 64, 141, 147
pre-existing social hierarchies 3
Privatisation 36, 63, 66, 72, 74, 77, 108, 115, 120
Proxy role 135
Public Interest Litigation 40, 71, 77
Public-Private Partnership 5, 125
Punchi Commission 132 f., 138
Punjab 31, 70, 100, 102–104, 106 f., 137
Purchasing Power Parity (PPP) 58

Quasi-confederal 101, 109

Index

Rajiv effect 58
Rajya Sabha 136
Rao, Narasimha 71, 99
Rashtriya Swayamsevak Sangh (RSS) 121
Rayalseema 113
reflexive society 7, 127
Reforms i, xvi–xviii, xix, 3–14, 23 f., 26, 28 f., 36, 39, 55, 58 f., 61, 63, 71, 78, 87, 93 f., 96–101, 108, 110–112, 115, 119, 121–123, 125–132, 135–141, 143–147
   3 'Ds' of India's reforms 146
   institutional reforms 89 ff., 146
   macro-economic reforms 3, 7, 99, 138
   structural reforms 5, 126
   land reforms 137 f., 146
   local government reforms 7, 126, 128, 132, 135, 144
   economic reforms xvi, 6–9, 13, 26, 63, 71, 78, 99, 108, 111, 138, 141, 143
Regionalism 10, 13, 35, 111 f.
Religion 28, 37, 83, 99, 108, 110 f., 113, 122 f., 133, 143 f.
Reserve Bank of India (RBI) 60
Revolution 2, 22, 63, 81–83, 88, 99, 142
Information Revolution 42, 44
Right to Education Act (RTE) 140
Right to Information Act (RTI) 38, 41, 62, 67, 138, 140 f.
Rights i, 6–9, 13, 21, 32, 35, 37, 56, 59, 62, 66–71, 74–76, 86, 89, 97, 101 f., 108, 112, 114, 119 f., 122–124, 128, 134, 136, 141
   caste rights 128
   civic rights 97
   human rights 6, 35, 37, 67, 86, 102, 108, 136
   minority rights 101, 108
Rural India 13, 60, 91, 127 f., 140

Sarkaria Commission 130 f.
Scheduled Caste (SC) 26, 57, 70, 79, 116, 124, 128, 130
Scheduled Tribe (ST) 26, 57, 70, 76, 79, 116, 124, 130, 142
Sen, Amartya 1, 3, 6, 59, 63, 139
Separation of powers 68 f., 76
Singh, Manmohan 71
Sixth Schedule 104
Social exclusion 37
Social welfare 7, 70 f., 96, 137
   social welfare state i, 2, 11 f., 55, 139, 145, 147

Socialism xvi, 11 f., 37, 72, 76, 142
   dissonance between socialism and liberalism 76
   shift away from socialism 146
Society i, xiii, xv, 2–11, 13 f., 27, 31, 33, 35, 37 f., 52 f., 55, 62–64, 70 f., 73, 76, 78, 80, 83, 87–90, 93, 95–99, 111, 121, 128, 131, 133–136, 138, 140–145, 147
   civil society xvi f., 4, 7, 14, 22, 38, 43, 64, 87, 89 f., 97, 99, 138, 143, 147
   political society 147
   reflexive society 7, 127
Special Economic Zones (SEZs) xvi, 7, 13, 63, 80 f., 85, 143
SEZ Act (2005) 117, 124, 138, 141
Spivak, Gayatri 87
Srikrishna Committee 116, 124
Star Network 49
State Finance Commissions (SFCs) 25
state-capital alliance 146
States Reorganisation Commission xviii, 102 f., 114
Stiglitz, Joseph 1, 65, 111, 139
Strong state 3 f.
Structural Adjustment Programmes (SAPs) 4, 112, 123
Supreme Court of India 40, 56, 64, 69, 71, 74, 115, 124, 142

Tamil Nadu 100, 107, 135
Telangana 13, 103, 107, 113–116, 123
   Telangana movement 113–115
   Telangana Rashtra Samiti 118
Telugu Desam Party (TDP) 118 f.
Territorial pluralism 101 f., 105, 108
Terrorism 2, 36, 80, 84
   foreign-sponsored terrorism 37
   international terrorism 95
   Islamic terrorism 95
Thatcher, Margaret 96
Third Space 51 f., 140
Trade Mark Act (1999) 75, 141
Trade-Related Aspects of Intellectual Property Rights, Agreement on (TRIPS) 75
Transformation 2, 9, 35, 98, 110, 112, 128, 142, 145, 147
Tribals (adivasis) 32, 37, 46, 61–64, 78–86, 90, 99, 102, 105, 127 f.
Trickle-down effect 37
Trinamool Congress (TMC) 15, 82, 134
Tryst with destiny 56, 144 f., 147

Unemployment 32, 60, 63
　Unemployment rate 100
United Nations Development Assistance Framework (UNDAF) 56
United Nations Development Programme (UNDP) 14, 23, 95
United Nations Millennium Development Goals (MDGs) 60
United Progressive Alliance (UPA) xvii, 24, 36, 38, 61, 118, 124, 147
United States of America 2, 19, 39 f., 42, 45, 47–49, 51–54, 64, 68–73, 87 f., 101, 109, 139
Urbanisation in India 24, 27, 79
US-AID 6
USSR 12, 36, 68, 72, 96
Uttarakhand Kranti Dal (UKD) 120
Uttarakhand 13, 56, 105, 111–113, 119–124, 143
　Uttarakhand movement 111, 114, 119, 121 f.
Uttar Pradesh xvi, 41, 56, 100–103, 105, 107, 112, 119 f., 135

Vidarbha region 60 f.
Violence xv, 32, 37, 61, 78 f., 81, 84–86, 128, 142
　communal violence xvi, 37, 61 f., 64, 95, 140
　Maoist violence 79, 81 f., 84–86, 142 f.
Vishalandhra 114
voter turnout 33 f.

War on terror 2
Weber, Max 53, 94 f.
Welfare state i, xvi, 2, 4, 9, 11 f., 55, 72, 109, 139, 145, 147
West Bengal 15, 62, 65, 79, 81 f., 90, 93 f., 100, 103, 107, 112, 130 f., 133 f., 136, 146
Westernisation 42, 51
Westminster model 39
　loss of relevance of the Westminster model 34
World Bank xvi, 5, 13, 23, 65, 126, 128, 136, 145
World Trade Organisation (WTO) 20 f., 75